Virtue and Values

for the Twenty-First Century

Jedediah Smith

VIRTUE AND VALUES FOR THE TWENTY-FIRST CENTURY

Renewing America's Character and Spirit

EDITED BY

J. Nelson Hoffman

Library of Congress Cataloging-in-Publication Data
Hoffman, Nelson.
Virtue and values for the twenty-first century:
renewing America's character and spirit.
ISBN 0-9715037-0-2
LCCN: 2001096083

Cover statue *Apron Strings* by Don Huntsman, photo by Steve Mundinger
Page ii statue *Jedediah Smith* by Don Huntsman
Cover design by Debbie Galloway
Book design by Jane Raese

PRESENTATION PAGE

This book is presented to:

Pitkin County Library

On this day: *New Year 2002*

On the occasion of: *First Publication*

By: *J Nelson Hoffman*

May the inspiration of my fellow authors bring a renewed sense of community to Aspen & the Roaring Fork Valley and a raised spirit to the reader.

Nels

For Joan, our children, and our grandchildren,
and for the contributors and their families.
Without them, this book would not have been possible.

In memory of my mother, Isabelle Hill Hoffman,
whose unquestioning love, example, and
memory inspires this book.

And for my grandfather, Frank Nelson Hill,
whose character, example, and mentoring
provided a lifetime model of leadership
I can only attempt to follow.

And to all who have shaped my faith and beliefs.

CONTENTS

--- *SECTION TWO* ---

Home, School, Places of Worship, and Work:
Opportunities to Build Values   57

The Threads of Individual Choice, the Fabrics of Society
J. Nelson Hoffman   59

PREFACE

THIS BOOK SEEKS TO INSPIRE a new American Revolution—not a political revolution or an economic revolution, but rather a revolution of the spirit.

The main inspiration for this book came in 1992. My wife Joan became concerned that the wonderful recipes from the great cooks in her family and mine would be lost to future generations. She created a cookbook of those recipes and added the favorite recipes of our children and friends. That book cemented old friendships and created many new ones.

Using her idea as a model, I have authored this book. Instead of food recipes, I have collected recipes of the lifelong values my contemporaries and I have tried to follow. These values came from our parents' generation. My wife and I, in turn, have tried to pass on those values, adapted to the current world, to our children and grandchildren. We believe these values and virtues are eternal, not subject to the vagaries of style, changes in the economy, or the inventions of new technologies.

The second inspiration for this book comes from Alexis de Tocqueville's *Democracy in America*:

> I understand here the expression *moers* in the sense that the ancients attached to the word *mores [morality]*; not only do I apply it to mores properly so called, which one could call habits of the heart, but to the different notions that men possess, to the various opinions that are current in their midst, and to the sum of ideas of which the habits of the mind are formed . . . I therefore comprehend under this word the whole moral and intellectual state of a people . . .

A final inspiration came from observing a multitude of bad examples of character and leadership in virtually every part of our society:

- Politicians—city, state, and national—who engage in personal conduct that disgraces their professional lives and their office, destroying public respect for government.
- Local policemen and authorities who surrender to the drug trade, victimizing the citizens they are paid to protect, destroying community confidence in law enforcement.
- Business leaders who lie to their employees, their customers, their creditors, and their stockholders.
- And even clergy who abuse their followers, sin against their vows and their faith, bringing disrespect and scandal to their calling.

These negative examples of character are then compounded when the media in our country promotes and presents the most sensational, evil, or scandalous news story available that day, applying pressure to the other news media to match this cycle of exploitative behavior.

Disturbed by conduct such as this, I began this book.

I long for a return to the strong moral leadership that inspired my life. It is the type of leadership that came from John F. Kennedy when he intoned, "Ask not what your country can do for you, but what you can do for your country." It is the type of presidential leadership Ronald Reagan displayed when he challenged the leaders of communism in his farewell address. And it is the leadership found in the inspirational words of Franklin Roosevelt's 1941 Inaugural Address:

> . . . A nation, like a person, has a body—a body that must be fed and clothed and housed, invigorated and rested, in a manner that measures up to the objectives of our time.
>
> A nation, like a person, has a mind—a mind that must be kept informed and alert, that must know itself, that understands the hopes and the needs of its neighbors—all the other nations that live within the narrowing circle of the world.

And a nation, like a person, has something deeper, something more permanent, something larger than the sum of its parts. It is something which matters most to its future—which calls forth the most sacred guarding of its present.

It is a thing for which we find it difficult—even impossible—to hit upon in a single, simple word.

And yet, we all understand what it is—*the spirit—the faith of America*. It is the product of centuries. It was born in the multitudes of those who came from many lands . . . mostly plain people, who sought here, early and late, to find freedom more freely . . .

At the turn of this new millennium, our country's future is challenged. And that challenge requires a response by all Americans. So ask yourself:

- Do you have any sense of the noble nation Roosevelt described?
- Do you know a young single parent who struggles to provide a good home for one or more children, one who feels overwhelmed by the challenges of being the sole wage earner, home maker, and both male and female role models to their children?
- Do you know young couples who, as dual income providers, are faced with jobs that demand evenings and/or weekends away from the family?
- Do you know an overworked teacher who, facing demands for greater performance from his or her pupils, is also called upon to provide training in discipline, honesty, work habits, and respect normally taught at home?
- Do you know of a troubled youth who, at the most vulnerable stage of life, is following anti-social examples and exhibiting self-destructive behaviors?

This book is devoted to providing help and direction for these people through the guiding inspirations and life experiences of the fifty people who have written for this book. It is a group that have followed their beliefs, pursued the American Dream, and have been successful in their lives. They are extraordinary people whom you meet on the street, work with in business, pray with in your place of worship. They have persevered and negotiated the challenges they faced in life, and now they wish to give something back through their collective experience. All are interested in helping families, especially children, with the urgent and difficult challenges they face every day.

CHARACTER

"Every man is the creature of the age in which he lives; very few are able to raise themselves above the ideas of the time."

—Voltaire

Voltaire's quotation provides one of the essential ingredients of this book. It is my belief that there is currently a crying need in our country for adults and institutions to take a leadership role in instructing youth in the importance of character. To me, Voltaire's quote on the importance of individual action rings true for the time in which we live. Too few people in our modern society are able to act against what is popular, stylish, or fashionable, even if that conduct or behavior is uncivilized, rude, or ignorant. Today, many anti-social behaviors are accepted. This acceptance has a cumulative negative effect on both individuals and our communal life. And the acceptance of such behavior is unconsciously passed on to children.

NURTURING

On the cover of this book, Don Huntsman's sculpture, *Apron Strings*, shows a young boy clinging to his mother's dress—portraying the trust and love in parenting that is one of the most precious gifts in life. Nurturing is a concept we use many times in this book. But in addition to the parenting context, we wish to show the positive possibilities which occur when families, houses of worship, and communities nurture each of their members.

A prime example of this group nurturing concept is the actions of the generation that came of age during World War II. They survived the decade of severe economic hardship called the Great Depression. Then they had to fight fascism, anti-Semitism, and communism in World War II and in Korea. In putting the hardship they endured behind them, they created a period of growth and prosperity for their children in this country and with the Marshall Plan provided the tools and capital to rebuild Europe. Here at home, their gratitude to the returning soldiers was manifested in the GI Bill that changed college education from a privilege reserved for the wealthy to an accessible possibility for people of all incomes. And low-cost loans were provided to returning soldiers to spread home ownership and redirect our own economic focus.

As has been stated by many observers, Americans have a marvelous ability to pull together when things get tough. This book wishes to spread that same spirit in these prosperous times.

ACKNOWLEDGMENTS

$\mathcal{M}$OST BOOKS CONTAIN A formal bibliography at the end. This book begins with a recognition that the content has been significantly inspired by the ideas of others: First and foremost are the contributors who have written of their experiences and insights. Second are the authors who are interested in the nation's standards of morality—authors interested in guiding children to create the most successful lives they can.

Tom Brokaw's two books, *The Greatest Generation* and *The Greatest Generation Speaks*, remember the tremendous sacrifices made by the generation that came of age during World War II and the moral fiber and "lifelong lessons" that they possess because of it. Steven Spielberg's two movies, *Saving Private Ryan* and *Schindler's List*, accurately detail the trials they endured and the evil brutality that they fought to defeat.

I have long been a fan of Bill Bennett, and his three books on classic and current values—*The Moral Compass*, *The Book of Virtue*, and *The Index of Leading Cultural Indicators*—have substantially influenced my thinking about the necessity of each generation passing on their values to succeeding generations.

John Wooden's *A Lifetime of Observations On and Off the Court* summarizes the perspective of the very accomplished and beloved coach from UCLA. His unaffected comment about being "just a simple man who lives by his beliefs" could serve as the inspirational backbone for this book.

Robert Bellah and his co-authors inspired me to look at our nation and our culture with a wider perspective. *Habits of the Heart—Individualism and Commitment in America* and *The Good Society* look not just at individual morality, but the significance of changes in the major institutions of our society (school, work, family, and community) and the effect these changes have on the values and formation of character in our young people. It is a perspective, which was offered by Alexis de Touqueville in the first half of the 19th century in his treatise *Democracy in America*, and it provides a template for evaluating a nation and its culture that I have tried to follow in writing this book.

There are three other books that have probably received smaller readership but have played a seminal role in shaping this project: Lawrence Steinberg's *Outside the Classroom* cogently describes the need to think about all the influences that affect youth outside the schoolroom and the futility of placing unrealistic expectations on schools.

Dr. Peter Benson's *All Kids Are Our Kids* develops a comprehensive picture of the significant links between healthy families, healthy youth, and healthy communities. It is increasingly apparent that as Americans seek individual wealth, and as the disparities in wealth distribution become greater, the need for institutions to assist economically disadvantaged families and individuals becomes ever greater. It is interesting to note that these problems are not unique to urban poverty areas. Recent disasters, such as those at Columbine High School and in other recent school shootings, teach us that moral issues affect every community, rich and poor, suburban, urban, and rural.

The recent prosperity in America has created a tendency for many to have a more isolationist view of the world. I believe the more international outlook of *Deliver Us from Evil—Peacekeepers, Warlords, and a World of Endless Conflict* by William Shawcross will be necessary for our nation to adopt in this new century. His book portrays the difficulties the United Nations faces each day attempting to maintain peace in the world and the reason why our nation should take a leadership role in this effort. Kosovo, Sarajevo, Somalia, Cambodia, and Sierra Leone are festering conflicts where racial and religious hatred cause daily torment, and there is a constant potential for the fighting to spread into surrounding countries.

For those readers interested in the role of the public school in teaching character, I would recommend *Finding Common Ground— A First Amendment Guide to Religion and Public Education* by Charles Haynes and Oliver Thomas.

For those who wish to understand the basis of religious freedom in America, I discovered a pivotal writing from 1637—*The Flushing (Quaker) Remonstrance*, a protest letter written by the inhabitants of Flushing for their local governor Peter Stuyvesant, Governor of the Dutch colony of New Amsterdam.

Five books I would recommend about the African-American experience are: *In Our Own Words: A Treasury of Quotations from the African-American Community* by Elza Dinwiddie-Boyd, *Black Heroes of the American Revolution* by Burke Davis, *American Women of Achievement* by Phillis Wheatley and Merle Richmond, *The Freedom Writers Diary: How Teachers and 150 Teens Used Writing to Change Themselves and the World Around Them* by The Freedom Writers with Erin Gruwell, and *Our Character, Our Future—Reclaiming America's Moral Destiny* by Alan Keyes.

In addition to submitting their own contributions, some of my co-authors also submitted works of inspiration from other writers. I would like to thank Carol Quinn for the Diane Loomans poem *If I Had My Child to Raise All Over Again*, Ann and Bill Guiffre for the Dorothy Day excerpt from *Why I Am Still a Catholic*, Jack McKearin for the quote on "trust" and the quote on never saying "I can't," Jack MacAllister for the poem *The Guy in the Glass*, and Al Fetters for the quote on "commitment" by W.H. Murray.

And finally, in writing this book I have used the services of several literary arts and graphic arts professionals. I wish to thank Cindy Hirschfeld, Steven Alldredge, and Nancy Roach for their editing and proofreading skills, Jane Raese for designing the page lay-out of the book, and Debbie Galloway for designing the book jacket.

INTRODUCTION

"In a higher world it is otherwise, but here below to live is to change, and to be perfect is to have changed often."

—John Henry Cardinal Newman

In the Preface, I spoke of a spiritual revolution. At the turn of the last century, a wave of fervor, now called Victorian and Puritanical, took place. America paused in its drive into the Industrial Revolution to refresh its moral and civic direction. In earlier history, the turn of a century marked a time of reflection on the current state of affairs, a more philosophical and spiritual perspective and a more deliberate attempt to look at the future.

Now, at the turn of this millennium, many authors have written of the progress of science and the economy. However, the topic that seems of more serious concern is the loss of society's cohesion, sense of belonging, community, and mutual purpose that has marked America throughout our history. It is significant that a land made up mainly of immigrants has become the standard bearer of democracy. Our melting pot is an example to the world. But in spite of our strengths, disturbing new trends which illustrate our weaknesses have emerged in the past few decades. Robert Putnam, a Harvard professor, describes this condition in his book *Bowling Alone—the Collapse and Revival of American Community*. Putnam describes the changes in America over the past 30–40 years and uses the term "social capital" to refer to the connectedness that is declining in many parts of society: church, community, and nation. Former Colorado Governor Richard Lamm, in his two contributions to this book, writes of the decline in values and the loss of "social glue."

Both of these learned men focus on the essence of the problem, and I heartily agree with their research and perspective. But my intuition leads me to include a path of inquiry that emphasizes the spiritual as well as the social, political, or economic dimension.

RENEWAL

Our country's capacity for periodic renewal has been one of our greatest strengths. To some, renewal suggests economic, political, or military renewal. This book focuses on none of these. Instead, it centers on the spiritual renewal of America—the examination of our collective conscience—what we believe in and what we stand for: the ideals, values, goals, and causes we are committed to supporting.

At the beginning of this new century, we have moved from the Industrial Age into the Information Age. Around the globe, shifts in industries have caused macro changes in national economies and the social order, and new technologies have created enormous new opportunities, as well as new questions and concerns. Our home and family lives and our educational, business, and spiritual institutions have struggled to adapt to these new challenges.

This book explores how individuals, families, and communities can positively respond to these changes, how thoughtful people can affect and influence the moral and ethical conduct of young people in these difficult times, and how leaders can help create healthier and safer families and communities.

CONTRIBUTORS

To better understand how ethical principles and leadership skills are transmitted from one generation to the next, I began to seek out men and women who had, in Voltaire's words, "raised themselves above the ideas of the times." I looked for the insights and experiences of these people. I considered how I could pass on their wealth of leadership and wisdom to the young people who will be assuming positions of responsibility in this new age. The responses to this inquiry provide the substance of this book.

In these pages, you will find the thinking and principles of an array of wonderful people who have affected my life and my wife Joan's life. Mostly born in the 1930s, 1940s, and 1950s, they came of age seeking the "American Dream," and they were very successful in attaining that dream. Now, they are concerned about many of the changes they see in our communities and our families, and they are concerned about the effect those changes have on raising healthy children.

The contributors are my partners in this collaborative effort. They bring ideas, experiences, and perspectives far wider than I could have presented on my own. They are successful in a variety of occupations, including business, politics, religious life, education, medicine, and the military. They include doctors and nurses, business executives, clergy, and educators from elementary schools to the faculty of some of the country's top universities. There has been no political, religious, or philosophical litmus test for inclusion in this collection. The binding criteria are a concern for children and the desire to pass along "lessons learned."

Many of our contributors' "lessons" will surprise even those who know them well. While it probably will not surprise the students who went to high school with Sister Elaine Kolesnick that she elected to follow her spiritual call to the religious life, I think it will surprise parishioners of St. Francis of Assisi in La Quinta, California, to learn that their pastor Jack Barker was both a rocket physicist *and* a concert pianist. In Rochester, New York, thousands of mothers, who had Dr. Dick Fullerton see them through their pregnancy and delivery, will learn of Medical Corpsman Richard Fullerton, who began his career as a healer by tending to the casualties as our fighting men battled across the islands of the Pacific. Students at a San Diego high school will learn that their wise and gentle principal was Navy jet pilot Commander Wayne Connell, who led his squadron back to the pitching deck of an aircraft carrier off Vietnam over 400 times! Or, it may surprise many Ford dealers and distributors to learn that Arthur Cerre, the creative, talented advertising executive who managed their accounts, is a much decorated Marine Captain and the survivor of the battles for Guadalcanal and the ensuing island battles that led to Japan's defeat.

It is my hope that principles and leadership skills can be learned from the stories of our diverse contributors.

OUR LEGACY

To my children and grandchildren, this book is my legacy to you. It is a gift, not in terms of money, but in terms of knowledge and experience. It conveys the spiritual and moral principles that Joan and I and our contributors have tried to follow.

The substance of this book focuses on my belief that character and leadership are cultivated at home. What happens elsewhere is a bonus. It is sad to see how many families have not accepted this fact and attempt to shift the burden of this responsibility to schools, civic groups, religious institutions, and community organizations.

We begin the book by focusing on the concept of leadership and the importance of transferring life skills and values from one generation to the next.

When I decided to move forward with this project, Governor Lamm's warm encouragement captured the exact tone and message I wanted to pass on to my family and other families. It was best expressed in one of his letters to me:

> I believe that a country's status and prosperity are like starlight—
> the light you see from a star is a delayed reaction from an image that
> started perhaps 10,000 years ago. And you may say the same thing
> for today's prosperity because it depends upon how well our parents
> and previous generations planted the competitiveness challenge,
> saved capital, [and] invested in infrastructure . . .
>   There's an old Arab saying that 'True wisdom is planting a tree
> under which you know you yourself will never sit.'

Governor Lamm's concern with the importance of each generation passing on the best of what they have to the next generation struck a chord deep within me. It encouraged me to try to understand the changes which have occurred in our nation over the last fifty years and to understand how those changes have affected our public school system, children, families, communities and our nation's culture.

ORGANIZATIONAL OVERVIEW

My wife and I believe the book illustrates that life's choices provide the opportunity to practice different values. In Joan's words, "The *choice*s you make in life *determine* the life you live."

In the course of this book, we examine this premise from many perspectives, and we show how making the right choice nurtures character and leadership and renews communities and our country.

In my business life, I often had the responsibility to examine the marketplace for our products and the responsibility to specify the significant changes impacting our products and services. Next, the task was to describe and forecast the new products that would be required in the future and later to identify the organization, skills, facilities, capital, and technology required to produce these new products. Calling upon that experience, I have organized the contents of this book in a similar fashion.

Section One: In partnership with the contributors, we look at the large, global forces that have affected life in the last half of the twentieth century. We reflect on how those forces affect the thinking, the morality, the educational process, and the climate of public opinion in America today.

Section Two: Following a model used by the 19th century philosopher Alexis de Touqueville in drawing a civic, political, social, and economic profile of America, we look at some of the main institutions of our lives. We explore how these institutions provide learning opportunities for nurturing character and leadership.

Section Three: We present the consensus values and skills our contributors believe are the principal components in the formation and development of character. These values are drawn from the Judeo-Christian heritage that inspired our nation's founding fathers. The contributors and I believe they are fundamental, unchanging priorities in raising young people. They are essential in helping them understand what it takes to lead successful lives, and these values and ideals should be unaffected by style, technology, or economic cycles.

Section Four: We hope that examples from successful lives will inspire a new generation of leaders. We believe the problems that have arisen in the recent past can be solved by concerted, communal action. Governor Lamm presents his ideas on rebuilding communities; his insightful suggestions provide a challenge for all of us to consider. We propose a few action items for the public agenda, offering suggestions and solutions for parents and communities.

Dick Hartl, one of our contributors, cited the following bit of wisdom he picked up from a pediatrician, "List all the desirable traits you'd like to see in your children—now go out and live them each and every day!"

So, to parents and grandparents, educators, the business community, and the clergy—lead by example. It is not necessary for you to adopt the ideas in this book. Determine what is important to you and your family, recall the wisdom of your culture and heritage, and pass along your own "lessons learned." It will help instill character and leadership. It will help create healthier families and communities. And it will help renew our country with the virtues and values which have made our nation great.

Virtue and Values

for the Twenty-First Century

SECTION ONE

America 2001

Family and Communal Values

— 1 —

LEADERSHIP
From One Generation
to the Next

———

W HEN THIS BOOK BEGAN, I addressed letters to friends
whom I felt had achieved success in their lives and possessed
strong leadership abilities. My letter asked them for their own personal "recipe for success." Who were their mentors? What were
their sources of inspiration? What had sustained them through
tough times?

Their answers form the foundation of this book. Like me, many
of them believe that a healthy democratic society depends upon its
citizenry to pass along the values of character and leadership from
one generation to the next. Virtually all of them believe that those
valuable lessons begin in the home with family.

Leadership—Part One

J. NELSON HOFFMAN

$\mathcal{F}$OR MOST OF MY ADULT LIFE, I have been a student of leadership. My interest in the subject can be traced back to the deep bond of affection between my grandfather, Frank Nelson Hill, and me. He is a marvelous example of a great leader. With my dad off to war, my mother also taught me many of the principles of leadership that have stayed with me to this day. My mother is a great example of the single mothers who struggle to raise their families and support themselves on their own.

As an only child, I was the focus of my mother's love and attention. "Nelson, you are something special," was the message I heard from her over and over. She taught me a work ethic, thirst for knowledge, initiative, and persistence.

It was my grandfather who added a note of responsibility in this message:

"Nelson, you have been blessed by being born tall and you have a good mind. But remember, everyone is born with special gifts and everyone is different. Some people are born with a special gift for caring—they become wonderful nurses and doctors. Some people have a talent for numbers—they go into business or banking. I was born with great physical strength, so I enjoy hard work and I can protect myself. (He was a good amateur boxer.) The most important thing is to remember that you have an obligation to use those gifts as well as you can. The greater the gift, the greater the obligation."

My grandfather was never interested in making a lot of money. During the Depression, he helped relatives, neighbors, and his fellow Masons survive those terrible years. When he died, my grandmother had to pay off several loans for banknotes Granddad had cosigned years earlier. He would give money when needed; his preferred method was to call it a loan, rather than a gift.

During the Depression, one of the greatest casualties was the loss of dignity people suffered in all economic classes. During those years, I watched as his selflessness gave people the critical help they needed without them ever feeling a loss of respect or self-worth. It was an invaluable lesson in generosity and in leadership.

In the ensuing years, I've probably read hundreds of books on management and leadership, attended countless hours of training classes and seminars, and tried to make the right decisions in my own life. But my actions pale in comparison to the indelible example I learned from my grandfather's life. What was his greatest leadership skill? He knew how to put others first.

How I Was Introduced to Abraham Lincoln

J. NELSON HOFFMAN

*H*AVE YOU EVER THOUGHT ABOUT how you became the person you are? Have you thought about the people, the events, the organizations, the groups that shaped your character and attitudes—parents, teachers, schools, packs and troops, clubs, teams, fraternities, or gangs?

I am blessed with many vivid memories of people and events which have been influential in shaping my life. One in particular stands out:

Imagine a cold, dark assembly hall of 300–350 seats with a raised platform at the front. In the center of the platform, an eleven-year-old boy stands at the podium on a box to see over the top of the lectern.

The hall is empty except for the boy and an older gentleman seated far away in the back row. The boy begins to speak in a quiet, hesitant voice, "Four score and seven years ago, our forefathers brought forth on this continent . . . "

He continues on for a minute or two, reciting the words in a dispassionate tone.

In the back of the auditorium, the old man rises from his seat and moves slowly down the aisle toward the front as he listens. Reaching the stage, he interrupts with a warm smile.

"That's fine, son. You've memorized the words just fine. But I'd like to give you a few suggestions that will help the audience react to the meaning of those words."

"I'd like to have you think about what Abraham Lincoln had in mind when he delivered this speech. *The Gettysburg Address* will go down in history as one of the greatest speeches ever written in our nation's history. Why? Because it tells the story of America. It tells the story of what America's values are and it tells the story of what America believes in and is willing to fight for."

"Let me give you a few tips. Before you begin, look at the audience, give them a big smile, and take a deep breath. Pick out a lady in the right front row and deliver the first phrase to her."

"Four score and seven years ago, our forefathers brought forth on this continent . . . "

"Say the word 'forefathers' slowly and clearly. Do the same with 'on this continent' . . . "

"Pause, take a breath, and pick out someone else in the audience, someone about the middle of the left side. Now, deliver the next phrase to that person, with a great deal of force."

"A New Nation, conceived in Liberty, and DEDICATED to the proposition that all . . ."

"Say that word very loud and very clear. Emphasize and dramatize it."

"ALL men are created equal."

That old gentleman was my grandfather, Frank N. Hill, an accomplished speaker, raconteur, leader, and grandfather supreme. He spent two or three hours with me, coaching, encouraging, and demonstrating how to give a two or three minute recitation of Lincoln's speech. The following Saturday evening, when I delivered the speech to our local Grange chapter, I felt the warm response of the audience and the satisfaction that came with it.

By passing on his skills to me he was modeling the traits he hoped I would acquire. His leadership and love encouraged me, created a sense of pride, and gave me the confidence to continue developing my speaking skills.

Those skills created a number of opportunities in later life that led to good jobs and financial security. Like my grandfather, I aspired to become a leader of men. Later, when I approached my retirement years, I thought about the gifts I had been given and Granddad's coaching was one of the first that came to mind.

I thought about how I might I might return that gift to the next generation—to "give back" in my retirement years. It occurred to me that there were young people who might not have these public speaking skills and that I could help them gain this advantage in the same way Granddad Hill helped me.

My Legacy—Community Service

CATHY BUSCHER

THERE ARE CERTAIN PERSONS who will always stand out for having had a large influence on me while I was growing up. My parents came from families of different religious denominations, economic status, and social levels. Both families, however, shared similar morals and values. When I think of my family as a whole, I remember the characteristics of goodness, honesty, and kindness demonstrated by every member.

Each of my parents' families was faithful in practicing its particular religion. Church on Sundays was always an important event. My staunch Episcopalian paternal grandmother and my very Catholic mother clearly demonstrated that their belief in God and the promise of a hereafter helped them get through various tragic circumstances. After their husbands died suddenly (both in their fifties), these women stoically plunged ahead with their busy lives, shunning self-pity and refusing to be a burden on those around them.

At age twelve, I was inspired by the actions of an uncle who returned to civilian life from World War II. He had achieved an impressive record during the war and suffered numerous injuries while fighting for five years. Obviously, he had been deeply touched by his experiences. In order to give thanks for peace and in memory of the brave men and women with whom he had fought, especially those who did not return, my uncle initiated a day of prayer in all of the city churches.

At certain times, I feel the need for strength and assistance. Like my grandmother and mother, I, too, am convinced of the power of prayer, especially during periods of duress. For example, my husband and I have been blessed with four healthy children, following what were considered risky pregnancies. We have tried to instill in our children a personal sense of faith, so that during stressful or painful situations they can turn to it for guidance and comfort, instead of feeling alone and helpless. It is so easy to get caught up in the trivia and complexities of daily existence. Our religion continually reminds us of the really important things in life. I pray that our children, by example, will pass on to our grandchildren the benefits and joys derived from a strong faith and unwavering religious beliefs.

One of the most important lessons passed on to me focused on the idea of contributing to one's community. If you are blessed with good fortune, it is your responsibility to share your time and resources with those less fortunate. It was my family's way of life, and I grew up believing that everyone lived this way. For example, during a trip to the local United Way office, I noticed pictures on the wall of various relatives who had volunteered for the organization. Actually, the entire Twin Cities community of Minnesota stressed the notion of helping the state's other towns and cities. One large local company, for instance, emphasized the importance of contributing to and supporting nonprofits in order to enhance the quality of life for their communities and citizens. Apparently at that time the Twin Cities raised more money per capita for nonprofits than any other location in the U.S.

Over the years, I have come to realize what a real privilege it is to serve on various community boards and committees. Each situation has been a learning experience, as well as a chance to contribute. Although today's young adults are often swamped with demanding jobs and family schedules, I hope they will always try to support their communities in some way. If they cannot do much now, they will have time later in life and will find it very rewarding. Many schools, in fact, require their students to perform community service in order to graduate, recognizing that our country was founded on the idea of volunteerism.

In today's society, the family as an institution is under tremendous pressure. I continually think back to how important the family was when I was growing up. In those days everyone in my two immediate families lived in the same city. The elder members were definitely the heads of the family. The younger members usually acceded to the opinions of the elders, whether they really agreed with them or not. Set traditions, such as the weekly Sunday luncheons at one grandmother's house, were not broken without a good excuse.

The desire for closeness and loyalty within families is more of a challenge today. Rarely do relatives all live in the same place. In this age of independence, not only have many children moved to new areas, but numerous parents have also decided to retire in different surroundings. Keeping in touch requires desire and work on everyone's part.

Reunions reaffirm our connection with past generations. Older family members are reawakened with past memories that they are eager to pass on. At same time, younger members can see the seniors as role models, learn about family history, and take pride in their family's past.

We are convinced that our offspring will continue to maintain a strong sense of our family heritage. Our daughter and three sons have always shown interest, concern, and support for their siblings and for their parents. Their actions demonstrate to their own youngsters that belonging to a loving and caring family is indeed a marvelous and precious gift.

For Cathy Buscher, her active volunteer life is a blessing and a legacy from her parents.

Living a Luxurious Life

Dr. Ann Ehringer

IT IS VERY DIFFICULT for me to think about success without thinking about values. As I have thought about that for these many months, I have reflected not only on what I have learned about living successfully, but from whom and from what experiences I have learned.

I have a luxurious life (and I use that word thoughtfully). It is luxurious because I have had the benefits of a wise and loving parental family, a broad, superior education with caring instructors, and finally, a splendid family of my own with a husband and grown daughter, son, and now a grandson, who are the lights and the prides of my life. It is luxurious because I have been blessed with wonderful relationships among friends whom I greatly admire and respect. It also is luxurious because I have been invited, time after time in my working life, to take on new challenges, new work, to learn new things, and to learn how to think new things. Within the luxury of all these new opportunities to learn, my life took paths I had never envisioned, and now I find myself in the most enviable of positions, concurrently owning a successful small business, serving on a board of directors, and teaching in a fine graduate business school with an open-ended charge to help young people become entrepreneurial and successful in business as well as life.

It is clear to me, as I reflect on what I teach my students, that I have learned from all of the people in my life. I am the student, and they are the teachers, and lifelong learning at the instruction of wise family, children, friends and challenging opportunities is what I call luxury. This is what I have learned (sometimes painfully, of course); this is what I teach my students. I also teach them that the single most important quality of a successful life (and successful business) is personal integrity. Without it, nothing else matters. With it, anything is possible, and once it is lost, it is almost impossible to regain. Personal integrity is based on core values and deeply held personal beliefs, and it is built on the small, often invisible, daily decisions we make about what we do, how we act, and how we treat other people.

The other important qualities that define a successful life, ultimately, are meaningful relationships and meaningful work. It will not be money or things or monuments by which we measure our lives at the end. It will be whether we have created and maintained good, strong, meaningful relationships—from family and friends to colleagues and employees. It will be whether we have contributed in some life-improving way, some meaningful way, to our organizations and communities, and world.

The most important reason to participate in anything is to contribute at the maximum of our talents, abilities, and resources, and in some personal way, to lead by action and example. The most important reason to own an organization is to build something which will sustain itself and endure and succeed beyond us.

The most important determinant of an organization's success or failure is its leader, the owner or president. The company will become whatever their core values and personal principles are, and the most important skill sets your leader may have are those of self-awareness, decision-making, the ability to work with other people and empower them, and the ability to listen and to lead.

The owner/president/leader's most important attitudes are being positive—seeing the world in a benevolent way, full of opportunity and promise—and possessing self-awareness, humility, and patience. Qualities of vision, commitment, and perseverance also are necessary for success in life and business, but they are not sufficient, or even primary. We can only steer through the webs of increasing information and complexity and change which surrounds us through conscious self-awareness—understanding what drives our decisions (our core values and personal principles), and understanding how we deploy our unique strengths and weaknesses, including the recognition of when our strengths become weaknesses. Only with humility can we acknowledge that "none of us is as smart as all of us," and no one of us can accomplish anything alone. We need the expertise, the involvement, and the commitment of other people to succeed at anything we want to achieve. (Even the most virtual of companies is dependent on a vast array of others.)

Only through patience will we be able to listen, teach, and coach other people, as well as give ourselves permission and encouragement to fail, which is a necessary part of trying and learning.

Having unshakable personal integrity, building meaningful relationships, and making meaningful contributions are imperatives we learn from family, friends, and colleagues. Having self-awareness, humility, and patience are among the life-changing lessons of learning to be a parent and a team member (as well as a team leader since leadership is sometimes far easier than followership for many of us). There are lessons learned especially from my children, and now shared with them in valued relationships as special adult friends, and there are lessons learned from my students. I believe these lessons are fundamental to leading a successful life, and I know that lifelong learning and the opportunities people have afforded me are what defines my life as luxurious.

An accomplished entrepreneur, corporate executive, CEO advisor, college professor, and friend, Dr. Ann Ehringer was also a member of my company's advisory board.

The Dorr Recipe for Twenty-First Century Success

DR. LARRY DORR

No THRILL SUPERSEDES SUCCESS, no matter the size. In fact, many small successes bring greater happiness than the heavy responsibility of one great success. I have often thought about why I have achieved success, and I have concluded that almost all of my achievements are due to my family—the values I learned from my parents, and the many lessons I've learned from my wife and children.

I believe each success has three ingredients in common—creativity, productivity, and stability. However, these ingredients will not promote success until they are mixed with the values of honesty and true concern for others. Creativity is the key ingredient. I wonder sometimes if there is a gene for this because the spark for true creativity is so much stronger in some than others. However, I think this characteristic is at least partly a training of the mind. I have always thought that my creativity was spawned by my years as a small boy in Dayton, Iowa, when I had to create my own play activities. I was a great cowboy who jumped rivers (a small creek) and swam lakes (the yard) to win the great battle and be a hero.

I believe a high ratio of children's play must be creative, as compared to TV education. My recipe to young people, and parents of young people, is to devote time to develop creativity of the mind and confidence in their creative pursuits. Listen to your mind (and heart), and follow your creative nature so that you can experience the happiness and thrill of your creative success. Creativity is not truly successful unless it benefits others.

I believe creativity doesn't work without productivity! How many good ideas have withered or been accomplished by someone else because there was no confidence in the creation, or no one would take the risk to be the leader?

I learned about risk from my father who preached and supported world peace during the early 1950s McCarthy persecution era. My father had the inner strength to stand against severe criticism, and it pleases me to know that I learned from his example. In spite of the criticism I heard, I am proud of being a leader in many facets of joint replacement medicine.

To bring your creation to fruition, you must develop courage to take a risk and then be willing to work harder than anyone. Courage can be learned by trying hard. With each success, confidence builds, and with each failure, the resolve to be successful next time hardens.

There is joy in work and particularly in the work to fulfill your own creativity. That is why surgery is so satisfying to me; each operation is my own creation of artistic accomplishment. I have been a leader in total joint replacement surgical techniques. Bone ingrowth fixation, hydroxyapatite fixation, and metal-on-metal articulation are procedures which came from my creative instincts. But the success of these creative instincts occurred only because of the productive work ethic I learned from my parents and my desire to do what was necessary to accomplish my creative goals.

A necessary ingredient for true success is the sustenance of creativity and productivity. A single successful idea or project is wonderful, but soon the spiritual strength gained from that success fades. The most successful people are those with the energy to endure the mixture of success and failure to continue to create future successes. To have this high positive energy requires stability. Otherwise, too much energy is expended to resolve negative aspects of life.

Stability means positive energy dominates your thinking time, and it is not drained from you by negative events. Therefore, you must spend much positive energy in your personal relationships so you have happiness and a high energy for creativity and productivity. I have experienced my own times of family or business turmoil, and, during these times, so much energy is spent on anxiety, worry, and negative thoughts that no energy is left for creativity, and productivity is low. It is my wife who has created stability for me over the years. She has straightened my course many times when, by myself, I may have floundered.

My recipe of creativity, productivity, and stability will require strong values and different "portions" of the ingredients, according to one's life and career. The more one's life and career are independent and centered around individual talents, the higher the creativity must be. Enthusiasm for productivity is quintessential to happiness. Enthusiasm for productivity in life will directly influence stability at home and work.

But in the end, everyone must become his or her own chef, to mix these ingredients into the right proportions for their own "potion" of success. I believe my understanding of these ingredients, and my own proper mixture, has resulted in my success.

Dr. Larry Dorr is a world-renowned orthopedic surgeon who replaced both of my hips in 1986, giving me a new life. He is the founder of Operation Walk and offered the first contribution to this book.

— 2 —

1950–2000
Fifty Years of Change

————

J. Nelson Hoffman

IN THE PAST FIFTY YEARS we've seen revolutionary advancements and changes in our nation and its people. We've become
more wealthy than at any time in our history as business and industry have benefited from new advancements in technology and new,
global financial opportunities. But at the same time, the culture and
health of some communities—urban, suburban, and rural—have
declined. And this decline has had a negative effect on our nation's
children.

During this period, the development of new technologies has influenced every aspect of our lives, changed how we communicate
with one another, and even altered the way we think of communities. Less obvious, but more insidious, is the fact that our spiritual
and moral lives are also affected. Violence in the media and the re-
lentless exposure of our nation's children to media inappropriate for
their age group are only two of the new problems created in the age

of the Internet. New moral, social, and religious concerns are faced every day.

How did these negative trends begin? How can we change them for the better? What are some solutions to those struggling with these same issues at the turn of this new century?

In the 1830s, philosopher Alexis de Tocqueville analyzed the roots of American culture and character by looking at the major institutions of a person's life—family, schools, business, and religions. Following his model, we look at the state of American communities and our culture as we begin the 21st century. We look at how people define success and express their priorities. We compare the strengths Tocqueville found 170 years ago to those of our current society. And we conclude that the hopes and dreams of our children depend upon our ability to convey and pass along positive ideas, nurturing the formation of character and values. Excellence of the spirit must accompany intellectual excellence, if not precede it. And, as this book will demonstrate, we must improve the strength and health of the essential institutions of our lives.

Over the past fifty years, many changes have had a dramatic effect on our families, communities, and the lives of our children and grandchildren. In the following pages, I look at five of them.

A GLOBAL ECONOMY

The 20th century began with our nation evolving from a rural, agrarian economy to the new industrial age of mechanization, assembly lines, and people moving from the country to cities.

At the dawn of the 21st century we are now living in the information age, and our economy is dependent upon new technologies and a global business environment.

The computer has changed the production of goods in significant ways and many manufacturing companies are now shifting their high labor costs from the small towns and cities of our country to the lower costs of undeveloped, unregulated nations.

This adjustment to the information age has a major impact on family and community life across America. As global ownership replaces local ownership, the decision on where goods are produced becomes a pure economic decision. The health of a local economy and its effect on a community and its people is frequently over-looked or never even considered.

In this global environment, the production of services is becoming as important as the production of goods. Knowledge and education are replacing raw materials as the principal ingredients in many businesses. As a consequence, the undereducated are at an even greater disadvantage in this 21st century global economic environment.

ADVANCING TECHNOLOGY AND THE COMMUNICATIONS REVOLUTION

Increasingly, family life and family values must compete with a multitude of entertainment media and new communications technologies. In this environment, parents, schools, and religious institutions are forced to compete with technologies that are conveying values, morals, and virtues to our young people in the guise of "free speech" and "free markets." The line between news and entertainment has grown less distinct, and even the democratic political system that is the foundation of our country has become dependent upon television and the values of special interest groups.

Though it has an enormous capacity to entertain and educate, modern television, driven by profit motive, has not measured up to the positive expectations many had for it in the 1950s. With its unfortunate, invasive nature of injecting the least-desirable aspects of private and public behavior into our homes, television has not helped parents convey the best of humanity to children. Instead, rude, crude, and stupid have become all too frequent themes.

Now, the Internet has created even more challenges, particularly to parents, educators, and people of faith. Our country was founded upon the principle of freedom of speech. But how free are we if the health and future well-being of our children and future generations is adversely affected by a steady diet of entertainment programming which is inappropriate for a child's age group? Does freedom require that the content be loaded with trash, poor manners, anti-intellectual bias, and challenges to traditional values? As predicted by Marshall McLuhan in 1964, technology *has* changed social relations and mental attitudes. The medium *is* the message.

THE FEMININE REVOLUTION

Another significant change in the last fifty years has been the increased opportunities for women in our society and their changing role. It blossomed with the suffrage movement at the beginning of the 20th century. The drudgery of housework was eased with the invention of electric appliances such as the washing machine, the electric refrigerator, the dishwasher, and vacuum cleaner. The opportunities for women grew dramatically during World War II as women joined the work force in record numbers to assist in the war effort. And it reached full bloom in the 1960s with the women's movement.

Now, women work outside the home in significant numbers. In many cases, they are a family's primary wage earner. Women's pay rates still trail men's. But there is more equality in the work force, and women are free to pursue virtually any career a man might pursue.

New technologies, such as the birth control pill and other scientific advances, have given women more control over choosing the timing of the birth process, and in many cases, they are choosing not to have children at all. But some of these new technologies create religious and social dilemmas for women and men alike, and children are now faced with issues unlike any earlier generations had to deal with.

Various factions debate the changing role of women in our society. We are still trying to understand the effect this has had on men, families, and children. However, most people laud the human rights advancement of women the last fifty years as one of the greatest achievements in our nation's history.

But there is one consequence of the changing role of men and women in the work force the last fifty years that both sides can agree upon:

Over the last several decades an increasingly larger portion of home making and child rearing tasks have been delegated from parents to other care givers. In both rich and poor families, it is children who are most affected by the increased work demands of both men and women in our changing economy. According to a Public Radio International report on *Marketplace,* parents in 1996 spent an average of twenty-two hours less each week with their children than parents spent with their children in 1969. A thoughtful reader might consider both the qualitative, as well as the quantitative, dimension of this report.

SPIRIT AND INTELLECT

Over the course of the last three to four centuries, beginning with the Renaissance and the Reformation, there has been a growing trend for mankind to give primary emphasis to the intellectual and material world, de-emphasizing its spiritual nature.

This trend seemed to accelerate in the last half of the twentieth century as science and economics preempted spiritual interests. Materialism, humanism, nihilism, and "meism" have replaced communism and socialism in competing with traditional religions.

In a substantial part of our society, there have been declines in the stability of families, schools, companies, and our sense of community. There has also been less emphasis in our faith in a communal divine God and a measurably steady decline in our faith in each other.

I believe the growth of humanism has been accelerated by succeeding Supreme Court rulings on the separation of church and state. In the book *Finding Common Ground*, John Seigenthaler makes the following point:

"In a world where each new advancement of communications technology moves us closer to relationships with peoples and cultures across the globe, our public systems of education are failing because they are not teaching our students about the world's major religions and their effect on human history and experience. At the same time, the lack of religious education deprives young people of a reliable moral compass."

A MOBILE SOCIETY

The European immigrants who founded America were in many cases fleeing poverty and religious persecution. They created the American tradition to move and change when times dictate.

During the Great Depression, waves of migration rolled across our nation—from the dustbowls of Oklahoma and Arkansas west to California; from the south to cities in the north. This migration accelerated during World War II as Americans flocked from the farm to factories in cities to build the goods of war. By the end of the war, we were a much more urban society.

As prosperity grew, citizens began leaving the inner cities for suburbia. Tax revenues and civic interest declined in the inner cities and problems with crime, education, and drugs increased. As the exodus to suburbia continued, the automobile became the center of the economy, and during the 1950s the pessimism and fear that dominated the 1930s drained away.

In the last half of the twentieth century, the movement west continued, and whole new industries were created. Silicon Valley became as big a center of finance and wealth as Wall Street. American goods represented a significant fraction of global production. As corporations of all sizes grew, families were moved and careers and markets flourished.

For example, my jobs required six moves over a forty year period. It wasn't until we stayed in Los Angeles for twenty-five years that we felt rooted in a community. I have been told that the average person entering the work force this year can expect to change jobs six times during his working life.

The consequence of the growth of suburbia and job moves has had mixed effects. For most suburbanites with children, their neighborhood serves as the center of their family social life. But, frequent moves make it more difficult to become part of the community. In Los Angeles, most of the suburban homes are surrounded by slump stone walls. Robert Frost once said that "good walls make good neighbours." I find them a real barrier to creating and maintaining good neighbors. In these times, it is vital that we consider the strength of a neighborhood as well as the strength of the individual family.

— 3 —

THE
CONSEQUENCES OF
THESE CHANGES

———

Success in modern America is defined primarily in terms of individual success: wealth, power, and fame. These values are very different from the values of fifty years ago. Those values were defined much more in terms of the success and the strength of the organizations that a person was part of: family, church, community, and nation. The strengths of the groups were derived from strong individual character. Strength of individual character and strength of the organization were intimately intertwined.

In their *Flight from Values*, Governor Richard Lamm and Eric Caldwell lament the overemphasis on individual rights in our society over the past few decades, citing Rutgers Professor David Popenoe:

Fundamentally, what emerges from these cultural shifts is an ethos of radical individualism in which autonomy, individual rights, and social equality have gained supremacy as cultural ideals. In keeping with these ideals, the main goals of personal behavior have shifted from obligation and commitment to social units (families, communities, religions, and nations) to personal choices, lifestyle options, self-fulfillment, and personal pleasure.

Their article details the failure of our schools to measure up to standards of past performance, and it details the dismal performance of our schools in comparison to the schools of the nations with which we compete economically.

The basic message of the Lamm/Caldwell article is to show how changes in our society and culture are trending negatively for an unacceptable percentage of Americans.

Ten years have passed since the following article was written, but many of the problems have not changed, and the solutions offered seem as relevant as if it was written today—

The Flight from Values

Richard Lamm and
Richard A. Caldwell

Early in his first term, Franklin D. Roosevelt proclaimed: "The moneychangers have fled from their high seats in the temple of our civilization." Three years later he stated, "I should like to have it said of my first administration that in it the forces of selfishness and of lust for power met their match. I should like to have it said of my second administration that in it these forces met their master."

For Roosevelt, the forces of greed and self-interest were a worthy, if insuperable, opponent. Roosevelt knew that successful public policies were rooted in a society that valued the common good—a society that was willing to forgo the pleasures of the moment in or-

New Jersey Bell Journal, 1990.

der to achieve higher goals. A society's real strength is the strength of its values.

Consider the American scene at the beginning of a new decade. Problems and pathologies seem to be everywhere. Japan and Germany are poised to challenge America for economic leadership. We are now the world's largest debtor nation. The Japanese yen is battling the dollar for world supremacy while British, Dutch, and Japanese business interests buy up American companies, real estate and technology at fire-sale prices.

In our streets, there are drugs, gangs and the homeless. Our inner cities look like war zones, locked into a perpetual struggle for turf and money. In our Congress, there is scandal and paralysis. In our skies, earth and waterways, there is pollution. And in our schools, there is a pervasive sense of disorganization, uncertainty, and failure. If the 20th century was the American century, will we be able to say the same about the 21st?

A great democracy is built on a sense of shared values; so are the schools. But the debate about schools is complicated by the fact that ours is a pluralistic system, one in which it is not easy to secure even a modest level of shared commitment to achieve difficult collective goals. Schools are a symbolic mirror in which we see reflected the problems of our entire nation. They are the generation way station in which we glimpse our future.

Simply stated, our future depends upon the quality and competitiveness of our educational system. The quality of our schools will determine whether or not the United States can compete in the profitable technologies and industries of the 21st century. Will we become a faltering society—one with great differentials in wealth and educational level from top to bottom, divided along race and class lines, competing in subsistence industries against the underdeveloped countries, and running up huge international debts to consume what we no longer produce?

Seven years ago, the eloquent words of the National Commission on Excellence in Education (*A Nation At Risk*, 1983) rang true and they continue to do so today:

". . . If an unfriendly power had attempted to impose upon America the mediocre educational performance that exists today, we might have viewed it as an act of war . . . We have, in effect, been committing an act of unthinking, unilateral educational disarmament."

Here is a brief catalog of America's educational disorder:

- Adult illiteracy ranges from 10 to 30 percent of the U.S. population, depending on one's definition of "illiterate."
- A decade ago, U.S. students (people who are now entering the work force), when matched against their counterparts in other advanced countries in 19 educational disciplines, never finished first. They did, however, finish last in seven categories.
- In standardized tests given between 1983 and 1986, American high school seniors came in last in biology among students from 13 countries. They were eleventh in chemistry and physics. Nearly half of U.S. high school graduates never completed a year of either subject. Only 6 percent of American students study math at all beyond the tenth grade. Less than 40 percent of U.S. high school students complete three years of math and science, compared with more than 90 percent in Japan, West Germany, and the Soviet Union.
- Out of 29 categories of college-level pursuits, high school students planning study in the field of education finished fourth from the bottom in scholastic aptitude tests.
- The anemic rise in average SAT scores since 1980 (which, in turn, has to be viewed against the backdrop of a 90-point decline between 1963 and 1980), is offset by the fact that between 1972 and 1981, the absolute number of high school seniors scoring above 600 on the SAT verbal section dropped 40 percent—from 116,630 to 69,612.
- The most recent National Assessment of Educational Progress told us that two-thirds of our 17-year-olds do not know that our Civil War took place between 1850 and 1900 and 70 percent do not know that Jim Crow laws were designed to enforce racial segregation.
- In spite of decades of civil rights legislation, nationwide efforts to integrate the schools, a War on Poverty, the highest per capita expenditures on schools in the developed world, and the economic boom of the 1980s, one-fifth of all chil-

dren, 50 percent of black and Hispanic children, and one-fourth of all preschoolers live in poverty, according to the House Select Committee on Children, Youth and Families. "What we're seeing," according to Gary Bauer, president of the Family Research Council, "is the inevitable result of 25 years of family breakdown, moral relativism, and a flight from values. We don't think there are particularly liberal government programs or conservative programs that can save America's children until the country gets serious about addressing the behavioral roots of these problems."

WIDENING THE EDUCATION DEBATE

For the past seven years, America has been engaged in a great education debate. But we maintain that this debate has been a narrow one, focused largely on the wrong issues. The reasons our children are not learning and are not competitive on an international level are found more outside the classroom than inside. The roots of our educational failure lie mainly in a deterioration of American values and culture, in the breakdown of the family in all socioeconomic categories, and in antieducation attitudes that pervade certain subcultures.

Schools, as many in the education establishment might like to believe, are not separate from the supporting social and political environment. The reverse is more true: schools are largely the products of their environments and the fundamental determinants of educational success or failure are found in the larger social and valuational setting in which the school operates.

There has been some developing consensus on the substance of educational reform. Corporations have been leading the reform because they know that just as American industry must compete globally, so, too, must American education. Most educators and corporate executives agree, for example, on the need for a common core of learning and for fundamental literacy skills at the center of every child's education.

But there has been plenty of conflict also: some reformers want to see the end of "social promotion" through the grades, arguing that it is a betrayal of educational standards to promote students from grade to grade who have not mastered basic content; other argue that increasing graduation and promotion standards increases the dropout rate for minorities and turns the public schools into bastions of middle-class Anglo values.

These assertions speak to our beliefs about due process and equal protection-ultimately to the core of our values surrounding the concept of fairness. Prescriptions for more of the "old-time religion" more homework, a tougher curriculum, more discipline, longer school days, a longer school year, and higher standards for educational attainment—will not work, however well-intentioned, because they treat the symptoms of educational decline, not the causes.

Tragically, this period of educational malaise parallels the worldwide ideological ascent of capitalism, or at least the exciting idea of a free marketplace. Everywhere, communism, socialism and what [financial author] Peter Drucker calls "salvation by society" are waning paradigms—the last preserves of dictators, authoritarians and party hacks. If America fails to press its advantage, we have only ourselves to blame.

THE "CIRCLE" OF CONSUMPTION

Our schools—the schools that are failing the nation—are the products of our society and its deepest values. Since the 1950s, our values have changed. American society is different. It may be better for some people; it may be worse. But value changes akin to those in the table (at the end of this article) have very real consequences. We have become a society that cares more about spending than saving, more about personal pleasure than community, more about leveraged buyouts and "paper entrepreneurialism" than investment in the future, and more about instant fame than lasting achievement.

In contrast, both Thomas P. Rohlen and Merry White, experts on Japanese educational practices, point out that Japan's schools produce a highly competent and competitive high school graduate because Japan, at root, is a society devoted to children and to learning. There really are no mysterious cultural forces or exotic curricula at work. There is, instead, unswerving support for education. The progressive malaise of American schools stems from a lack of clear public standards, underscored by a series of dysfunctional value changes over the past 40 years.

Do Americans have a purpose? Yes, says ethicist Laurence Shames, but that purpose is consumption as an end in itself. In *The Hunger for More* (Times Books, 1989), Shames writes:

> . . . Consumption without excuses and without the need for justification—the beauty part was that it finessed the irksome question of values and of purpose. During the past decade, many people came to believe that there didn't have to be a purpose. The mechanism didn't require it. Consumption kept workers working, which kept the paychecks coming, which kept the people spending, which kept the inventors inventing and investors investing, which meant that there was more to consume. The system, properly understood, was independent of values and needed no philosophy to prop it up. It was a perfect circle, complete in itself and empty in the middle.

THE LAS VEGAS SYNDROME

The acquisition of knowledge depends on an individual's willingness to delay gratification for greater gains in the future. Without question, the 1980s for many were a decade of pure, unmitigated greed. For some, this was exactly what America should have stood for. Why keep desire in check when there was a fortune to be made? Why be shameful or worry about a sense of ethics or guilt when having the best was within such easy grasp?

In *Circus of Ambition* (Warner Books, 1989), social critic John Taylor observes:

> . . . In a few short years the values of industrious labor and thrift and the values of the Protestant work ethic, celebrated by Benjamin Franklin and accepted as the key to success by the American middle class for generations, were replaced with what Paul Blumberg called the Las Vegas Syndrome. Life had become a gamble; success went to the lucky speculators. Most people, of course, including many who had worked hard and grown up expecting to be rewarded for it, were not lucky. They experienced "downward mobility, " the perceived and in many cases actual decline in living standards. Their disappointed

expectations spread the belief that, as Jimmy Carter once remarked in a telling moment of his presidency, "life is unfair."

Is Edward Gibbon describing the new America when he observes that "the greatness of Rome was founded on the rare and almost incredible alliance of virtue and fortune"? But now, he says, "this native splendor is degraded and sullied by the conduct of some nobles who, unmindful of their own dignity and that of their country, assume an unbounded license of vice and folly." (*The Decline and Fall of the Roman Empire*, Penguin ed., 1981)

The study of emerging American values is the real key to understanding the functioning of basic American institutions and complex organizations, such as the schools. Through comprehending dominant values and social trends, together with their rate of change, one can see the relationship between individual success and the common good-between what sociologist C. Wright Mills called "private troubles and public issues."

PRISON CAMPS AND HOLDING CELLS

We are in an historic struggle of tremendous importance over which specific values will come to dominate our national life. Either we are moving toward a new synthesis between traditional commitments and new forms of personal fulfillment, or we are approaching a fragmented, anomic society, wherein the family is a shambles, the work ethic has collapsed, personal freedom is restricted, and the economy is increasingly uncompetitive. At that point the schools, which should have been the civilizing and integrating forces within our society, will be reduced to prison camps, and the classrooms will be holding cells.

As the table "The Great American 40-Year Value Shift" indicates, some of these value changes have been profound. One can argue about their functionality or dysfunctionality. In a relativistic world, one person's freedom is another person's license. America, after all, is the kingdom of the individual. But as University of Tennessee President and former Tennessee Governor Lamar Alexander observed at the recent opening of the first Japanese high school in the United States, the Meiji Gakuin High School in Sweetwater, Tennessee:

The Great American 40-Year Value Shift

1950s	*1990s*	*Consequences/Results*
Saving	Spending	Federal debt; Trade deficit
Delayed gratification	Instant gratification	Narcissism
Ozzie and Harriet	Latchkey kids	71% high school graduation rate
Certainty	Ambivalence	Marriage counseling
Investing	Leveraging	Low rate of productivity growth; Michael Milken
Unionization	Bankruptcy	Middle class decline
Lifetime employer	Outplacement	Look out for #1; Alienation
Neighborhood	Lifestyle	Community failure; Single-issue politics; Age segregation; Ethnic conflict; Gentrification
Middle class	Underclass	Drugs; Gangs; Teenage grannies; Colombia
Export	Import	Acura; Infiniti; Lexus; FAX; VCRs
Containment	Economic Security	Trade sanctions; Managed trade
Deterrence	Terrorism	Metal detectors
Upward mobility	Downward mobility	The homeless; Shrinking middle class
Duty	Divorce	Despair
"We"	"Me"	"Them"
Sexual repression	Affairs	Celibacy
Equity	Renting/leasing	Balloon payments
Organized religion	Cults; TV preachers	Authoritarianism
Heroes	Cover girls	Cynicism
Public troubles	Private issues	Greed; Fear; Insularity
B-52	*Challenger*	Pessimism
Internationalism	Isolationism	Personality politics; "Psychiatrization" of foreign leaders (Mikhail and Raisa Gorbachev as role models)
Money	More money	Even more money

(continues)

The Great American 40-Year Value Shift   *(continued)*

1950s	1990s	Consequences/Results
"Do what you're told"	"Do what you want"	"You do it"
Young	Middle age	Old
Public virtue	Personal well-being	Decline of polity; Voter alienation
Civil rights	Affirmative Action	Lawsuits and lawyers
Press conference	Photo opportunity	*People* magazine
Achievement	Fame	Political polls
Manufacturing	Service	Mitsubishi buys Rockefeller Center; Sony buys Columbia Pictures
Value-added	Mastercard	Five-year car loans; Repossessions
Problems	Pathologies	Analysis paralysis
Hope	Happiness	Preference by L'Oréal
Bomb shelters	Crack houses	Drug Czar William Bennett
Organization Man	Murphy Brown	Androgyny
NATO; Godless communists	Commie capitalists	Trading blocs; new alliances
Psychoanalysis/ neurosis	Support groups/ serial killers	Big book sales
Cheeseburger, fries shake	Cheeseburger, fries, shake	American cultural hegemony
USA	Japan	"Japanaphobia"
Regulation	Deregulation	Re-regulation
Cash	Credit	Cash

"Japanese students take more courses in three years than ours do in four. They go to school 230 days a year while ours go 180 days. They go to school one more hour each day, take home three times more homework, and take harder courses. They go to school on Saturdays while our doors are closed . . . "

We can't blame that on our teachers or administrators. It's because our students, parents, and communities don't want a better education. Those doors can be open, the school days can be longer, and the schools can be open during the summer—if we want them to be.

At some point in the near future—and that point is rapidly approaching—we will have to decide as a society that we want the schools to produce literate, informed, and competent citizens, ready to serve the national interest and the common good. The progressive failure of American schools stems from a lack of clear public standards and values-standards, values that are deeply felt within our society and that represent a commitment to the future vitality of our community and nation.

GIVING UP THE
MADISON AVENUE FANTASY

Diane Ravitch, one of America's foremost education critics, suggests that we will get the schools we deserve. In *The Troubled Crusade* (Basic Books, 1983), she writes:

> Despite our dissatisfaction, we will soon transform our educational system. It is not that it can't be done. The problem is that we lack consensus about whether there are skills everyone should have. If we believed that it was important to have a highly literate public, to have people capable of understanding history and politics and economics, to have citizens who are knowledgeable about science and technology, to have a society in which the powers of verbal communication are developed systematically and intentionally, then we would know what we wanted of our schools. Until we do, we get the schools we deserve, which accurately reflect our own confusion about the value of education.
>
> In our view, if America defaults on her responsibility to educate for competition, others will take our place. But will these others share our disdain for excess power concentrated in either the hands of government or the corporation? Will the Soviet Union grow to love human rights as we do? Shall we entrust our basic constitutional freedoms to the Japanese? Can we be sure that the Germans, this time, will seek out only what is best in the European experience?

Presented in these stark terms, most Americans should be inclined to give up the mesmerizing fantasy of an endlessly-rich America, pouring out a steady stream of ever-increasing entitlements. Americans need to awaken from a dream where nothing has a final price and where everything is available on a limitless line of credit. How can we educate our schoolchildren if the entire society lives in a Madison Avenue fantasy world?

Americans must stop defining the world purely in terms of cash flow and start thinking about long-term success—about the satisfaction that comes from exerting full effort on a task.

Americans need to think about quality and value as well, not just about quarterly dividends, leveraged buyouts, and the fashions of the moment. American leaders in both the public and private sectors need to help us redefine the nature of our lives and our perceptions of what is worthy or unworthy, honorable or dishonorable. When this happens, our schools and our society will thrive as never before.

THE CULTURE OF LEARNING

Having the right values to support education is important, but it is not the whole story. Values can take hold only in a supportive culture—a social heredity that represents the total legacy of group behavior effective in the present. Values exist in a cultural context, not in a vacuum. Culture itself is learned—it is not an automatic or instinctive heritage, but must be won anew by each succeeding generation.

So why do some nations succeed while others fail? Why did the Japanese and Germans rebuild their war-torn countries into industrial giants while Brazil, Argentina and Mexico, who have far more resources, fail to construct wealth-creating economies? Why are there virtually no economically successful countries south of the border?

These are complex questions with more than one answer, but one common theme is "culture" and the maintenance of inherited vitality. Countries (and subcultures) that stress education, economic and political freedom, delayed gratification, mutual trust and hard work create wealth. Those that do not stay poor.

Even within American culture, those groups like the Japanese, other more recent Asian immigrants such as the Vietnamese, and Jews, whose culture stresses hard work and learning, succeed in disproportionate numbers despite discrimination, while other cultures give off different signals that too often lead to disproportionate rates of failure. It is not lack of talent or some inherent inferiority, it is lack of values in a supportive cultural context that too often results in failure. Culture has the potential to overcome discrimination, poverty, even racism, if it sends the right signals.

STRESS IN THE CHANGING FAMILY

The condition of the American family is an indicator that cultural norms are failing. The American family is undergoing significant change. More families are headed by women, especially in the black community; this was the case in nearly 45 percent of the black households in 1986, compared with 28 percent in 1968. In 1986, 26 percent of white families were headed by women, as compared with only 9 percent in 1968. More and more families are headed by single parents. Only about 80 percent of white children lived with both parents in 1988, and the proportion of homeless children in shelters rose to 40 percent in 1983 from 21 percent in 1984.

Divorce plays a major role in the number of single-parent families. An economy that requires two wage earners per family plays a role in increasing the stress among parents and the time children are kept in day care centers. Drugs and poverty also play a role in producing an unstable environment.

In an article in the Fall 1989 issue of *Family Affairs Journal*, Professor David Popenoe of Rutgers put it this way:

> Fundamentally, what emerges from these cultural shifts is an ethos of radical individualism in which personal autonomy, individual rights, and social equality have gained supremacy as cultural ideals. In keeping with these ideals, the main goals of personal behavior have shifted from obligation and commitment to social units (families, communities, religions, nations) to personal choices, lifestyle options, self-fulfillment, and personal pleasure.

James Fallows, in his book *More Like Us* (Houghton Mifflin, 1989), says that "in the long run, a society's strength depends on the way that ordinary people voluntarily behave." The sum total of voluntary behaviors is what Fallows means by culture. Sociologists have made a similar distinction between primary and secondary mechanisms of social control. In general, when primary institutions, such as the family, fail, secondary mechanisms, such as schools and the police, have a hard time keeping up with deteriorating values. "Successful societies—those that progress economically and politically and can control the terms on which they deal with the outside world-succeed," Fallows continues, "because they have found ways to match individual self-interest to the collective good."

But some cultures are more supportive of appropriate and useful "voluntary behaviors" than others. Lawrence Harrison, author of the provocative book *Underdevelopment Is A State Of Mind* (Harvard, 1985) spent many years as an official in Latin America attached to the Agency for International Development. He has summarized the seven ingredients of what he calls a "useful" culture. These, he says, are the "conditions that encourage the expression of human creative capacity:"

- The expectation of fair play
- Availability of educational opportunities
- Availability of health services
- Encouragement of experimentation and criticism
- Matching of skills and jobs
- Rewards for merit and achievement
- Stability and continuity

Today, the main American educational failure is with all our children. Too many of our children know too little and are poorly motivated and prepared for the competitive society of the future. No group, majority or minority, is succeeding in sufficient numbers to save America from decline. However, black and Hispanic failure rates are disturbingly high and require special attention.

THE "ENEMY WITHIN"

The almost universal explanation for minority failure is racism and discrimination. But there are powerful cultural factors at work as well. As Glenn C. Loury, Harvard economist and author of *From Children to Citizens* (Springer-Verlag, 1987), recently put it:

> It is now beyond dispute that many of the problems of contemporary black American life lie outside the reach of effective government action and require for their successful resolution actions that can only be undertaken by the black community itself. These problems involve at their core the values, attitudes, and behaviors of individual blacks. . . . Too much of the political energy, talent, and imagination abounding in the emerging black middle class is being channeled into a struggle against an "enemy without" while the "enemy within" goes unchecked.

In *A Place on the Corner* a fascinating study of ghetto street life, University of Pennsylvania sociologist Elijah Anderson focuses on the growing gap between the ghetto and the rest of society (including middle-class blacks):

"Two competing lifestyles vie for the hearts and minds of the young person in the ghetto underclass community. The stable nuclear family with its belief in upward mobility provides one. The street culture which revolves around sex, babies, and other antisocial behavior provides the other."

We would hasten to add that other subcultures in American society can be equally dysfunctional. For example, the upper middle-class suburban culture, with its emphasis on status, money, peer pressure, and materialism, often sends exactly the wrong message to high school students from even the "best of families."

Of equal importance is the possibility that outcomes some would ascribe purely to cultural factors may have other origins. For example, Herbert L. Needleman, M.D., writing in the *New England Journal of Medicine* (January 11, 1990), describes the negative effects of long-term, low-level lead poisoning on children's academic progress and cognitive functioning. Lead poisoning is far more prevalent in lower class environments, being positively correlated with poverty itself:

Exposure to lead, even in children who remain asymptomatic, may have an important and enduring effect on the success in life of such children . . . early indicators of lead burden and behavioral deficit are strong predictors of poor school outcome . . . Higher levels of lead in childhood were also significantly associated with lower class standing in high school, increased absenteeism, lower vocabulary and grammatical reasoning scores, poorer hand-eye coordination, longer reaction times, and slower finger tapping.

Schools can do only so much to counter broad cultural trends. Schools, in the case of lead poisoning, can do only so much to combat environmental unfairness, itself a product of lower socioeconomic class. Schools can reinforce values, but they cannot correct for all cultural deficiencies. The American school system today is as much a victim of cultural and environmental failure as its students are of uncontrollable shifts in national values.

LAYING CLAIM TO THE NEXT MILLENNIUM

We cannot assume that past success will ensure future success; past strengths will not be enough. We must overcome our problems. They will not cure themselves. We must find real solutions to our obvious educational failures, especially the failure of our brightest and most talented youngsters from every socioeconomic class to perform to the best of their ability. We must act now to reverse decline and to counteract value changes that are heading us in the wrong direction. We must not allow negative cultural forces to overwhelm the best parts of the American experience. Above all, we must be realistic and not hide behind political slogans or vague promises that shield us from the truth.

America can maintain its greatness. Our schools can succeed. But if we do not bring our best values to the fore, this generation's legacy to the next will be a poor one indeed. It will be a legacy of diminished hopes and disappointed dreams. The choice of futures is ours. We must learn to care again about the common good. If we do not, the next millennium will belong to someone else.

Richard Lamm served two terms as the Governor of Colorado and continues his public service as a scholar at the University of Denver. His capacity for articulating public policy issues, particularly in the fields of health and education, have earned him a national audience.

The Key

WILLIAM A. GUIFFRE

Prejudice,
Key unique,
Locks in—
Locks out—
Yet never turns the other way.

Bill Guiffre has devoted his life to teaching young people. During his career, he was a teacher and administrator. Now, in retirement, he writes children's stories and poetry.

The Balkanization of America

J. NELSON HOFFMAN

I AGREE WITH GOVERNOR LAMM on his views of the need to build community. Like him, I am concerned that many of the very well-meaning people who promote the cause of diversity may be unintentionally creating forces which separate us as a nation, not unite us.

My thinking on this issue goes back fifty or sixty years—to my childhood, when I learned all the ethnic epithets that people use when they are in the "them" vs. "us" mode. I played on a street with black playmates, and as I grew up, the "N-word" became more objectionable and I didn't like jokes built on that word.

At the University of Rochester, I learned a word that has become more significant, more important to me as I matured. That word is Balkanization.

I want to make sure my children teach that word to my grandchildren. I want them to understand the hate, the wars, the persecution, and suffering that other nations endure. And I want them to understand several related words:

stereotype
anti-Semitism
racial discrimination and hatred of:
    Afro-Americans
    Hispanics, particularly Mexicans
    Asians
gender bias
economic class hardships.

I learned the meaning of the word Balkanization from an economics professor visiting from England. The point came up in a discussion of how currencies were affected by international politics. I believe he was as much historian as economist since he took us well outside the boundaries of our economics textbook.

The professor wanted us to understand how the historical conflicts in southern Europe affected the current political and economic climate. For example, both Greece and Turkey have proven stalwart allies of America, yet century-old rivalries prevent any sort of enduring peace and goodwill between them. The hatreds of the religious groups found in the various nations created at the end of World War II were below the surface and kept in check by the rivalry of the West against the Soviet Union. When that competition ended, the Balkans once again became a battleground of ethnic and religious hatred and war. With the end of the Cold War, ancient animosities blew up, and the Balkans once again disintegrated into armed conflict.

The professor made the point that whenever a political entity is divided into fragments, the whole is no longer strong enough to keep its integrity.

That is the root of my concern in the present day.

In the sixties and seventies, the civil rights movement was about winning equality and integrating black America into the mainstream. Now, I see various leaders promoting separatism. I think that is very unfortunate because of the great benefits of integration. I have seen how it can bring black Americans into every profession, political office, or new business opportunity that this nation offers.

Similarly, my company made every effort to bring immigrant Hispanic workers fully into the work force—to move them from the factory floor into the front office. We stressed the learning of English and thought of ourselves as a bicultural company. It is clear that the language of international business is English, and opportunity in our company was related to gaining a command of this important communication skill.

The university campuses are another place I see diversity emphasized, at the cost of unity. When I was in college, there was concern that black or Jewish students would be excluded from social life and from the Greek system of sororities and fraternities.

Now, 50 years later, I see a voluntary resegregation occurring as Hispanic, African-Americans, Asians, Orthodox Jews, and many other cultural and religious groups, seek separate housing, schools, and social clubs.

I certainly respect everyone's right of free association. But it seems to me the college years are a time to get to know people from outside one's own race and economic background. In an increasingly closer and interconnected world, it is important to take those opportunities to meet people from other nations and cultures.

Stereotypes. It is easy to understand how negative stereotypes get started. Drama, both live and on television, exaggerates and emphasizes the strengths and weakness of a given race, class, or nationality of people. Comedians create humor by playing on the perceived traits of races, age groups, and stereotypes. I have learned to be suspicious of any attempt to group character or characteristics to race, nation, sex, or gender.

Anti-Semitism. In the last 20 years of my life, my best friend and business partner has been a man of the Jewish faith, Bruce Greenbaum. I love him like a son—our families enjoy each other's company, and the bonds of trust, concern, and affection are strong. Bruce and I created a great company and a wonderful life together.

When I hear remarks based on racial and anti-Semitic stereotypical terms, my blood boils. Thirty years ago, when I was helping my children in learning about their Catholic faith, I had great difficulty with the portions of the Bible I regarded as promoting anti-Semitism. Today, in Bible study groups, I still meet people who blame the Crucifixion on the Jews. Recently, I was pleased when the current Pope brought this problem to the surface and acknowledged the errors of the past.

Racial Discrimination.   I believe our society is truly sensitized to the inherent injustice of racial discrimination and the information age presents both an opportunity and a challenge: Those who study and learn will benefit, independent of race, color, or sex. But if individuals get stuck in old models of racial stereotypes, those who are left behind will become poorer, less educated, and less able to participate in the nation's future.

Gender Bias.   I will continue to take flak from my oldest daughter Karen when I refer to young ladies as girls, and when I encourage my grandsons, but not my granddaughters, in sports. I would like to think that I have taught her well, but the truth is, I am learning from my daughter in this instance.

As part of the industrial establishment that recognized the role young ladies wanted to play and were prepared and motivated to play in the 1980s and 1990s, I am acutely aware of the career ambitions and fulfillment for young women that comes with achievement in the professional world.

I am equally aware of the tremendous blessing I have in a wife who chose the career of spouse, housewife, and mother to our children.

I am grateful I lived in a less complicated world. I can hardly imagine what the new technological age will mean for the opportunity and choices both sexes will have.

Economic Class.   In the history of the world, the United States has brought more people a better standard of living than any other nation or any other economic or political theory. I also share the pessimist's concern for the poor people who have not been able to get aboard the train of economic and knowledge progress.

My life began in 1933 at the height of the Great Depression. My generation was driven by the fear of poverty and propelled by the economic miracle that occurred after World War II. Education provided the levitation. Yet, many could not, or did not, take advantage of the available opportunities.

Now, as we face this new millennium, the stratification of our society is aggravated if young people cannot, or do not, achieve the knowledge base and skills necessary to earn a decent living in the new world of technology that is being created. Joan and I thank God for the educational experiences we had.

Joan and I have traveled over much of the world, and every time we come home we thank God for being Americans. To our children and grandchildren I say, "Be a fighter to shape the society you live in and fight for a tolerant and unified America."

The words of Martin Luther King are truths for all time:

> When we let freedom ring, when we let it ring from every village and every hamlet, from every state and city, we will be able to speed up that day when all God's children, black men and white men (and women), Jews and Gentiles, Protestants and Catholics, will be able to join hands and sing in the words of that old Negro spiritual, "Free at last! Free at last! Thank God Almighty, we are free at last . . .
>
> . . . I have a dream that one day this nation will rise up and live out the true meaning of this creed—We hold these truths to be self evident: that all men (and women) are created equal.

When that day comes, a word like Balkanization will be used to describe a past problem we solved successfully.

As we've created a nation the last fifty years that struggles with the equality of its people, we sometimes lose sight of what is most important.

Valuing Things More Than People

JAY THOMPSON

A COMMENT BY A LOCAL RADIO ANNOUNCER has helped me focus on an important lesson I learned during my formative years. The announcer's exact words are gone, but the essence of his thinking remains with me. He expressed the idea that in today's society, compared to that of fifty years ago, we seem to value things rather than people. As a parent and a public educator I say, "How true!"

My childhood in a small, then-rural town during the post-recession and war years was certainly more simple and basic than the affluent lifestyle that youngsters enjoy today. But those lean times forced us to know and rely on the people in our lives. After all, that was about all we had.

With few, or none, of the material things that children today have, we were left to our own devices to create a life. We interacted with family, friends, and other townspeople of all ages and positions in our small, restricted geographical area. We learned to respect those folks for their commitment, their work ethic, their dedication to family life, and their willingness to devote time and effort to help growing children develop into responsible citizens.

Family life for me during those early years was a three-generation affair—grandparents, parents, and children were all under one roof. Everyone in the family had to share the burdens in order for life to be enjoyable. My father spent long hours at work, including Saturdays, and then found time to plant, weed, and harvest a large "victory garden" as our part of the war effort.

My mother spent the entire work week keeping the house and family operating smoothly. She planned and prepared meals for seven in between spending one day in the washroom, a day and a half at the ironing board, and two days housecleaning. It was obvious that making our house a home was a long, sometimes tedious task. My mother felt that being a homemaker was her greatest responsibility and didn't join the outside-the-home work force until all of her children were past high school. Dedication to family was important, no matter the time and effort spent.

Those days afforded much time to know and converse with each other. A yearly treat was being taken out to dinner by my grandparents, since we rarely dined at others' homes, and already had a full table at our own house. After school, conversations happened easily as my mother had warm cookies ready for hungry students, who were in those years eager to reflect on the day's encounters. In our small town, supporting your children in their activities was easy. Everyone knew each other, so each gathering was almost like a large family group. Parents were there to support their children at home and at play. And they did!

Children also played a part in the tasks of a homeowner. We weeded gardens, mowed lawns, washed and dried dishes, and kept our rooms neat. We did all this rather willingly, for that was the model our parents set. But there was also the chance to play with and enjoy our peers. We had time on our hands, and no televisions, computers, or video games to occupy us. What to do? That was not a problem, for we had developed a mutual respect among our friends and for their ideas and ingenious ways of creating recreation.

A small town center gave a generation of growing boys and girls a variety of ideas and venues for fun, and there was always time to curl up with a good book or visit the community library. We made our own fun and were supported in this by our peers and our parents. Much could be done right at home—in the yard, on a porch, or in a playroom—and our home was not an exception. We had a large backyard, ideal for playing baseball or croquet, as well as evening games. There were summers of pinochle games and playing among the pillars of the porch. We developed a "grocery store" in a deserted chicken coop and a "rodeo," using an overstuffed elephant, for our parents to attend. These experiences helped us become interdependent and appreciative of others.

Lasting friendships develop when you know people better than just to wave to in passing. With the number of students, teachers, neighbors, and service people young people see in their busy lives today, is it any wonder they can't remember the name of their first-grade teacher or the local bus driver? Sixty years ago, we knew and respected the town librarian, grocery store clerks, and the local barber. We knew them by name, and they knew us. They kept us on the right path as we grew up, and we could appreciate the hard work they did. We knew where they lived and where they worshipped; we mourned them when they died.

Knowing people well helps us value them, whether as family, as community, or as friends. How much have I succeeded in passing this idea on to future generations? Perhaps this is done in many ways without even thinking. For example, it is easy for a teacher to gain the confidence of students by being open and fair, as well as working hard at his or her job. The same goes at home, when a parent models a strong work ethic. Each adult in a young person's life occupies only a very small percentage of a day. But with a little effort, you can really get to know young people and let them get to know you. Then it is easy to let them see through your actions that there is a wonderful reward to valuing people rather than things.

Jay Thompson, a former high school classmate of mine, is an elementary school teacher. I believe he's right on target with his assessment of our consumer-driven society.

Whatever Happened to Sin?

JAMES RYAN

IN EARLY DECEMBER 1991, a lead editorial in the *Wall Street Journal* talked of a twenty-five-year sexual revolution and the hopes of many that a counterrevolution was somewhere on the horizon. In the previous few months, a nationwide audience of the American people watched and listened as a U.S. Senate committee discussed aspects of a porno film, listened to a nephew of President John F. Kennedy tell the evening news about a sexual incident he had been involved in, and watched while the New York Board of Education handed out condoms to adolescents.

The *Journal* article noted other bits of evidence that would strongly attest to a moral breakdown in our society, concluding that perhaps all of this had something to do with a concept alien to our contemporary culture—namely, sin.

I was fascinated by this article, for here was the *Wall Street Journal*, a popular, nonreligious periodical, talking about sin! I hadn't heard sin mentioned either in church or in polite conversation for at least twenty years. And I had often wondered how such a concept— one that made a significant impact on me—had just disappeared.

What follows is pretty much a personal lament framed by a modest amount of research on the subject. It isn't meant to be a learned treatise on the historical or theological aspects of sin, but rather a heartfelt expression of something that is very much a part of my psyche.

I suppose we all look back on our upbringing and attempt to understand the origins of our personality and, especially, of our value system. I believe my values, as for most people, came from my family, in particular an Irish mother who spoke often of sin and morality. These were interwoven into her own philosophy, which was both pragmatic and dogmatic. Those raised in the Catholic faith during that era, and especially those who attended Catholic schools, know the attention that was paid to sin. There were the venial sins and the "killer" mortal sins. And while much of it seems overdone in retrospect, I suggest that we've thrown the baby out with the bath water, not just modifying but virtually eliminating the very guidelines that promote a moral lifestyle.

WHAT IS SIN?

To me, sin relates to the Ten Commandments and the seven cardinal, or "deadly," sins: anger, greed, pride, sloth, envy, lust, and gluttony. Putting definitions aside, it seems to me that sin represents a dramatic turning away from God, a selfish focusing on ourselves and choosing our way rather than God's. St. Augustine described it as turning "away from the universal whole to the individual part."

Kevin Kelly, in *The Changing Paradigms of Sin*, attempted further refinement of this understanding. The "turning away" from God also became a turning away from other people, and he labeled this paradigm "person injuring." Sin could also be understood through direct communication with God rather than relying on how others define it. Kelly called this "heart condition." A third paradigm was what he called "historical-cultural realism," wherein institutions and social structures "act" in ways that are dehumanizing to others. It is, in other words, a culturally conditioned behavior with a moral void. Slavery fits this definition, for while it was sinful in its exploitation of blacks, it is often seen as a collective guilt of "the times" rather than a personal guilt. Kelly added to the definition of sin with a focus on disobedience, both the obvious disobedience of authority (the Commandments, cardinal sins, church authority) and the feelings of guilt that have no relation to real life—the concept of original sin—which he labeled disease.

The definitions of sin and the nuances of understanding it are many, but I want to move on to the question that really perplexes me: Whatever happened to sin?

THE DISAPPEARANCE OF SIN

While I am unaware of any recent public discussions of sin, I fully expected my library research to be fruitful in understanding its disappearance. I naturally anticipated that the *Catholic Periodical and Literature Index* would have numerous references to sin, and I wasn't disappointed. Most of it, however, was heavy reading and so focused in interpretation that it was of little value to my generalist approach. What I wasn't expecting was the paucity of material relating to sin in the *Reader's Guide to Periodical Literature* as well as a complete "strikeout" in the *New York Times* index. The latter produced not one article on sin in the past five years, although there were at least fifty references to Frank Sinatra, who was next in line alphabetically.

It seems sin has just up and disappeared from common usage. It used to be a proud word, a strong word, a serious word. Now it's a word we either use not at all or apologize for. It was a word used often by United States presidents, from Lincoln through Eisenhower. The word sin was last used by President Eisenhower in 1953; according to one reference I found, no president since then has used this word to describe a national failing. They have talked of pride, self-righteousness, moral decay, and a number of other shortcomings but have avoided using the word sin. And just a week ago during a penance service, I listened to the priest use words such as alienation and supreme alienation in place of venial and mortal sin.

As I ruminate about the disappearance of sin, I can't help but tie it to what I perceive as a morality gap in today's society. Is it coincidental, or is there some cause and effect at work here? Have moral values diminished because we no longer talk of sin as a guideline, or has the moral breakdown eroded our sense of the importance of sin?

To the extent that sin is the "flight from responsibility," as eminent psychiatrist Karl Menninger noted years ago, then perhaps it is our cultural abandonment of responsibility that almost mandates that we expunge sin from our consciousness—otherwise the guilt would be too extreme.

We older Catholics have witnessed a dramatic change in morality, from the painful demands of an earlier era to today's "anything goes" outlook. Much of this has to do with a contemporary view of God that has resulted from several mixed-blessing changes that have affected our church. The liberalization of the church through the pronouncements of Vatican II, the demythologizing of scripture, the change from Latin to English, the giving back of the church to the people with an emphasis on fulfilling the will of individual conscience, the defection of the clergy, and American's ambivalence about the church's position on birth control have all undermined the institution's credibility and authority. At the same time, youth have encountered in the homilies and hymns a Jesus who was all-loving and wanted them to "be not afraid," as He would right all wrongs. If Jesus is all forgiving, without even requiring an apology, is it any wonder that there is no such thing as sin anymore?

Pope John Paul II has noted another reason for the disappearance of sin in our society: an attitude that trivializes human responsibility for our actions. "On the basis of certain affirmations of psychology," he has said, "concern to avoid creating feelings of guilt or to place limits on freedom leads to a refusal ever to admit any shortcomings." He has also advised that, "the restoration of a proper sense of sin is the first way of facing the grave spiritual crises looming over man today." Pope Pius XII, in an earlier time, used the same kind of reasoning to conclude that "the sin of the century is the loss of the sense of sin."

If in the past examining our consciences led us to see sin everywhere, today we have trouble recognizing it anywhere. You may remember a Woody Allen movie called *Crimes and Misdemeanors*. It is the story of Judah Rosenthal, a successful opthamalogist who seems to be leading the perfect life as husband, father, and pillar of the community—until his mistress threatens to tell all to his wife. Though not a religious man, Judah seeks advice from his rabbi, who urges him to confess to his wife and to God. But Judah is unwilling to take the risk; he is not looking for forgiveness but an escape. Thus he plots the murder of his mistress. After the terrible deed has been done, Judah teeters on the brink of confession or of a nervous breakdown but succumbs to neither. As time goes by, he is amazed that his wife never discovers the affair and the murder is blamed on a burglar. His business and marriage both prosper, and he learns to lie to his rabbi. At one point he summarizes how the world seems to work: rationalize sin, deny guilt, and life will go on better than before.

This movie is really the story of two murders—that of the mistress and of a man's conscience. In a systematic fashion, Judah got rid of God by denying His existence. Once God was out of the way, Judah could redefine his standard of justice, a system where right and wrong no longer served as absolutes. Once God had been displaced and justice redefined, the tiresome, heavy-handed guilt that seemed so prevalent just disappeared. In a way this movie serves as a metaphor for my thesis that sin has been erased from our language, and we have redefined our standards to suit our not-always-noble purposes.

Sin certainly didn't disappear overnight, although it seemed so to me. Some of the references I found suggest that several scientific discoveries around the turn of the century have played a role in the disappearance of sin. Hypnosis, psychoanalysis, and the conditioned reflex phenomena all, in one way or another, suggested that an individual wasn't fully responsible for his or her actions, and, therefore, sinful acts could be beyond one's control. Hypnotic suggestion provided evidence that one could be induced to do or think something without even realizing it. Psychoanalysis revealed the conscious and unconscious love and hate attachments that dominate our basic personality structure. And the conditioned reflex phenomena, which later became the basis of behaviorism, essentially removed much of the sin/guilt attachment from the human condition. Pavlov—and later B. F. Skinner—realized that internal determinants of an act (a conditioned response) could affect notions of intention, motivation, and premeditation. In short, you could be "conditioned" to sin by factors beyond your control, just as Pavlov's dogs were conditioned to salivate when a bell rang.

Other social scientists and the like would argue that the disappearance of sin was the manifestation of a new human compassion, which was unwilling to impose the severity of old and harsher penalties to the transgressions of a modern era. In the old days, penalties for displeasing those in power, whether parental, civil, economic, or divine, were heavy handed. This intertwining of sin and penalty was ingrained in society. The idea of sin, however, began to disappear because it "violated" the current standards of decency and comfort. Rather than modify the penalties for sin, it was easier to forget sin altogether.

Other theories abound on the vanishing concept of sin. One suggests that as sins have been converted into crimes, with the passage of new laws, they still exist but are called by a different name. It has become the civilized custom to attempt to legislate morality and coerce virtue through the court system. The less tangible concept of sin became less important, then, as the number of behavior benchmarks (laws) proliferated.

Similarly, over time sin has been converted into a symptom or symptoms of disease, and diseases, as we know, are hardly sins. When a man killed a stranger years ago, it was considered not only a heinous crime, but also a very grievous sin. As medical science evolved and we began to explore human behavior and its abnormalities, murder has been redefined as a symptom of a deranged personality. If a person could be proved insane at the time of a murder, then there was no criminal intention and, hence, no sin committed. This theory has produced a conflict between hard-core moralists, who believe that most, if not all, behavior is conscious and voluntary, and those who see behavior as involuntary, automatic, and reactive—a symptom and not a sin. When you think about it, is anger a sin or a symptom? How about kleptomania, obesity, or addiction? And aren't we more likely to excuse bad behavior by thinking of it as the symptom of a stressful lifestyle?

Another theory focuses on the transfer of responsibility for irresponsible actions from the individual to the shoulders of many. If a group is made to share responsibility, the heavy burden of guilt and the perception of evil are diffused. Perhaps nowhere is this more clearly illustrated than in the morality of a "just" war, in which individual actions of murder, mayhem, arson, sabotage, and cruelty are collectively exonerated. The individual action, sinful in its isolation, is acceptable when considered under the umbrella of a group's morality.

A similar analogy relates to the sins of the corporation, for example, the insider trading scams of Boesky and Milken where the corporate shield protected immoral behavior. Before the shield collapsed, it was easy to point a finger at the actions of Corporation A and Corporation B to justify your own corporation's similar indiscretions or egregious behavior.

In all of these theories, a dominant theme emerges: that the ideas of sin and guilt, which formerly served as a restraint on action, have been eroded by the presumption that the individual has less control over his or her behavior than previously assumed, and thus any sense of personal responsibility or guilt is inappropriate. This idea gives comfort and relief to some and becomes an alarming threat to others.

WHAT ARE THE EFFECTS?

What are the effects of this new moral philosophy? The obvious one, of course, is the erosion of the idea of sin itself and the transference of blame and guilt. New models of child rearing and teaching have resulted from these changes in customs and standards. There are no "bad children" anymore, only "bad parents," and a new emphasis has been placed on tenderness and love in child rearing. Words like bad, wicked, and immoral have been dropped from our parenting vocabularies, for they are considered threatening and old-fashioned.

The suggestion that a particular behavior results from determining forces and factors outside of the individual has led some to doubt that such behavior can be easily controlled or modified. And the old sinful acts are no longer deemed immoral or wrong. If a behavior is really wrong, it is termed a crime or a disease.

I, for one, don't believe that sin can be explained away that easily. While acknowledging the impact of these theories of disease, deviancy, and behaviorism, I still believe that most of our behavior results from the exercise of free will and that the guidelines embodied in the "old" concept of sin still provide appropriate parameters for a moral lifestyle today.

CLOSING THE MORALITY GAP

Along with the disappearance of sin, we have created a morality gap in our society. The statistics that support my theory are overwhelming. While I don't want to fill this essay with numbers, just recall the incidents of "wilding" that became part of the ever-increasing crime statistics; the AIDS pandemic that so dominates our news; and the public disclosure of our political leaders' immoral or indiscreet behavior.

A survey of incoming freshman at St. John Fisher College, which was part of a national survey conducted at other colleges and universities, summarized the evidence of a morality gap. In answer to one of the questions, more than 52 percent of the respondents felt that having sexual relations was okay, even if you had known your partner for only a short period of time. Another survey, taken in Europe in 1985 and reported by a Dutch sociologist, revealed that 40 percent of those interviewed had never experienced any feelings of regret about their actions—a lack of moral awareness on a frightening scale.

The relatively new field of "therapeutic psychology" places the emphasis on being pleased or gratified with yourself, not on being saved. Because there is a certain psychological fragility to this condition, the theory goes, a therapeutic cannot live with any sense of his or her own sinfulness.

The question arises, What can we do about this moral decline? Whose job is it to preach, teach, and live by example? While I think we all need to play a role in this revolution—parents, teachers, police, doctors, political leaders, the media—I believe the clergy should bear the greatest responsibility, as guardians of our faith and moral character. They have permitted, even encouraged, a slide away from the standards of sin because to do otherwise would have involved fighting the tide of secularism with seemingly old-fashioned and out-of-date clichés and ideas.

Let me close with a short homily from Dr. Kenneth Mauldin of the First Presbyterian Church in Topeka, Kansas, one who has spoken to the problem of moral decline and its solution with clarity:

> As one who previously took pleasure in believing that he was "liberal" and "progressive," it is not enjoyable now to be in the role of a "conservative" or a "puritan." Puritanism is so disdained today, and so jibed at, that one recoils from the very word itself as though it were some sort of disease. Yet, I doubt that the cure for Puritanism is impuritanism, and I have genuine difficulty adjusting to the blatant unrestraint of today. And a preacher must be true to himself, and proclaim what he believes to be true, whether it be popular or not.

We live in an undisciplined age. It concerns me that apparently our clamor is for right without responsibility, for privilege without painful striving, for cultural and intellectual shortcuts that should be described as self-deceiving.

The Greeks had a saying that the fair things in life are hard; that strength—be it physical, mental, or moral—was gained only by effort and self-discipline. Is this truth outdated? Must we not admit that, as a people, we are morally and religiously undisciplined? In the name of freedom and liberation, we have fled every yoke and every restriction as though work, art, study, and religion are disciplines we can do without.

The very concept of self-discipline has come under attack, and my personal conviction is that this is one reason that for many people life has lost its dimensions. The heights and depths are gone, and life has become flat and dull and cheap and frivolous. The pleasures sought are the pleasures of a smoking heart and a pulsating nerve and when the thrill is gone, the refuge is drink or drugs.

It may very well be that as adults we have been so captured by the cult of comfort ourselves that we are incapable of challenging our own young people with the great needs of a world that is bewildered, uprooted, beaten down, and more than half-starved.

Whose responsibility is it to spread the gospel of sin? Obviously, those who diligently search for wisdom and enlightenment—the philosophers.

James Ryan is a successful contractor and lifelong student of philosophy. We were high school competitors in Rochester, New York.

The Sexual Revolution:
A Message to My Grandchildren

J. NELSON HOFFMAN

*A*NOTHER MAJOR CHANGE in the last fifty years has been in the area of human intimacy. The term "sexual revolution" brings to mind a number of meanings depending upon one's life experiences. Let me attempt to explain what I mean.

I do not mean to include the "feminine revolution," which I strongly support. The historical view of men being superior to women is thankfully dead.

The "revolution" I can not support is the one where there is a confusion of standards of what is private and what is public in relations between a man and woman.

The "revolution" I rebel against is the one where traditional standards (in western Judeo-Christian terms) have been discarded, and there are seemingly no prohibitions against premarital sex, adultery, or virtually any kind of sex in general.

The "revolution" I find demeaning is the one where the view of intercourse is something that is not sacred, not limited to marriage, and oftentimes treated as a recreational sport.

The "revolution" I am against is the one where we provide condoms to teenagers rather than credible rationales for deferring sex.

The "revolution" I find troubling is the one where there is a constant sexual stimulus in most advertising, entertainment, and in many daily dialogues. What was mysterious is now profane.

The truism "familiarity breeds contempt" is seen in the frequency with which double entendre has become the standard of television and movie humor. There is a de facto contest to see which set of writers and producers of TV shows or movies can push the censors to the limit! They call it artistic license; I call it licentiousness.

My view of this change in society—this "sexual revolution" is really a "sexual dissolution." In the end, it will have the same destructive results as the Communist Revolution: Millions of people will end up destitute after living through decades and generations of confusion, and the relationships and institutions that could have made their lives meaningful and significant will be destroyed.

My views are grounded in Genesis. As part of God's plan for creation, he gave to woman and man the power to create new life. He intended that act of creation to be an extension of his love for humankind. And it is my belief that all life is sacred.

The science of all things related to man's mind and body is growing at an ever-accelerating pace. In my lifetime, the issue of birth and birth control has been altered by new advances in medicine and new technology. Now, we have new detection methods for determining the time of fertility, the sex of an infant, or any potential defects the new baby may have. With this new information, comes new responsibilities and new questions about the rights to privacy.

Each day, new breakthroughs in science challenge us to reexamine our beliefs and values. In *Time* magazine (March 29, 1999), Frederick Golden discussed the impact of in vitro fertilization:

"These innovations have freed women from the tyranny of their biological clock, triggered an explosion of multiple births, even made the sex act irrelevant in conception, all the while setting the stage for still more unsettling spectacles to come, such as human cloning."

Given the present circumstances, one could conclude that the act of bringing children into the world, as a supreme pledge of the love and commitment between man and wife, is now obsolete. I do not think so. As stated by Melody and Bob Durham later in this book, "Raising healthy, responsible children is one of life's greatest privileges, and greatest responsibilities. But raising children is also one of life's greatest pleasures."

To my grandchildren, I would like to speak about the dual concept of privilege and responsibility:

You are at the most privileged time of your life—your parents provide food, shelter, and clothing, your teachers and coaches are focused on your learning and your future success. Society is structured to help you succeed. If, I repeat, *if* you are willing to accept responsibility. As you become an adult, the period when you are provided for ends, and one must accept the responsibility of becoming a provider. It is a time when one must exercise self control, not give in to passions and impulses.

In this age, where the expression "sexually active" is used so loosely, let me offer a few thoughts. Teen-age years are a time of growth, testing, and preparation for your life's work. It is a daunting time, when the sexual drives are building momentum, while at the same time, your educational challenges are the greatest. In our educational meritocracy, education must be pursued in depth, so studies rightly assume center stage during these years. An end comes to your days of childhood and you now have the responsibilities of being an adult. But you also receive the privileges of being an adult.

When I was growing up, my father and grandfather instilled in me the importance of becoming a "head-of-household" provider. Granddad was a great example of a highly skilled craftsman, and Dad began his work life as a textile worker.

Today, in the information age, the emphasis is on intellectual skills over manual skills. Women are pursuing the same goals and careers as men, with the same responsibilities, and the role of "provider" no longer rests exclusively on the shoulders of males.

The lesson that I was taught was: a happy and successful life is built on a good education. That education was paid for by the deferral of sexual passion. That deferral of sexual passion, the chance to act responsibly with self-control in spite of your naturally-occurring sexual passion, is one of the greatest challenges you have at this point in your life. That is as true today as when I accepted it 50 years ago.

We hope the ideas presented in this book will help resurrect this "old-fashioned" message to young adults everywhere. We hope that all parents will be successful in showing their children positive alternatives to this concept of being "sexually active."

Let me set forth a premise that I believe is essential to changing the current situation:

"No child should be brought into the world unless the parents are committed to providing that child with love, the material necessities of life, and the willingness to educate, instruct and mentor that child on the skills it takes to become a healthy, moral, responsible citizen."

This is a huge commitment, not to be taken lightly. It is a commitment which takes twenty years to complete successfully! It is such a difficult task, and it takes so long, I do believe that the only time this commitment should be undertaken is within the institution of marriage, and only when the couple is committed to seeing the job through to success.

Anthropologists may say that man is a polygamous animal, but this will not sway my religious faith that God gave us the Sacrament of Marriage. Mechanical and chemical means may be available to prevent conception from occurring and abortion may be a legal choice for people to choose when unwanted conception occurs. These are not choices for me.

This is where the current confusion of language occurs: having sex and making love have become synonymous. I have a different view. Sex is the coupling of people interested in satisfaction not conception. That is quite different from two people who are showing their love for each other, are committed for life, and will sacrifice, even life itself, for their love of their spouse, and the support of any new life they bring into this world.

There can be little doubt that the exploding new technology of medicine will bring us more choices pertaining to the creation of new life. Let us hope that respect for the *sacredness of that life* guides our children in choosing among those options.

It breaks my heart to think of very young adults, at times, children having more children. As I look at poverty around the world, it seems to me that an unthinking act that creates new life lies at the core of the problem. I pray that in the new millennium the value of each and every new life will be treasured.

SECTION TWO

Home, School,
Places of Worship,
and Work

Opportunities to Build Values

IN THE LAST CHAPTER, Governor Lamm and Richard Caldwell
described how modern America has changed in the last few
decades. Success is now defined primarily in terms of individual
success: wealth, power, or fame. In contrast, fifty years ago success
was defined much differently, and an individual's success was more
intertwined with the communal values of their family, church, and
country. For example, fifty years ago patriotism was a treasured, essential value. Now, it is often criticized or ridiculed.

In Section Two, we follow de Tocqueville's model and look at how
the vitality of communities and groups of people who surround a

person's life—family, church, school, or workplace—affects the welfare of the individuals involved in those communities. How are these groups affected by the values and leadership of their members? How do these communities provide opportunities for an individual to formulate leadership skills and life values?

As we participate in our daily lives in families, communities, careers, and places of worship, two consequences result:

- We form our individual character.
- We create the health and well-being of the societies and communities which surround us.

In exploring these consequences, two metaphors come to mind: the spinning of thread or yarn and the weaving of cloth and fabric.

The Threads of Individual Choice, the Fabrics of Society

J. NELSON HOFFMAN

WHEN MAN DISCOVERED that the fibers of cotton, flax, or wool could be spun into interwoven continuous lengths, the result created new properties such as strength and warmth. The metaphor is used to illustrate the fact that yarns or thread create new performance because each of the individual fibers is intimately mixed, spun, and pulled together to create something stronger or different from the individual fiber.

In a similar fashion, as we go about our daily lives, we are spinning threads. We make intellectual, emotional, and spiritual choices, all interwoven to create our character and personality. If the spiritual fiber is missing or weak, the thread is less strong. Perhaps that is why people speak of an individual having a strong moral fiber as part of their values.

In the movie *Gandhi*, one image has significant meaning for me: Gandhi sitting on a mat with a spinning frame on his lap. This wonderful, humble man, with huge problems facing him, spent part of his day in the simple, ancient art of spinning thread from cotton fibers. As he worked, he prayed and thought about ways to bring together the contentious people of his country. He didn't seek power, fame, or money, yet he became one of the most influential individuals of the past century.

The invention of the loom and the process of weaving created cloth or fabric which provided a whole new set of opportunities for the ancient societies which used these new inventions. Woven cloth or fabric could be fashioned into clothing to provide warmth, sewn into containers for the transport of grain, or used to create sails for ships and armies to travel great distances.

WEAVING THE FABRIC OF SOCIETY

Our second metaphor employs fabric and the process of weaving to illustrate how our individual decisions determine the effectiveness of the principal communities of our lives.

We view communities as opening up new opportunities not available in our individual lives. We group communities as they occur in life. Our first group consists of family, tribe, or neighborhood—places where our first learning and nurturing begins. Our second group is geographic—city, county, state, and nation. They provide the framework from which we derive our security and sense of freedom. The third group is the academic institutions—from elementary school through college or university—which provide us with knowledge. Places of worship, where we strengthen our spiritual life and find the philosophical direction we need, constitute the fourth group. And the final group is the workplace, where we make a living and seek fulfillment in a rewarding career.

In thinking about how each of these institutions relate to the individual members in these organizations, I find the image of a loom and the process of weaving as a helpful metaphor. Stretching from top to bottom are a regular array of taut threads called the warp threads which provide the structure and foundation of the fabric.

In each of the main communities of life there are a few basic common threads—or common actions—which make that group successful. The first is the *sense of belonging and connectedness* that flows between the individual and the team, family, or worship community. The second is the *sense of commitment*. We generally think of this as a characteristic of the individual, but the loyalty the individual shows to the institution must be returned. The third thread is a *nurturing thread*. It involves growth, nourishment, training and education, love or affection, and the providing of necessities. The fourth is the *capacity to know good and evil*, both individually and collectively, and to act accordingly.

The process of weaving involves working the horizontal threads through the vertical threads. It is this action, this process, that creates fabric. Similarly, most of the actions we take in cooperation with other like-minded people creates the "fabric of societies" which surrounds us.

There is a wide range of fabrics for every kind of purpose: from a lightweight, delicate silk of great beauty to a sturdy, heavyweight canvas which provides strength and durability. In our metaphor, each of our individual and collective actions—at home, in the family, at work, or as a volunteer in the community—weaves the fabric of our life values.

Peter Drucker, one of America's most respected business scholars, has stated that organizations are defined, not by what they say or talk about, but rather by *what they do*. Unless a group's vision or mission statement is implemented with action, then it is mere rhetoric.

In Section Two, we present the thoughts and actions of our contributors as they discuss their participation in the institutions and communities which are the main focus of their lives.

NURTURING HEALTHY FAMILIES AND RESPONSIBLE CHILDREN

The Critical Role of Parenting

—————

WHILE FAMILIES COME IN ALL COMBINATIONS in our modern society, I believe that the role of parenting is such an all encompassing job and so important in the formation of a child's later success, that this role is best performed by a couple in a stable relationship.

— A GOOD MARRIAGE —

Where does successful parenting originate? To me, it starts with the foundation of a successful family—a good marriage. While there are many successful, single parents who are raising healthy children, it is my feeling that modern life demands so much of our time that it takes two parents to keep up with active children. It is the parents' challenge to motivate their children. Ideally, it is two parents who are committed to this challenge and committed to making a good marriage.

Marriage: One + One = One

WILLIAM A. GUIFFRE

Not I or my
Nor me or mine;
Not you or your
Nor thee or thine;
For if a marriage is to be,
Then mine is ours,
And I is we.

My Life as Husband and Father

ROBERT PILE

I WAS BORN IN THE SMALL TOWN of Friedens, Somerset County, in Western Pennsylvania. Except for the forty-six months I spent in the Marine Corp during World War II, I've lived my entire life in Friedens. My parents were Ross I. Pile and Lucy Alice Hensel Pile, of German and Dutch descent.

I do not remember much about my early childhood except that I always had a place to eat and sleep. I was the seventh born of eight children, six boys and two girls. We had our spats, and we pulled pranks on one another, but in the end, we seemed to get along fairly well. I do remember sleeping in a baby crib with my youngest brother until the age of six. Then the two of us moved into a double bed and shared it with an older brother. The girls had a room, my parents had a room, and we all shared one bathroom. Fortunately, we did have indoor plumbing, but we all had to line up to use that one bathroom, so we only took baths and changed underwear on Saturdays, as was the general custom of most families in the 1920s.

As I think about growing up in the '20s and '30s, I remember that my parents didn't pay much attention to their children. Mother was busy with housework, and Dad was always at work, so he spent very little time with his family. He owned a creamery that he loved and put in long hours. His motto was, "The early bird gets the worm" so he went to work every day early in the morning and was there until bedtime.

I attended a four-room schoolhouse, two grades to each room through eighth grade. What we didn't have, we didn't miss. In spite of it all, we learned to read, write, add, and subtract. I didn't like school, but I never refused to go. The schools did not furnish recreation equipment to elementary grades, so our playground excitement consisted of three swings and a basketball hoop. I never saw a basketball. Occasionally, some boy would bring a baseball to school, and we would hit it with a stick or board we had found.

High school days were a little different. There, we had a small gym with basketballs, volleyballs, and baseballs. It was a small high school. In the four grades, there were fewer than 100 students, but it provided a good education. I still didn't enjoy school except for the sports. But I never quit. Even though my parents never encouraged us kids in school, my brothers and I all finished high school.

In the small town where I lived, the poorest families were coal miners. They truly did "owe their souls to the company store." Farming families had enough food, and I worked at a farm as a boy. I looked at work as something that was expected of mankind. My father did it, and I enjoyed it too. I worked the whole summer for a pair of tennis shoes. After graduation from high school, my first job was at my father's I.X.L. Creamery.

I went to Pittsburgh to enlist in the Marines, and a week later I was sent to Paris Island, South Carolina, for three months of boot camp. I was then sent to Washington, D.C., and my wife Theda joined me there. We had an apartment and jobs working for the government.

There was always a fear that I would be sent overseas because I had been told more than once, "be ready in two weeks." Each time, my orders were changed, and in the service, you follow orders and don't question them.

Although many people close to me served overseas during the war, I remained in D.C. until the Normandy Invasion. In 1944, we were sent to Cherry Point, North Carolina, where we remained for two years.

After returning to Friedens in 1946, I resumed work at Dad's creamery. While my father loved to work, I never resented him or regretted his lack of time with us. Instead, I had that same love for my work.

Theda and I bought a house. I was able to work right beside my home and family, and I had no further ambition than to do my work and provide for my family.

When Dad died, I became one of four brothers to own and run the creamery. During the 38 years I worked in our family business with my brothers, there was no resentment or major arguments. I am proud of that. In 1975, we sold the I.X.L. Creamery.

Having and raising children provided the happiest times in my life. Theda was a good mother, and we were very content and happy.

I always felt that it was important to be involved in my childrens' lives and to advise them the best I could.

I never looked at life in terms of challenges. I just did what came. If you never have something, you cannot miss it. Theda and I were, and are, happy with what we have. Anything more or less would not have made us happier.

Time can be an ally or an enemy. In my life, it has fortunately been an ally. The Lord is in charge and He provides. Accept it and go with it. If a person has good morals, he should be willing to work for what he needs and work to attain what he desires. What we inherit from our parents should be passed on to our kids, and anything else we can do to help other people should be done.

Theda and Bob Pile are modern Good Samaritans. They took Joanie and me in during a blizzard that closed the Pennsylvania Turnpike in 1967, and that long weekend has grown into a lifelong friendship.

My Life as Wife and Mother

THEDA CONNOR PILE

I GREW UP IN FRIEDENS with two sisters and a brother. My parents were wonderful. My father was a coal miner throughout the 1930s. We had a cow named Molly at home, thus always had milk, cottage cheese, and churned butter. We had chickens that Dad raised, killed, and dressed.

We were poor but never went hungry, thriving on love and caring and God-fearing parents. In fact, I never knew how poor we were until years later.

We were happy and had what we needed. About 1931, when I was ten years old, Mother sent to Sears Roebuck for a catalog. She bought me two dresses for one dollar, and I was thrilled! For my sister Dot's graduation in 1932, she got a dress for $3.98. We got what we needed from the company store. Getting a bag of candy was true excitement.

I always enjoyed school and did well. Bob and I started dating when we were 16. I graduated from high school in 1938, and he graduated in 1939. At that age, we weren't concerned with the economy or politics. We just thought that was how it was. We had what we had and were happy with it.

We were married on December 28, 1941. Bob entered the Marine Corps in July, 1942. They had started drafting men before we were married. Although we did have access to a radio, we were not fully aware of the scale of the war until Pearl Harbor was bombed.

When the war was over, it was such a joyous time for everyone. There was hugging and parties everywhere. We packed up and returned home to Pennsylvania in April, 1946. On the way home from visiting friends, we saw our first television in New York.

We decided to have children after the war. We bought our first home next to the I.X.L. Creamery that year for $1500. Our first baby, Linda Kay, was born in January, 1947. Barbara Jane was born in 1950, and James Robert in 1957. We had a wonderful life just enjoying our children and neighbors.

We faithfully attended Friedens Lutheran Church all of our lives. I sang in the choir and taught Sunday School, and Bob was Sunday School Superintendent. Because we were poor, we wanted our kids to have more. We wanted them to excel. We wanted to be good examples to our children.

We celebrated our 58th wedding anniversary in December, 1999. What a great 58 years we have had! The years have produced 3 children, 10 grandchildren and 5 great-grandchildren. My prayer for them is that they will always follow Proverbs 3:4: "Trust in the Lord with all your heart and lean not on your own understanding; in all of your ways acknowledge Him and He will direct your path." It is so important to have a personal relationship with the Lord. It is also important to be kind. You never know how much people are hurting. I pray that I can always live by the motto my mother lived by: "Do all the good you can, to every person you can, in every way you can, as long as ever you can, because you only pass this way but once."

❦ ❦ ❦

— EFFECTIVE PARENTING —

A truism picked up forty years ago from my friend Jack McGraw says it best, "The problem with parenting is that by the time you are any good at it—you are out of a job."

Then you get a golden opportunity to be a grandparent. As a grandparent, you watch as your children struggle with parenting issues. When they face a problem, it is easy to reflect back on what you did in an earlier similar situation.

Sometimes you can help your children by giving advice. But actions usually speak louder than words in this instance, and your children will act as you did under similar circumstances years earlier. It is my hope that, with this book, the ideas and paths which are suggested can be used so that the mistakes made by my generation are not repeated. We have included some positive ideas and useful models from earlier generations so that those who are now parents may pass along the best of what we have to offer to future generations.

Since our focus is children and young adults, I believe the examples of leadership and inspiration must begin at home. My son-in-law David Wunderlin has a ritual with his children that I believe is a great illustration of raising children with this in mind. Each night as he tucks my granddaughter into bed, David tells her, "Julie, you can be anything you want, as long as it is worthy of you."

If I Had My Child to Raise All Over Again

DIANE LOOMANS

If I had my child to raise all over again,
I'd finger paint more and point the finger less.
I'd do less correcting, and more connecting.
I'd take my eyes off my watch, and watch with my eyes.
I would care to know less, and know to care more.
I'd take more hikes and fly more kites.
I'd stop playing serious, and seriously play.
I'd run through more fields, and gaze at more stars.
I'd do more hugging, and less tugging.
I would be firm less often, and affirm much more.
I'd build self-esteem first, and the house later.
I'd teach less about the love of power,
And more about the power of love.

On Raising a Healthy Child

MELODY AND BOB DURHAM

"Train up a child in the way he should go: and when he is old,
he will not depart from it."
—Proverbs 22:6

Raising healthy, responsible children is one of life's greatest privileges and responsibilities given to human beings. It can also bring great joy or sadness. Like other responsibilities, it is accompanied by risks and benefits. Most parents embark on this journey with great expectations for being "good" parents.

WHAT IS A GOOD PARENT?

First and foremost, it is one who puts the child's best interest first. This will mean investing heavily in the marital relationship which, in turn, supports and nurtures the child. It means balancing work and family to provide quality time for spouse and children.

It includes a lifestyle centered around core values such as honesty, kindness, fairness, hard work, and a central belief in a personal God who is involved and interested in our daily lives.

Secondly, a good parent models healthy and responsible behavior for a child to emulate. This includes effective conflict resolution and communication skills. It means honesty and integrity in all relationships, i.e., work, home, church, friends, and government.

Thirdly, the parents must be willing to shift responsibility to the child as they grow. This is often a difficult task for the parent. The tendency is to hold "responsibility" or control and "protect" the child. The very act of sharing and then giving responsibility is one of ultimate trust by the parent. It says to the child that their parent trusts them to be responsible and has expectations for their behavior and choices.

The rubber meets the road when a child chooses to be irresponsible in his behavior. A parent's knee-jerk reaction is to censure the child and take back responsibility. It is at this critical juncture that a parent must choose to let the child suffer the consequence of his choice and be there to love and empathize with him (not criticize). It also means giving the child the same responsibility again, so he has a chance to succeed and learn. If this learning opportunity (that is, try-and-fail experience) is provided at an early age, the child will learn quickly that all actions and choices have consequences. And, he will be less likely to make a bad choice, i.e., drinking and driving at age 18, and suffering injury, penalty, or death as a consequence.

It is imperative that both parents and child see "failures" as learning experiences. In this manner, a child views his parents as being "in it with him" and not against him. This combination of love, empathy, and consequences is the key to success.

Melody Durham heads the Cardiac Rehabilitation and the Nursing Education Programs at Aspen Valley Hospital. Her husband Bob has a private counseling practice.

Measuring Your Success as a Parent: Look at the Product

RUTH AND BUDDY GREENBAUM

*M*Y WIFE RUTH AND I have been blessed with three fine, loving, sensitive, and caring children. Along with all the other exciting and varied experiences in their daily lives, they are now experiencing firsthand the joys of parenthood.

When Ruth and I measure how successful our lives have been, we look at how successful, healthy, and happy our children are now. Have they led meaningful lives? Have they contributed to the communities in which they live?

We have wondered many times about the things we did in bringing up our children, and why they became the mature adults we had always hoped and prayed for. Each child is so different, and yet, very much alike in their morals, sensitivity, and values. Now, these same characteristics can be seen in our grandchildren.

When we think about the process involved in bringing up each generation, we ask ourselves: What prepared us? Where did this knowledge and ability come from? Our parents were never exposed to any formal or structured education on the subject of rearing and bringing up children or even the psychology of this very important subject, and neither were we.

Was it from the tales and stories of the past generation or our own experiences that we learned and passed on this information to our children? Did they inherit the right genes, or were we just blessed with lots of luck?

There's no doubt that environment, friends, and education were important ingredients. How did we successfully put all this together in a timely order? I'm really not sure, but I do know that each of these factors was a building block which contributed to our childrens' character and values, along with lots of good common sense.

More recently, I had the opportunity to pass along a little insight that had been given to me by my father when I went off to college. My first-born grandson was preparing to begin his first semester at the West Point Military Academy when he asked if I had any good advice.

My advice was basically the same that my father had given to me, and it was advice I had passed on to my children: *Make the utmost of this opportunity for an excellent education.* Study hard and learn all you can absorb. Remember the values your parents taught you, and at the same time, enjoy college and the friendships you make. But most importantly, when you find yourself in a situation where you are questioning your course of action, either alone or with friends, ask yourself, "Would I or my parents be proud to read about this in the morning newspaper?"

Ruth and Buddy Greenbaum are the parents of my business partner Bruce Greenbaum.

Unselfish Love

Warren Lien

I would like to take this opportunity to share some thoughts and lessons learned over the years. When our children were young, there was a need to work through many problems together. The underlying strength of our family relationship can be summed up in two related ideas: unselfish love and a willingness to give of one's self.

I recently heard a story about the value of giving. There are two large lakes in the Holy Land: the Sea of Galilee and the Dead Sea. Life flourishes around and in the Sea of Galilee, while the area in and around the Dead Sea is dead.

Why is this? Water flows into the Sea of Galilee from the upper regions of the River Jordan and out by the Jordan. This makes the lake very healthy for fish and fowl and fauna with agriculture and human life surrounding the lake. The Dead Sea has water coming in from the River Jordan, but has no outflow. The sea can not support any life. In other words, the Dead Sea does not GIVE; it only TAKES. This can also be applied to people, especially family members. Learning to give of one's self and not always having your hand out expecting something is basic to family life.

This example also applies to your relationship with the Lord; if you are a giving person, He will give you boundless blessings.

In business, don't separate your business conduct from the previous paragraph; business requires performance. In most cases, this comes down to providing a service/product in a timely manner. Pay your bills on time and people will give you whatever you want. This may seem rather simplistic, but it does work!

The President of Lien Rubber Company, Warren Lien is an active Catholic layman.

Ground Rules

John Lutz

A Father as Single Parent—John Lutz

John was the first single parent I remember. His role at home was drastically altered by his wife Phyllis' battle with multiple sclerosis and her death.

John's contribution describes the message for his daughter Cherie as she left for college. —Ed.

*H*EALTH IS A TOP PRIORITY IN LIFE. Sometimes, health is not a matter of choice, but circumstances. This was brought home in a major way to me when my first wife, Phyl, died of multiple sclerosis.

As a single parent, I raised my daughter, Cherie, for a number of years, and she successfully made it through high school. When she went to college at UCLA, I gave her three ground rules to follow:

1. Don't get on drugs!
2. Don't get pregnant!
3. Don't get married!

She graduated from law school, was very successful in business, and later got married, having the knowledge, experience, and wisdom to pick the right partner. She is still happily married, with two wonderful sons who are a tribute to the younger generation who will take over the future.

John Lutz is a retired DuPont sales executive.

—PROVIDING GOOD EXAMPLES—

For virtually every parent and grandparent, there is a desire to implant generosity and compassion in their children and grandchildren. The next four pieces describe memorable examples of how this is accomplished.

Giving

WILLIAM A. GUIFFRE

(written on my father's death at age fifty-seven)

As infant on his mother's knee
His every thought was just on he.
But time increased his thoughts you see
And soon his thoughts encompassed three.
Soon friends and brother, a sister, too
Away from him, his love they drew.
A wife, six children, grandchildren new—
and then his life of love was through.
He taught me this, just how to live.
To man, to God, yourself to give.

Mom Did It . . . Could I?

BONNIE HIRSCHHORN

WHEN I WAS A LITTLE GIRL, I would watch Mom and Dad go off to work, usually seven days a week. Dad worked as a taxicab driver for a fleet in the Bronx. Mom worked three jobs: as a clerk in the dry cleaning store around the corner during the day, as a baby sitter in the early evening, and as a home attendant for an elderly lady with multiple sclerosis most Sundays. Sometimes I would go to Mom's job and watch, especially the days she'd took care of the lady. I could never imagine, when I was nine and ten, that someone could bathe, toilet, and dress a stranger. Mom did it every week for years, until the lady passed away. We never talked out loud about her experiences working with this deformed, old woman. It was Mom's calm demeanor and caring influence that has stayed with me all these many years later.

During these times, we'd take care of each other. My brother watched me and I, in turn, watched our "baby" sister. We all had responsibilities to each other and to the family. To that end, we all knew what was expected in the house (i.e., a one bedroom, three-room apartment in a forty-eight-family building in Brooklyn's Crown Heights), in school, and in the community. Our extended family is enormous, and we had our duties toward them as well.

We were all expected to excel in school. As the second child, I was always told how good a student my brother was and how his precedent was to be my minimal goal. My sister was luckier.

Although we had not moved, the school district boundaries changed, and she went to a different elementary school than we did. She had only herself to compete against. For her, in school, siblings did not exist.

My brother and I had this academic competition which I did not recognize at the time. We had many of the same teachers in PS 221 in Brooklyn. We were almost always in the top class. Being in the "best" class was enough pressure in and of itself. My brother was always among the best students in his grade. I was somewhere in the middle of my group. I kind of plodded along, never quite reaching his level of success, but also not realizing how well I was doing for myself. Besides, I had other responsibilities in the house as the oldest girl. I had to help cook, clean, and watch our sister. Frequently Mom was not home immediately after school. Dad always returned after we had gone to bed.

By the time we went to college, and we all knew (from the back of our birth certificate upon which it was written) that we would go to college, my brother's path and mine were still intertwined. He had spent time in the army, and when he returned home I had almost caught up to him in our college studies. We are five years apart in age, a gender and a generation apart in societal expectations.

I recall one teacher in a college math class who was committed to giving him a higher grade (even though we had the same average) because "boys should get better marks than girls in math." It mattered not that I was helping my brother from time to time. He got the "A."

My brother went on to become a teacher of science and ultimately a supervisor. He has since retired and has recently become a grandfather. I became a teacher of history, did a stint as a supervisor, and am currently working as a school counselor. Our sister majored in art, hated teaching, and went to work for corporate America until she retired to be a full time mom.

Mom and Dad were the hardest working people we knew. Everyone thought that we were rich. We always had enough to eat, clean clothes and our health. When we walked out of the building on a rare family outing, we were a sight. Many of the clothes we wore were recycled, but always clean, crisply starched and ironed (including our underwear). As a matter of fact, I do not recall shopping for any clothing, except shoes, until I was in high school. And then, my clothes were purchased with money I earned from part-time jobs. I recall sharing nylon hose with Mom. I'd wear them first, when they "ran" she would wear them under slacks to her job in the dry cleaning store. It was not until many years later that I realized the many sacrifices Mom and Dad made so that we could have the few extras our family could afford.

So, what does this all mean?

I raised two sons of whom I could not be prouder. I love them completely and unconditionally. They, too, were brought up wearing hand-me-downs, alternated with brand new clothing. They attended the same schools and encountered many of the same teachers. Our economic situation was never Spartan. We always had more than enough for our needs and many of our wants.

I know that the way my parents cared for us had nothing to do with our possessions but only with what we had: love, respect, motivation, and expectations. I, in turn, tried to raise my children with the same regard.

In my work, I endeavor to treat other peoples' children with the same love, respect, and regard that I have for the children of my womb.

When I turned a certain age, I was finally able to appreciate what my family taught me. *We are all different. We are not equal. We are all special. We each have strengths and weakness. And, in the diversity that we have, we enhance each other and help each other to become better people.*

When adversity struck my nuclear family, it was the strength that Mom and Dad nurtured in me that enabled us to conquer and survive.

Bonnie Hirschorn has recently been promoted to the position of assistant principal at the Communications and Graphic Arts High School in downtown Manhattan.

Perfect Love

Debbie Galloway

God loves us. He loves us unconditionally. He loves us perfectly. I think He wants us to love each other perfectly—but that doesn't happen very often here on earth. But I'm here to tell you that sometimes it does. It happened between Grandmommy and me. We loved each other unconditionally . . . perfectly. And it was amazing.

It wasn't always that way. As a child I barely knew Grandmommy. I'd see her at family gatherings when she'd show up with her cheese grits casserole or wearing a Santa hat, on my birthdays when Granddaddy would magically pull silver dollars from my ears, and on various other occasions when I'd stop by her house to ask her to hem a skirt for me or search through her button box to find a rare button. I always liked her just fine.

But I grew up and Grandmommy grew old. And God, in His infinite wisdom, realized that we needed each other.

I say our love was perfect because it was so easy, so pure, so uncomplicated. It was just Grandmommy and me—engaged in an always delightful, always comforting relationship. God graced our relationship by encouraging us to give and to receive in an almost effortless way.

Grandmommy gave freely to me, and I was able to graciously accept her many gifts. And vice versa. I'd bring her dinner; she'd return the dish filled with her no-bake chocolate oatmeal cookies. She'd hem a dress; I'd weed her garden. I'd pick up a sack full of groceries; she'd teach my children to make a stuffed pillow or doll clothes. I'd carry boxes to her basement; she'd rock Mary to sleep. No keeping tabs on who did what for whom. It was all so easy. Easy to give and easy to receive.

So what was the secret to our love? How can we recreate that kind of love, again and again, in our lives? These are the questions I am asking. I'm listening hard for the answers.

Here's what I heard so far:

- Be admirers of each other.
- Put those you love at the top of your list.
- Enjoy each other.

First, *be admirers of each other.* Grandmommy and I formed our own mutual admiration society. In her eyes, everything I did was just fine. My lasagna was yummy. My children delightful. My haircut just right. My outfit so flattering. To me, Grandmommy was beautiful. Her costume jewelry was exquisite. Her butter curls the best. Her ability to produce just what I needed—whether tomato paste, evaporated milk, or a Japanese kimono bordered on miraculous. Surely the rest of the world wouldn't agree—but in her eyes, I could do no wrong, and in my eyes, she was the Martha Stewart of all grandmothers.

Second, *put those you love at the top of your list*—as in before dirty dishes or piles of laundry or work projects with deadlines lurking. This is the hardest lesson for me and the one I struggle with the most. The hallmark of Grandmommy's and my relationship was our willingness to put the other first.

Before the days of cellular phones, I'd be running like a mad woman into Kroger. I'd stop, deposit my quarter into the pay phone, and dial Grandmommy, asking if she needed anything at the grocery. She'd always say "no," and I'd always go on talking to her about anything I could to keep her on the phone. Pretty soon, she'd say "Well, you could pick me up some milk," or "I finished my Grape Nuts last Tuesday," or "I've only got one banana left." I'd end up with a list of four or five things and she'd end up with food in her kitchen. Putting Grandmommy at the top of my list was easy.

But what she would do for me was truly remarkable, and it is the one thing I vow to emulate. Grandmommy was a very busy woman. She sewed for dozens of people; she kept house; she went to Circle Club, church, and Wednesday dinners; she attended Actors Theatre, the ballet, coffee concerts, and Homemakers Club. But whenever I'd call her and say "Grandmommy, what are you doing?" She would ALWAYS say, "Nothing. What do you want me to do?"

Talk about making it easy for me to receive her help! I'd tell her that I needed to run some errands and without hesitating, she would reply: "I'll be waiting at the end of my driveway." I'd buckle Mary into her infant seat, Jack into his baby car seat, Maggie into her booster seat and off we'd go to pick up Grandmommy, who sure enough, would be waiting with her thumb out. She'd hop into the car and off we'd go on our adventure. In and out of places all over St. Matthews: the dry cleaners, the drug store, and of course, Woolworth's. I'd shop and she'd sit in the car playing "Riddley, Riddley, Ree" and singing "School Days" with my three babies. I'd get more done in one hour than I could in a day without her. What a help she was! The icing on the adventure was when I would pull into her driveway to drop her off and she would thank ME. No, Grandmommy, it is YOU I thank for always putting me at the top of your list.

And finally, *we need to enjoy one another*. My times with Grandmommy were always joyful. Baking cheese straws wasn't a chore to be dreaded, but a much-anticipated time to spend a whole day together. Ringing Grandmommy's doorbell, sticking six small sweaty hands through her mail slot to let her know we had arrived, eating M&M's and drinking refrigerator-cold water while dancing to her music box was an outing of the best kind for my children and me. Visiting Grandmommy at the Episcopal Church Home was a joy—never an obligation. Petting the bunny, kissing the fish, playing bingo, performing an impromptu piano recital, singing old-fashioned songs at the sing-along were always fun—leaving me feeling uplifted after each visit.

Even visiting Grandmommy the last week of her life was joyful in an odd way. Holding hands, breathing in and out together, waiting patiently for the end of this life and the beginning of another was both reassuring and comforting to both of us. I watched Grandmommy endure the labor of dying in anticipation of the joy to be found in her next life. It reminded me of enduring the labor of birth in anticipation of the joy to be found in the creation of a new life. Yes, the circle of life is unending.

I grieved that whole week. It was hard watching Grandmommy struggle for each breath. It's never easy to say good-bye—or see you later to someone you love so much. When Grandmommy died, I was afraid that some part of me would die. But instead what happened is just the opposite: part of Grandmommy lives on inside me. Her spirit will be with me all my days. I can call on my memories of her anytime I need to be cheered or comforted or anytime I need to cheer or comfort others.

I can just picture her now, already settling in up in Heaven. And when God says to her "Mary, what are you doing?" She'll look up with a smile and say "Nothing Lord, what would you like me to do?"

Debbie Galloway is the president of a communications company in Louisville, Kentucky, and she is the designer of the jacket cover for this book. This tribute was delivered as an eulogy to her grandmother at her funeral.

A Country Doctor in Southern Maryland

Tom Tippett

*M*Y MATERNAL GRANDFATHER, Dr. Thomas L. Higdon, was a "horse and buggy" country doctor in a very isolated section of southern Maryland from about 1890 until the 1950s. He died at the age of 92, with few material possessions other than his farm property, but he left behind a legacy that will last for generations.

About ten years ago, an elementary school close to where my grandfather lived was named after him. Dr. Higdon was honored for the many things he did to benefit his community. Dr. Higdon not only helped them with their physical health, but his compassion and dedication helped smooth the way for the social changes that happened in his community from the 1930s to the 1950s.

As a member of the Board of Education, he was a moving force in the 1930s in establishing the first high school for black children in southern Maryland. A southerner and a realist, my grandfather did not believe in integration at that time, but he knew the best way to help the very large, impoverished black population was to offer the opportunity for an education. The elementary school named for him is now integrated. I know he was able to foresee this as the end result of what was a bold step in its time.

Every evening my grandfather and my grandmother would gather everyone together. We would recite the Rosary and seemingly endless litanies before bedtime.

On Sunday, our excursions to church were a combination religious, social, and professional event. My grandfather would dispense medical help from his horse-and-buggy, then his automobile, or he would find a space for privacy in a corner of the church hall.

On the way home, he would make house calls for the shut-ins. He would arrive home weighted down with produce, canned goods, baked goods, or shellfish in lieu of cash payment. The maximum I ever remember my grandfather charging for a house call was $5.00. The fee was mainly based on ability to pay rather than services rendered.

Most of the black patients, who constituted over half of his practice, paid "in kind," if at all. However, if on a Saturday night a group of men came to his home office to get stitched up after a barroom brawl, my grandfather would refuse to treat them if they did not have the cash. He believed that if they could waste their money on alcohol, they could afford to pay for medical treatment.

I had the good fortune to spend most of my childhood and teenage summers with my grandparents. Their influence on my sense of right and wrong and on social responsibility was immense.

My grandfather taught me that although all men are created equal in the eyes of God, they are not all equal, given the same talents or opportunities. It is therefore the responsibility of those of us who have received abundantly to give to those who have received less. The Bible says: *Those to whom much is given, much is expected.*

Hopefully I have been successful in passing on this concept to my children and grandchildren. If I am remembered as kindly as my grandfather Dr. Higdon has been, I will consider my life a success.

Tom Tippett operated a marine supply business in central California. In retirement, he has taken an active role in SCORE (an organization staffed by senior retired executives) and other volunteer organizations.

— 5 —

PARENTS +
SCHOOLS +
TEACHERS =

A Formula for Educational Success

———

Among the lessons of the past few decades concerning public education in America is the idea that success in educating our youth is like a three-legged stool: parents, schools, and teachers are all essential. We begin this chapter describing our major expectations for what a school system should accomplish. We follow with articles on the significance of preschool preparation and stories by and about teachers. Finally, we close with the role of the arts in the education process.

Among the various organs of education, the school is of outstanding importance. In nurturing the intellectual faculties which are its special mission, it develops a capacity for sound judgment and introduces the pupils to the cultural heritage bequeathed to them by former generations. It fosters a sense of values and prepares them for professional life. By providing for friendly contacts between pupils of different characters and backgrounds, it encourages mutual understanding. Furthermore, it constitutes a center in whose activity and growth not only the families and teachers but also the various associations for the promotion of cultural, civil and religious life, civic society, and the entire community should take part.

Splendid, therefore, and of the highest importance, is the vocation of those who help parents in carrying out their duties and act in the name of the community by undertaking a teaching career. This vocation requires special qualities of mind and heart, most careful preparation, and a constant readiness to accept new ideas and to adapt the old.

—Declaration on Christian Education,
Vatican II

PRESCHOOL PREPARATION: A PARENT IS A CHILD'S FIRST TEACHER

As the Vatican Encyclical and the following writing by Jim Trelease so eloquently point out, it takes a combination of support from both parents and schools in order for a child to be empowered by his educational achievement. In too many cases today, it seems that parents are sitting back, demanding that our schools educate our children and teach them what character and values are. But schools should not be institutions where parents delegate their responsibilities. Instead, they should be partners with parents.

Earlier, we pointed out the fact that our society is now living in an information culture, dependent upon a well-educated work force. But study after study of our nation's educational system shows that our students score worse than almost all other industrialized nations in math and science.

How can parents help their children compete academically? They can become their childrens' first teachers. I know my mother was for me, and it inspired in me a lifelong love affair for reading and for learning.

Excerpts from
The Read-Aloud Handbook

JIM TRELEASE

*T*HE FOLLOWING EXCERPTS are taken from *The Read-Aloud Handbook* by Jim Trelease (Penguin Books, 1982)

> *"If we would get our parents to read to their preschool children 15 minutes day, we could revolutionize the schools."*
> —**Ruth Love**
> **Superintendent of Chicago Public Schools (1981)**

> *"You may have tangible wealth untold:*
> *Caskets of jewels and coffers of gold.*
> *Richer than I you can never be—*
> *I had a Mother who read to me."*
> —**"The Reading Mother," Strickland Gillilan**
> from *Best Loved Poems of the American People*

Taped inside my copy of *Charlotte's Web* are a note and a photograph of a little boy beside a cake. They were sent to me by a stranger named Kelly Kline, a parent in Cleona, Pennsylvania. "Dear Mr. Trelease: I heard you speak at Lebanon Valley College, Pennsylvania, last month. I was the mother who had just finished reading *Charlotte's Web* to my three-year-old son, Derek. We thought you would get a kick out of our 'Wilbur' cake. I forgot to mention, when I finished reading the book, his next four words were, 'Mom—read it again!' Guess what we're doing? You got it—we're on Chapter 17."

Upon investigation, I learned that Derek's mother did not start reading to him when he was three. Beginning with the day he was born, she did not let a day go by without a book—often more than one. She began with Jack Prelutsky's *Read-Aloud Rhymes for the Very*

Young, along with nursery rhymes. What started as a handful of books from the library grew into bags full of books, so by three he was ready for his very first novel. By four years of age, he had taught himself to read, [not] with a commercial phonics program, however. One thing can be said in favor of such products: they're right when they say, "There are only forty-four sounds in the English language." And all of those forty-four sounds—every ending, blending, and diphthong—can be found in *Goodnight Moon* and *Make Way for Ducklings* and *Charlotte's Web.* Which is just the way Mrs. Kline gave them to Derek. Although she was trained as a teacher, she did no formal teaching with Derek other than to answer his questions and read to him.

Now I want you to jump ahead to the day Derek sat down at the kindergarten learning table for the first time. Think about the dozen novels he'd heard by that day—the thousand picture books he'd heard, as well as the ones he'd read himself, and the tens of thousands of words he knew from all those readings. And then I want you to think about the child on his left and the one on his right— who, if they were typical American kindergarten children, had heard no novels and only a handful of tired picture books over the last five years.

Which child had the larger vocabulary with which to understand the teacher? Which one had the longer attention span with which to work in class? . . . Mrs. Kline brought a child to the classroom ready and willing to learn . . .

I recently called Kelly Kline to see how Derek was progressing at age six. He now reads picture books to his mother and she does novels with him. They'd just finished *Maniac Magee* by Jerry Spinelli and Roald Dahl's *Matilda.*

Imagine how bright a world we would have if all parents behaved like Derek's. Extensive research has proven that reading aloud to a child is the single most important factor in raising a reader. It is also the best kept secret in American education.

[Italic added for emphasis. —Ed.]

Mom Loved to Read to Me

J. NELSON HOFFMAN

I THINK MY MOTHER'S LOVE OF READING originated with her dad, who wanted his children to go further than he had. Granddad Hill worked very hard during the day, but in the evening after he had washed up and had dinner he read to himself and to his children. His role model was Abraham Lincoln. Though Granddad could not continue his formal education past the seventh grade, he thirsted for knowledge and reading about politics, history, and industry satisfied this need.

My mother, the second of three girls, loved to read classic literature. A teacher at East High School, Ellis Sergeant Smith was a strong influence on her, and after Mom and Dad were married Ellis Smith stayed a friend and mentor. The books that he suggested were either ones he thought she would enjoy or books for her to read to me. An early favorite of mine was *The Secret Garden*.

Mom read to me as if every story was exciting. She read with drama, fun, and she got me involved. When a story reached a particularly important point, she would stop and ask, "What do you think happens next?"

It is only after much reflection that I have learned that she never thought about teaching me to read. She was more interested in making reading exciting, fun, and adventurous so that I would want to learn to read.

My grandfather aided her in buying books for me. I have fond memories of the knights and ladies of King Arthur and his Court and a book with the stories of the great explorers: Perry and Amundsen, the Johnsons, Stanley and Livingston. In the days before television, these stories vividly described the explorers' adventures. They stimulated my quest for exploration, and I don't think it's a coincidence that I went on to become a scientist. Even today, fifty years later, I suspect my hobby of reading about the adventurous mountain men who opened the west is a continuation of my early reading interest in explorers.

When I approached retirement, I wanted to help increase children's reading skills and motivation. Since reading is one of the great gifts and blessings I have received, I felt this would be a good "give back" for me to work on.

This is how I learned of the National Center for Family Literacy, whose headquarters are in Louisville, Kentucky. Its innovative founder, Sharon Darling, recognized the problems facing a young parent who lacks the ability to read, so she started a program which allows both parents and child to learn to read together. The great success of her program created a model that is being copied nationally.

The second resource is the writing of Jim Trelease, who discovered the need for a reference to help young parents locate literature appropriate for different age groups. His *The Read-Aloud Handbook* is a great asset for young mothers and fathers.

The key to success in school comes well before the first classroom. I know of no greater legacy than reading to children and teaching them the pleasure, the adventure, and the joy in books and reading. I will always be indebted to my mother for giving me this great gift.

Wonderment

WILLIAM A. GUIFFRE

Where has the why gone?
Who has stolen the wonderment?
Can no one take time to watch
a spider weaving webs,
a blue jay building nests?
Is there no longer joy on puffing on dandelions, white bloomed?
Would you live?
Watch the child,
wide eyed,
wondering.

No weed the dandelion, but a miracle of softness.
The spider's web a lighted lace.
The jay, a bird, but more, a blur of blue.
And life . . .
the wonderment of love
the love of wonderment.

Parental Responsibility—
Dr. Amitai Etzioni

J. NELSON HOFFMAN

$\mathcal{P}$HIL DEMARTINI, Headmaster of St. Francis School, Louisville, Kentucky, called to my attention the writings of Dr. Amitai Etzioni—pointing out the importance of parents and schools working together. Dr. Amitai Etzioni is a scholar and the author of nineteen books including *The Limits of Privacy* and *The New Golden Rule: Community and Morality in a Democratic Society*. He was also a senior White House advisor during the Reagan presidency and a leading public policy expert.

According to Etzioni:

Helping children develop the moral and intellectual faculties needed to make responsible decisions when they grow up is what raising kids is all about. As I see it, parents and teachers have not merely a right but a duty to find out what their charges are reading, screening, or playing with. They have a duty to help shape the educational environment of their children, help them choose which books they should read, which music they should listen to, which TV programs they should watch, and which they should avoid. Anyone can provide room and board, and love comes naturally. But developing a child's character is a parent's highest duty, one they share with educators, who often do stand in for parents. . . . There is very little in our collective lives that is more important than saving the lives of our children. We should dedicate more of our energy and resources to doing so even if we have to proceed one child at a time, for helping one child may save fifteen.

As a child grows older, he develops those moral and intellectual faculties Etzioni wrote about with the help of strong mentors. One of the first people to make me understand the value of good mentoring was a bright high school student, Jim Pritts. I helped Jim win a scholarship to the University of Rochester, and he not only played basketball, but followed me into a career in optics as well.

Later in the chapter, a career elementary school teacher, Carol Quinn, provides insights from her thirty years of teaching, including writings from her students and quotes from historical figures who inspired them.

Admiration and Respect for Teachers

JIM PRITTS

 ELS ASKED ME TO WRITE about life-changing insights and values. One that came to mind quickly was the value of admiration and respect for those who teach. I don't know exactly how this value came to be instilled in me. I do know that it is a value I have held starting as early as nursery school and kindergarten. Perhaps it was partially the result of being raised in an unhappy marriage which led to divorce when I was 10. My father spent little time teaching or nurturing my two brothers and me. It was natural to accept teachers (who were ready to offer acknowledgment and praise) to fill the void.

As a child, I do remember clearly that I admired and respected my teachers far more than either of my own parents. However, as I got older, I came to realize how hard my parents worked and how they both deserved respect and admiration, in spite of their short-comings as parents. I also realized that my mother's only real dream in life was to have her sons get a college education and get out of Somerset! Perhaps it was her dream (which has come true far more than she had ever wished) that became the seed for my life's work.

I began developing special relationships with teachers starting in elementary school and continuing through college. I was even in-spired to spend a few years teaching part-time at the University of Rochester after I got my MBA, a job I enjoyed immensely. From 7th grade on, I became especially interested in getting to know my teachers and spending time with them after class, sometimes walking home with them, talking about wide-ranging subjects. Also, during that time, I became frequently confused and upset with the treatment these same teachers received from other students. Misbehaving in class, mocking, personal attacks, unrolling toilet paper all over their lawns and homes, and even more became the "in" things to do to gain standing and recognition from other students.

I could not (still can't) understand how they could be so cruel to those who were dedicating their lives to helping us all in so many ways—all the ways that teaching improves our lives. I am afraid not much has changed in this regard, with today's teachers not getting the appreciation, respect, or pay they deserve.

A former vice president of Revo Sunglasses, Jim Pritts now heads the World Sun-glass Association.

Thirty Years of Teaching

CAROL QUINN

AT THE DAWN OF OUR NEW MILLENNIUM, we seem to be at a tremendous crossroads in education. Powerful forces, both inside and outside the school, vie for control of its destiny.

Someone once described our classrooms like this: "If a band of Martians came to Earth and observed our schools, they would go home and describe the process as one person standing around doing something, and a whole bunch of other people sitting there watching them do it!"

This idea was so outrageous that new strategies such as "cooperative learning" and "whole language" were offered throughout the country. Now, the pendulum has swung back to basics, at least in the northeast.

I have been teaching elementary school now for over thirty years! I am still as eager to begin each day with as much enthusiasm and imagination as ever. I love my students, which I guess says it all.

I was honored to be included in the 1998 edition of *Who's Who Among America's Teachers*, nominated by a student from China.

The pieces on the following pages have been collected from my years in teaching.

A career elementary school teacher listed in the 'Who's Who Among America's Teachers', Carol Quinn also heads her local teacher's union.

Collaboration

Carol Quinn and Grade Three

Halidon Public School

"If at first you don't succeed—get your brother to do the work."
"Where there's smoke, there's pollution."
"If you light just one little candle, you definitely need electricity."
"April showers . . . drown the flowers."
"He who laughs last, doesn't have a very good sense of humor."
"If you put off until tomorrow, you will have a 'lotta' sorrow."
"Look to the left, look to the right, but don't look down if you're afraid of the height."

"Take time to smell the flowers and the coffee."

"Now I lay me down to sleep . . . wake me at five."

"When you wish upon a star, you're wasting time! Oh yes, you are."

"What the world needs now is . . . more Nintendo games."

"I left my heart in . . . a Wayne Hills Mall shopping cart."

"Just let a smile be your umbrella, and you'll get soaking wet."

"If at first you don't succeed . . . don't do it anymore."

"If you light just one little candle, you probably need new batteries."

"Look before you . . . sit."

"Take time to smell the flowers . . . and a bee will sting you."

"Just let a smile be your umbrella, and you'll find a good-looking fella."

"What the world needs now is . . . Charlie Brown."

Quotations

"There are only two lasting bequests we can hope to give our children. One of these is roots, the other wings."
—Hodding Carter

"See everything; overlook a great deal; correct a little."
—Pope John XXIII

"One mother teaches more than a hundred teachers."
—Jewish Proverb

"By learning you will teach, by teaching you will learn."
—Latin Proverb

"Never, never, never, never give up."
—Winston Churchill

"Failure is only the opportunity to begin again, intelligently."
—Henry Ford

Teachers—Sculptors of the Future

J. NELSON HOFFMAN

DICK LEARN WAS MY GENERAL SCIENCE TEACHER at East High School in Rochester, New York. A dedicated and enthusiastic man, he came from Pittsburgh where he had worked in the steel mills. Working in the blistering heat from the blast furnaces, he decided that education was the fastest path to escape such backbreaking labor. Because of his experience with such difficult work, he projected a passion for learning that he passed to all of his students.

Jim Pritts has written about how many teachers are unrecognized and/or unappreciated. Dick Learn was the inspiration of many future doctors, scientists, engineers—all who took the study and practice of science as their life's work. Their careers are a strong testimony to the long lasting influence of his guidance and inspiration.

Dick Learn developed his presentation of his subject around the life of Francis Bacon and his role in developing the scientific method. Mr. Learn was a storyteller, and the way he described Bacon's achievements was exciting, historical, and challenging. In order to make the laboratory experiments more interesting, he emphasized the way each experiment's data and conclusions were used in modern society. Whether the topic was biology, geology, physics, or chemistry, he tied the fundamental principles of an experiment to history, business, society, and current fields of study.

He began with the purpose of each experiment, the methods and procedures to be used, the equipment and apparatus, the data and observations, and then the conclusions and practical applications. To mark papers he corrected, he kept a red and a blue pencil. For passing, failing, or good, he used the red pencil to put the grade at the top. The blue pencil was reserved for **Excellent**. He used it sparingly, and I swear he had some occult power to measure the sweat you had pored into your work. That blue-penciled **Excellent** became my Holy Grail. I would put in hours and hours studying books and periodicals to flesh out the conclusions and practical application sections of my reports.

As an example, can you imagine a less-exciting experiment than determining the "latent heat of vaporization"? Mr. Learn found out my grandfather was a railroad man. He suggested that the amount of heat required to boil water was fundamental to the steam engines used to drive railroad trains. I can still visualize the hours I spent in the library learning the difference between fire tube and water tube boilers, understanding how the steam operated the power drivers to transfer force from the wheels to the track, etc. When the paper came back, the great big, blue **Excellent** at the top of that paper was a prize I never forgot.

In retrospect, my career as a scientist and engineer was probably launched in that class. Mr. Learn created curiosities that still endure, instilling the wonderful desire to understand how things work.

I learned one very valuable lesson from him: It is a true talent and great gift to be able to create curiosity and mystery about a subject. That is a real foundation stone to build motivation and desire, and is a prerequisite, in my mind, to achieving excellence in one's chosen field.

As we view the ever-spiraling salaries given to professional athletes and entertainers, isn't it tragic that teachers at most levels struggle to receive an equitable paycheck? When a vocation has such significant, fundamental impact on the future of society, isn't it sad that we value those who entertain us more than we pay those who shape our futures?

The Success of Military Base Schools

J. NELSON HOFFMAN AND

excerpts from WILLIAM RASPBERRY

IN THE DECEMBER 27, 1999, ISSUE of the *San Diego Tribune*, William Raspberry wrote of an important observation about the 71 schools on military bases. The eighth grade students of these schools in nationally competitive tests, ranked second only to Connecticut in writing skills, fourth in reading, and military base schools sent 13% more of their graduates to college. From the performance standpoint, they are at the top of the performance curve relative to the average state school.

In summing up the various solutions to the problems of public schools, he began by drawing a distinction between those individuals who are dead certain they know what to do to fix our schools, and a second group, including himself, as not so sure. He suggests the model of the schools located on military bases is a good place to start looking for proposed solutions.

Raspberry tests traditional causes—*poverty?*—over half the students qualify for reduced cost or free meals—*race?*—forty percent are Hispanic or black—*stability?*—new duty assignments and overseas deployment force frequent changes in schools—*single parent?*—most enlisted military families have one of the parents away frequently, sometimes for extended periods, and it is very common to find that both parents are working. Raspberry speculates that the involved presence of parents, particularly fathers, is a significant factor in the performance of their children in school.

But his primary conclusion is that "these children have parents who believe their own efforts—not race, not special gifts, not breaks are the chief determinant of their success." His conclusion is endorsed by researchers who study these schools in great detail:

> My guess, and that is all it is, is that people who believe *they can achieve based on their own efforts* raise children who share that belief ... Military children, I am suggesting, may have an unusual degree of academic success because they hold to an unusual degree the empowering belief that they are in control of their own destiny. (Italic added for emphasis. —Ed.)

When I look at all of the factors which help a child achieve in school, four observations occur to me:

1. In virtually all the pieces by our contributors, it is striking to note the frequency that the parents of our contributors placed living and teaching an empowering, positive ap-

proach to life. I haven't found any who projected a "victim mentality."

2. The quotation from my wife Joan—*The choices you make in life determine the life you live.*—reflects youth and adults who believe they are in control of their own destiny.

3. When I speak to young people, I ask them to repeat my mantra again and again long after I have left them: *We are the future of America! We hold the future in our hands!*

4. The impact that my military experience had on my life was very significant, particularly in learning about discipline. I discuss this subject in more detail later in the book.

THE IMPORTANCE OF ARTS EDUCATION

There is a growing consensus among educators, policymakers, and parents that children do better in school, perform more efficiently in the business workplace, are more self-confident, and achieve overall success if they exposed to an educational curriculum which incorporates arts education.

According to U.S. Secretary of Education Richard Riley: "The process of studying and creating art, in all of its distinct forms, defines those qualities that are at the heart of education reform in the 1990s—creativity, perseverance, a sense of standards, and above all, a striving for excellence."

As the Kennedy Center has documented in its ArtsEdge literature, arts education is, above all else, an activity of the mind, and arts can play a crucial role in improving basic learning skills like reading, writing, and math. Students of the arts continue to outperform nonstudents of the arts on basic SAT achievement tests. Creativity is naturally developed through arts education. In humanities programs which incorporated arts education, students had significantly higher class attendance and were less likely to drop out. With its emphasis on creative discovery, arts programs stimulate a variety of learning styles, engender enthusiasm and motivation for learning, teach discipline, the value of sustained effort to achieve excellence, and the concrete rewards of hard work.

The Importance of Art

Don Huntsman

Since the dawn of man, the need to create art has been a primary part of man's existence. The earliest cave people sculpted and drew and chiseled on their walls. They may have done this solely for decoration or to document their being or perhaps it was a religious act. Regardless, today we stand in awe of their creativity, and we all recognize the importance of their efforts.

Creativity is a part of everyone. The way we decorate our homes, plant our gardens, or arrange our tables, are all examples of art. The act of doodling while talking on the phone, sketching on our grocery list or in the margins of our notebooks or simply the way we dress fulfills our need to create.

An artist, however, does more than arrange for beauty or make order out of chaos. Why an artist creates we may only speculate. They may want to document life, tell a story, express their feelings, make a political statement, or simply create beauty. The difference between an artist and the rest of mankind is more than ability; the artist feels much more strongly and usually has a more intense desire to create. In fact, most great artists would create whether they were paid or not.

Traditionally, the artist takes lifeless material like clay, paint, stone, etc., and, like magic, breathes life into it. The result, depending on the subject, color, composition, technique and skill, is a wonderful object that is capable of stimulating the senses and even reaching the soul of those who come in contact with the work.

As an aside, some of today's modern art may or may not stimulate the senses, and this develops into a debate of what is art. Simply stated, many professional critics and gurus of modern art feel the idea expressed and exhibited is more important than skill or subject. For example, they contend dropping a few rocks, rugs, or other objects into a pile, which most anyone can do by accident, is considered art. They believe it is art because no one has done it before in a museum or in an exhibition environment. Others contend this work has to be explained, otherwise one might feel that the show is not yet completed. Some would ask why, without an explanation or discussion or response from a viewer, those rugs can be considered art.

Another discussion today concerns the importance of beauty in art. Some contend it is of the utmost importance, others say it doesn't matter, and still others feel that if art is beautiful, it is therefore trite and inconsequential. I just say art can be beautiful. The fact that it moves and touches mankind is the important factor to me.

It should also be pointed out that art can include the written word, all forms of music, as well as the performing arts, when we are talking about the importance of art to mankind.

There is almost an endless list of what a work of art can express. It can show an era and a lifestyle from bygone days, recording those times for posterity; it can be a symbol and pass an idea from one generation on to the next; it can express the madness of war, show the tenderness of love, or create a thousand other responses in the viewer.

Art can be important in documentation, as in the portraits of great artists like Rembrandt or the Brady Civil War photographs or in preserving the changing world as in the landscapes of Constable, Moran, and Innes, to name a few. Art can be educational, or it can be calming as in Monet's *Lily Pond* or in the sounds of Debussy or a simple haiku poem. It can be exciting as in the ballet *Rodeo* by Copeland, thought-provoking like Picasso's *La Guernica*, or gut wrenching as in Sorolla's peasant paintings. Art can simply put a smile on our faces. The examples are too numerous to give. It has even been proven that people in hospitals heal faster when there is art present.

One must also consider that what people respond to in a particular piece of art, and what they like, can be very different. The old adage "beauty is in the eye of the beholder" is the miracle of art. Even people who like the same kind of art, or the same piece of art, will differ in their responses to that work. This same work of art can evoke a thousand different responses in a thousand different people. Depending on our own personal experiences, our responses will vary, and the strength of our responses to that work will also vary. The wonder of art is that it can touch the soul of each and every one of us!

Thus, one can understand that art is, and always has been, one of the most important aspects in the life of man. We need to preserve the works of our past masters for generations to come. We need to educate the masses, especially our children, about the potential of art, and we need to support and encourage our young ones to create. We also need to support our museums, and make known our likes and dislikes. Most importantly, we all need to recognize and make known the importance of art to mankind.

An accomplished sculptor, Don Huntsman owns an art gallery in Aspen, Colorado.

Teach Your Child to Love Music and Singing

J. NELSON HOFFMAN

I WAS TRULY BLESSED WITH A MOTHER who had the spirit of a poet and musician. With an around-the-clock, optimistic attitude, she loved to listen to all sorts of music as she went about her daily tasks. Her love of music was so ingrained in me I am persuaded I must have begun hearing her hum or sing softly before I was born.

And as I was growing up, she would sing and then explain what she liked about the music playing on the radio or phonograph.

During the Depression, dancing was a favorite inexpensive pastime. The young people of today may not recognize dancing from the thirties, but steps such as the tango, the fox trot, or the rumba were very elegant. My parents were fabulous dancers, and I always admired the way they would glide across the floor, no matter the tempo.

My next exposure to music came in church and Sunday school. When Mom took me to church, she knew all the hymns. She sang with vigor and enthusiasm (within the boundaries of Episcopal decorum), and she encouraged me to learn the words and tunes and sing along.

In Rochester, the philanthropy of George Eastman was used to promote music education in the public school system, and in the fourth or fifth grade, everyone was tested for music aptitude. I was lucky enough to win a scholarship, which allowed me study piano and theory at the Eastman Preparatory school.

The next step of my music appreciation came in junior high when a classmate told me he was going to get paid to sing in the boy's choir at Christ Church, and he asked me to join him. Most of the hymns were familiar, and the formal training in voice was a real confidence builder.

Around this time in my life, a period of illness kept me at home. While recuperating, I developed a liking for the Texaco Saturday afternoon broadcasts from the Metropolitan Opera. My grandfather noticed this interest and gave me a copy of Milton Cross' *Story of the Opera*. I loved being able to follow the libretto, and although the lyrics were in Italian and German, I learned to follow the story and love the melodies.

When we moved to Penfield, a small town outside Rochester, New York, I found that many of my high school classmates were big fans of country and western music. When I lived in the city, we bought *Hit Parade* magazine so we could learn the lyrics of the popular songs. In Penfield, we listened to Eddie Arnold, Ernest Tubbs, and Hank Williams. The lyrics were corny, but they still linger in my memory. In fact, when Joan and I celebrated our 40th wedding anniversary, our choice for the first dance was Vince Gill's *Just Look at Us*.

We lived in California when State Proposition 13 was passed, and it wasn't long after that the budget-cutters decided that music and art were not really essential in the state's schools. Time has proven what a tragedy that decision was. I am a great admirer of the Galef Institute in Los Angeles, an organization which has demonstrated how critical music, visual arts, and drama are in creating motivated young minds to learn reading, writing, and arithmetic right along with the arts.

In the retirement phase of my life, I find it a great pleasure to just sit and become completely involved in a great piece of music performed by a talented artist: symphonies, Broadway show tunes, hymns, bluegrass, and opera.

I have treasured memories, some of which have survived for five or six decades: The Concertgebouw Orchestra of Amsterdam playing *Beethoven's 3rd* and *7th* at the Eastman Theatre; Victoria De Los Angeles singing *Un Bel Di*; the 75th Anniversary of the Boston Pops at Tanglewood, with a three-day celebration of Beethoven conducted by Leonard Bernstein, Seiji Ozawa, and Leopold Stokowski; an Up With People Concert in Evansville, Indiana, which I attended with my daughter Patty, and a Peter, Paul, and Mary Concert in Los Angeles. We live now in Snowmass, Colorado, home to The Jazz Festival and Aspen Music Festival, and it doesn't get much better!

The pleasures of music have been a big factor in enjoying my luxurious life, and music has been a key in opening up my emotions to my loved ones. I pray all parents will have an appreciation of how music can be used to mold and shape their children.

6

PLACES OF
WORSHIP

Developing the Spiritual Person

————

A SERMON BY Catholic layman Robert Matt was one of the spurring inspirations for this book. While our nation has enjoyed the greatest prosperity in our history the last several decades, we've also seen an over-emphasis on individual rights and needs and de-emphasis on concerns for the spiritual side of the individual.

In a letter to me, retired Navy jet pilot and school principal Wayne Connell presented his ideas on this subject: "The ascension of the intellect over the spirit has been going on for the past 300 years. It has accelerated in the last two or three decades as the framework of our culture has changed from humanism to relativism. All this is to say that the standards that create meaning and provide support are now being discarded in favor of each person making up their own rules, which are changed, as necessary, to fit any current situation."

I agree with Wayne Connell and find that this use of situational ethics to govern modern behavior deplorable. I find it ironic that as the baby-boomer generation ages and becomes parents, they are increasingly abandoning the "anything goes" attitude of the 60s and

70s. As they raise their children, they are turning back to traditional values and core beliefs, endeavoring to teach them right from wrong.

Joan and I have been blessed in our marriage with the guiding hand of our parish priest and our friendship with a number of clergymen. We value their friendship and are nurtured daily by their words, thoughts, and deeds.

As he expresses later in the book, Wayne Connell finds that life is too short to learn from experiences. Instead, he suggests that young people find a model or teacher and learn from their stories. But he also has an explicit test for these models. In his words: "If an honest to goodness real relationship with God isn't in the stories, then you aren't following the right model."

As this present generation of parents work diligently to instill their values in their children, there is a keen need for them to include institutions like a church, synagogue, or mosque in developing this essential part of their children's lives.

In this chapter we illustrate the nurturing quality of shepherds and the value our contributors place on developing their spiritual lives. We begin with a thoughtful article by Rabbi William Green, Dean of the College at the University of Rochester. We then present the inspiring words of Phil Hart, who has discovered his spiritual self in the simplicity of his daily existence and follow up with the writings by a number of clergy. We close the chapter with my thoughts on my chosen field of study—optics—and its relationship to my spiritual beliefs, reflecting the old adage, "He was blind, but now he could see."

Against the Grain:
On the Nature of Religion

RABBI WILLIAM GREEN

*I*F YOU WANT TO SEE just what religion has become at the turn of the Christian millennium, you have to go to your computer and open to web site at *www.speakout.com*. There you will find what the composers of this site call the Speakout.com Religion Selector. The Religion Selector lists a number of key questions about religious beliefs and supplies a set of alternative answers. You select the option that matches what you believe. At the end of the list, you push a selector button, and your computer will tell you which religion you should join. Here are two partial examples:

What is the Nature of the Deity or Deities (i.e., God, Gods, Higher Power, etc.)?

- Only one God, a corporeal spirit (has a body), supreme, personal God Almighty, the Creator.
- Only one God, incorporeal (not body) spirit, supreme, personal God Almighty, the Creator.
- Multiple personal gods (or goddesses) regarded as facets of one God, and/or as separate gods.
- The supreme force is the impersonal Ultimate Reality (or life force, ultimate truth, cosmic order, absolute bliss, universal soul), which resides within and/or beyond all.
- The supreme existence is both the eternal, impersonal, formless Ultimate Reality, and personal God (or Gods).
- No God or supreme force. Or, not sure. Or, not important.
- None of the above.

Why is there terrible wrongdoing in the world?

- Adam and Eve's original disobedience resulted in human sinfulness or a damaged nature or tendency to yield to Satan's temptations or evil inclination or the introduction of evil to the world.

- Not the above; rather, wrongdoing results from a God-given weak side to human nature, or drive to satisfy personal needs, which sometimes results in wrongful choices (or vulnerability to Satan's temptations).
- Ignorance of one's true existence as pure spirit and as one with the Universal Truth (or Soul, Mind, et. al.) can lead to wrongdoing. Or, spiritual/cosmic disharmony or imbalance may result in wrongdoing.
- Not listening to the voice of God, who resides within all, can lead to wrongdoing
- Egoism (self importance) leads to desire, craving, and attachments, which can lead too unwholesome thoughts and behavior, i.e., greed, hate, and violence.
- No supernatural or spiritual reasons. Human nature, psychology, sociology, criminology, etc. explain wrongdoing. Or not sure. Or not important.
- None of the above.

A student friend of mine, a Sikh from India, took this sample and then e-mailed the rest of his religion class saying that he was converting to neo-paganism because his preferences and Sikhism matched only 64% of the time!

So this is where the Internet culture of late capitalism is taking us. Religion is reduced to a set of truncated slogans that conform to our already established preferences. I wonder if you can get a money back guarantee if you are dissatisfied with your choice after 30 days!

Contrast this web site with a well-known biblical episode. Here, freely translated, is a portion from Genesis 22: "And it came to pass that God tested Abraham. He said to him, 'Abraham.' And he said, 'I'm here.' And he said, 'Now, take your son, your special one, Isaac, the one you love, and get yourself to the land of Moriah, and offer him up there as a burnt-offering on one of the heights, where I will tell you.' And Abraham got up early the next morning and saddled his donkey, and he took two of his young male servants with him, and his son, Isaac."

Something is wrong with this picture. God tells Abraham to sacrifice his one beloved son, and Abraham's response is not just to get out of bed, but to get up early to do it. What happened to him? Is this the same Abraham who talked back to God so forcefully in Genesis 1:8 before the destruction of Sodom and Gomorra? Is the same father who silently gets up early to sacrifice his son, the same man who can say to God, "Will not the judge of all the earth act justly?"

The contrast of these two examples should make us think. Why is the biblical story of Abraham and Isaac—like other biblical narratives—so arresting and affecting? What gives religion its capacity to instruct and to shape lives?

Surely the appeal and persistence of religion lies partially, if not principally, in its conviction of the fundamental correctness of its vision of reality, which both shapes and is generated by its adherents' experience in the world. Religion is compelling because of its affirmations of certitude and truth, because of its refusal to compromise on basic convictions, and because of the extent of its claims on the human person. Unlike other aspects of culture—politics or philosophy, for example—religion tends to extend its reach, to be comprehensive in scope. In nearly all societies religion exhibits enormous range of expression. For instance, religion attacks all the senses—not only in speech and writing, but also in art, music, and dance, in smell and taste, in ethics, sexuality, and intellect. Most religions have cosmologies and eschatologies, theories of nature, birth, gender, marriage, suffering, and death. Few political systems, social ideologies, or philosophies have such a reach or exhibit religion's capacity to make definitive demands on the total human being.

But there is more. Unlike our website example, religion is not important because it conforms to our whims and prejudices; it is important precisely because it does not. In so many ways, religion is effective because it runs against the grain, calls us to do what we don't want to do, and because it is counterintuitive.

Think of the ways, for western religions, biblical affirmations push people, call people, to do what their instincts and intuition might never on their own support.

Is it intuitive to believe in a deity who is invisible and incorporeal?

Is it intuitive to think that all life is interrelated when our experience tells us it is fragmented?

Is it intuitive to think that every action we perform and every thought we take has ethical significance?

Is it intuitive to honor our parents and to care for them when they can no longer do us any good?

Is it intuitive to live in hope when experience tells us that all is lost?

Because it is counterintuitive, religion draws us to self-consciousness and nudges us to engage and exercise parts of our humanity that otherwise would lie dormant. Because in so many fundamental ways religion goes against the grain, it moves us beyond the realms of instinct and appetite and keeps up from becoming victims of our passions.

Through stories, commandments, parables, laws, and rituals, the religions of the world call human beings to a kind of self-transcendence in which we can see ourselves—individually and collectively—from a divine perspective, so to speak. By asking us to live counterintuitively, religion requires us to live lives governed by mind and will.

Rabbi William Green is the Philip S. Bernstein Professor of Judaic Studies, Professor of Religion, and Dean of the College, The University of Rochester.

How I Live Today

PHIL HART

*M*Y STORY IS SHORT . . . I was raised in southern California in a loving, middle-class home. I graduated from high school in 1956 and proceeded to live the life I interpreted would bring me happiness. I married and was blessed with two wonderful daughters. I then founded a company which I directed until 1997. In all of that time that I found business success, I also did much to create deep happiness and serenity, but in the end, I found little of either.

In 1993 I had a spiritual awakening, and as a result of that experience, I now live a wonderful life of fulfillment and balance in a grove of trees in the mountains. I have found my bliss.

With this new awakening, I now realize that I am living fully when I am aligned with all four levels of my being. I see these levels as: my actions, or my physical level; my mental level, or rational belief system put into logic and words; my emotional level, which I simplify into fear, love, joy, anger, and sadness; and, my spiritual or higher self—where my higher power resides and there's a place of love without judgment.

To find this place of serenity and aliveness, it is necessary for me to be aware and evaluate where I am "in the moment." For me, the compass to "awareness" starts by checking out my emotions. Most of my life I spent denying these emotions most of the time. Once I am clear about the deepest level of emotion in the moment, I then look to the belief supporting that emotion my choice of action or behavior.

Until I did my "work" (a term I use for soul work) I lived in fear and anger, denied my feelings, and pursued a life of aimless striving. I searched for love and acceptance and found pain and loneliness instead. I lived in a place of "doing and acting" to prove myself to the world and to God. This took the form of work and alcohol addiction. For me, the emotional pain of inner loneliness became so great that I could no longer hide and suppress it.

In a moment of great darkness, I reached out for help from God and was divinely touched with trust. From that moment on, both people and programs became available to do my work and discover this new way of living.

What I have learned so far are these simple things:

1. I had taken on beliefs about myself, God, and the whole world which were not my own or true. These are what I term emotional wounds and shadow beliefs. Today, I have a new set of beliefs which are creating both love and community with myself, with God, and with all of creation.

2. Parts of me still believes in some of the old beliefs, and they still trigger fear and anger. Awareness of this gives me an opportunity to look at them, reconnect with what I know to be true, and move back to a place of love.

3. My emotions are my pathway to knowing where I am in the moment.

4. Principles are those beliefs I hold dear. These include: integrity, accountability, being present, and trust in myself and my higher power. I may not be able to maintain these all the time, but my intention is to increase the amount of time I am honoring these principles.

5. Next in importance to me today is to honor values. These values are those things I hold dear to me, and when I am honoring them I feel alive and congruent with life. These values include: marriage, family, community, friends, service, nature, music, personal growth, education, courage, compassion, wisdom, blessing, laughter, love, and acceptance.

6. I am blessed with uniqueness, and I have a special gift to give during this life. I listen to my inner truth (easier said than done). "Follow your bliss."

7. Until I truly am able to accept and live myself, I am not able to love those around me.

In conclusion, I wish to offer all of you a blessing and prayer as you walk the courageous path of life into a new millennium. You are blessed with the ability to find great joy and direction in your life in your own way. May you find it, embrace it, and pass that on to the universe.

Phil Hart sold his furniture retailing business and found his heart's desire in spiritual counseling.

Christ's Presence and Being Right

Father Roddy MacNamara

*T*wo ideas have had a profound effect on my attitude and behavior. The first came from a lecture by a Franciscan priest who spoke at a retreat I attended about twenty years ago. He talked about the presence of Jesus in the Eucharistic bread at mass and about the power of the priesthood in our Catholic tradition being passed on down through the centuries. This power, first given to the Apostles, comes from taking the bread and wine and saying the words, "This is my body and this is my blood" in obedience to Jesus' command. Then he spoke of the miracle of our faith: Jesus is truly present in the bread and wine because the priest has said the words of consecration. Believing this has given me a sense of awe of the priesthood, and, perhaps, was significant in leading me to become a priest.

As the lecture continued, the priest dropped his bombshell: "Jesus is not present because the priest says the words." He paused, and I puzzled over the statement. Then he continued: "Jesus is present because he said he would be when the priest said the words." What he meant sunk in. Any power we have is due to God. All power is in God.

I arrived at the second idea more recently. It came from my reflections on some of the happenings in this great country and in our world. I do not claim this idea as my own. I deduced it from looking at the abundance of conflict today: everything from the O.J. Simpson trial, to the turbulence in Kosovo, to debates in the House and the Senate, to our own arguments at home and at work. It seems that all news, and thus our lives, are framed as a story, with only two sides: right and wrong to every story. For example, if a city builds a new subway, or a bishop a new church, the telling of the story includes only those who agree and those who disagree with the choice or decision. It is painted as a conflict, with both sides claiming to be "right," and the opposition, of course, is "wrong."

Sometimes I find myself drawn into this way of looking at things. I am right; others are wrong. Being right becomes important and, thus, a goal. Is there something wrong with that? I think so. I do not believe that is why God put us on this great planet. I may act like He put me here to be right. But the truth is, I believe He put me here to be good.

Father Roddy MacNamara is the Pastor of St. John Eudes parish in Chatsworth, California.

Remember to Whom You Belong

FATHER MICHAEL GLENN

IN THE THIRTY-SIX YEARS OF MY LIFE, I have been privileged to live all over the world: Rome, Jerusalem, and throughout the United States. In that time, no one person has had more of an impact on me than the spellbinding preacher and radical rabbi from the north of Israel named Jesus. He revealed himself not only as a teacher of wisdom, but as the very Son of God. On the cross He showed to us the immense love of God that has served to bring us back to Him and reunite us with Him in every way.

Of all the teachings of Jesus, perhaps that which underlies almost all of the Gospels, is the reality that Jesus belonged to the Father. He invites us, too, to have just that kind of relationship—a profound sense of belonging to God the Father in Christ.

If there is a reason why most people lose their way in this world or struggle with their self-esteem or question whether they have a purpose in this life, it results from the reality that they have lost hold of this basic fact—they belong to God. The bond that holds us to God is nothing other than the very presence, love, and power of Jesus. If any one thing can sustain us through difficulty, doubt, and tragedy, it is that even when we are most alone, this fundamental relationship is always there to strengthen us. That relationship is the one that we have through Christ to God the Father.

From this teaching of Jesus flows one of the other great realities of the Christian faith: Christianity is not at its core a moral religion. It is not fundamentally about doing good. Rather, it is about realizing that God has loved us radically in Christ. He sent His Son to die upon the cross, and as we gaze upon that act of love, we know how much we mean to God the Father. Our moral life, our desire to do good, is nothing other than our response to this love of God that we discovered in Christ Jesus. Just as when two young people fall in love and their lives are radically changed by the love they discover in the other person, so it is when we discover Christ.

As we discover the love of Christ for us, our lives begin to change. We live in different ways, and we value different things; that is the

Christian moral life. Our values and judgments are formed not because we hope to be loved by God, but because we have already been loved by God. That love is so overwhelming that it changes us, transforming our minds and affecting our actions so that we live as people who are perceptibly touched by the very love of God. Our moral life should not be something that we abide by regretfully; it should be an outgrowth and reflection of our love for Christ.

The question that we must constantly ask ourselves when we fail is not does God love us? Because certainly God does love us. The question we should be asking instead is have we realized enough the love of God for us, and have we allowed that love to be reflected in what we say and do, and, ultimately, what we think?

The reality that will transform us is that we belong to God in Christ.

Father Michael Glenn is the former pastor of St. Mary's Church in Aspen, Colorado. He is now the rector of the seminary for the diocese of Denver.

What Is Conscience?

ROBERT MATT

I DO NOT INTEND to define the term *conscience* but rather give a pragmatic answer to the question from a philosophical perspective.

If we use the term *god*, it should be lower-cased and refer only to the supreme power that put this world together. We can stand on that philosophically with or without a faith belief.

Proceeding from that philosophical basis, we can say that in human nature are two inherent conditions that motivate our actions: the power for rational reasoning that is logically sound and the power of our emotions.

We can then answer the question, What is conscience? When emotion takes over and we act in a matter that deviates from our inherent ability to reason rationally, we create a conflict between our ability to think and our emotions. (This conflict is present to our consciousness.) The manifestation of that conflict in our consciousness is our conscience. This answer shows us where and what conscience is. How it got there is simply evidenced by the fact that it is there. Philosophically, all we can say about the origins of conscience derives from using the term *god*.

To reason rationally and logically is an acquired attribute. We all acquire it in different degrees, depending on our material attributes of genes, nurture, environment, and culture. Consequently consciousness varies. This means the conflict between reason and emotion varies, and thus conscience varies from individual to individual.

If we stopped with that statement, our consciousness and our conscience would be relative, solely determined by our material attributes, over which we have little control. That would mean being judgmental about an act—deeming it good or bad, right or wrong, or determining moral responsibility—would be based on relative opinion, not on truth as evidenced by a real knowledge and understanding of moral philosophy.

To overcome that involves two philosophical disputations that have been going on from the beginning of human recorded history.

The first is the matter of free choice. Practically all of philosophical history comes down on the side that human nature, without exception, has the ability to choose. This is almost a given. But: What do we choose from? And what is the basis for our choices? Do we choose from innumerable alternatives determined by our material attributes? Do we always have the ability to choose otherwise, regardless of what we have chosen?

From my study of moral philosophy, based on armchair thinking about human nature, I think there is overwhelming evidence that the second question relates to how we have the ability to act. This I call free will. It cannot be empirically proved, but, I believe, it is amply demonstrated in the human condition. (That is a another disputation too lengthy to be handled here.)

The second philosophical disputation that has been going on all through recorded history is: How do we determine what is the right thing to do?

To determine what is objectively good or bad, right or wrong to do, cannot be based on empirical evidence. However, it can be based on rational reasoning that is logically sound, for example, the self-evident truth of the proposition: "We ought to desire whatever is really good for us and nothing else." To understand this truth, I assume we make a distinction between natural and acquired desires, and between real and apparent goods.

The philosophical history of responding to this last disputation goes back to Aristotle's *Nicomachean Ethics* and is promulgated by Mortimer Adler in his book *Ten Philosophical Mistakes.*

If we come down on my side of these two philosophical disputations, then there is an objective morality. Determinism and relativism are wrong. There is a good or bad, a right or wrong, and a moral responsibility connected with our human acts.

Finally regarding the term *conscience,* from both a philosophical perspective and a theological one, you shape your own conscience.

From theology, at least Christian in principle, you shape your conscience from your belief in the revealed word and the role model of Christ. However, the tenants of theology can never violate philosophical truth. From a philosophical perspective, without faith belief, you shape your conscience from rational reasoning based on sound logic, starting with the self-evident truth of desiring what is good and nothing more.

A devoted Catholic layman, Robert Matt is the CEO of a chain of Ethan Allen Furniture stores.

Forty Years a Missionary

FATHER THOMAS DEL BARRIO

ST. MARK IN HIS GOSPEL 3:13 SAYS: "He went up the mountain and summoned those whom He wanted and they came to him." That has been happening from the very beginning. He chooses those HE WANTS.

I come from a very religious family. My father was a teacher (my first teacher). He had a brother who was a priest and one sister who was a nun. My father had been training to become a priest and after six years he gave up the training. I am sure he was not WANTED to be a priest.

I was the third born, but the second boy in the family. I was very naughty. So much so that people in the village used to say I would never become a priest.

The one who influenced my life was my father. We saw him praying every night after we all had gone to bed. He was a heavy smoker, and yet he never smoked a cigarette on Fridays. His faith and love for the Lord was great and he said, "How can I smoke on the day Jesus suffered for me?"

Neither he nor my mother ever told me to become a priest. I think they prayed that I would become a priest but never said a word. I remember them saying, "If that is what you want, do it. Think and pray to find out." I was a bit afraid because the year I entered the seminary was the same year my eldest brother gave up. If he, who was so good, gave up, what was I trying to do?

In those days, I lived at the seminary. Discipline was very strict, conditions very hard. In my second year I was among a group of the students who got pneumonia. I was sent home to be treated by the family doctor. After two to three weeks, my uncle, who was a professor in the seminary, said I was missing too many lessons and I had to go back (he was not teaching me). So I returned to the seminary, but I was not well, and within a few months I was feeling worse. I was tired and had lost my appetite.

They took me to the hospital, and the x-rays showed I had a shadow on my lungs and was declared a TB patient. I was told to have complete rest. For three years I was not allowed to stay at seminary. The family doctor told me that I had to give up the studies for the priesthood, as it was a clear sign I had no vocation. When God calls He gives the means to achieve it. But I did not give up.

It was during this time I heard a priest speaking about the shortage of priests in South America, and I started thinking about continuing my studies in a special seminary of foreign missions. After a couple of years of remaining at home with my parents, I told them of my intentions. I don't think they took me seriously. After all I was very sick and thin. I did not eat very well even though my parents would buy the best for me to eat. I loathed food.

I think it was during the summer holidays of 1949 that a statue of Our Lady of Fatima was brought to Spain. When my father heard about it, he wanted to take me to Madrid to pray in front of the image and ask the Mother for a cure, but he couldn't find me. When I came home in the evening, he was very disappointed, until I told him I was hungry, and his disappointment changed to surprise. From that time on, I have never lost my appetite. I was taken to a hospital for x-rays, and I was told that I had no more fever and was cured.

The next three years I felt very good, and I was told I could finally go to the seminary for foreign missions if I still wanted to. My parents and my uncle never said a word to discourage me, but some priests who were friends of my father and uncle spoke to them, then called me to say that I was out of my mind. They felt I was throwing away a great opportunity at home. I knew what they were thinking, but I thought God had called me and I wanted to go.

I completed my studies in 1956. After ordination I was assigned as assistant priest in Bilbao for four months. While I was there, I was assistant chaplain to the bull ring and had to go when there was a bullfight. It was an experience that I did not enjoy.

In December of 1956, we traveled by ship from Barcelona to Las Palmas (Canary Island) and then to Cape Town, South Africa. After traveling for another three days by train, we arrived in Rhodesia, which is now called Zimbabwe. We were three priests and two sisters, and we enjoyed the traveling except when we got seasick.

We arrived in Rhodesia on the 5th of January, 1957, and the same month I got my first appointment to a mission called Kana. In those days, we were not given time to learn languages. In May, I was told, "You are going to be a chaplain to the Dominican Sisters in Balawayo for three months and you must learn English and get your driver's license."

After that I was in charge of running schools and helping the teachers (very few were trained). My work was to go from one school to another, supervise the work done, and advise the teachers where I could.

It was hard living in the bush, sleeping in the schools with no windows or doors, eating what was there. While in that mission, I

was asked by the Apostolic Prefect to explore the north of the territory, and, with another priest, spent some time among tsetse fly, elephants, and all kinds of animals. It was very wild country.

In 1962 I was chosen to open a new mission in the territories I had explored. It was a very hard but a wonderful experience. To make 175 miles took me two days. With very poor roads, the last seven miles took me a whole day. To cross the rivers, we had to cut trees and place them across the water. I had two workers with me. We arrived in the afternoon and the grass was so high I could not see where I was driving. One of the workers walked in front. It was getting dark when we arrived and slept on the lorry. That night we heard the elephants coming toward us, and after that night we saw elephants passing by everyday. The locals said I had placed the mission in the house of the elephants.

The people of the Shangwe tribe were very simple and poor, but good. I was the first white to live there and some natives had never seen a white man before. I used a bicycle and many times they would stop me to look at me. They all said I had a long nose.

One day I shot an elephant that had been bothering us. The chief came to congratulate me as I had given food to his people. When he saw my cassette machine, he thought he could speak into it and reach the District Commissioner. He talked into the machine, but I don't know where I put that tape. What I can tell you is that the chief's people rejoiced having meat to eat!

After some time, I reported the incident with the elephant to the District Commissioner 75 miles away. I was brought to court and sentenced to sixty-five days of hard labor. But, in the end, the whole sentence was suspended.

In 1964 we had a very strong wind storm. I saw a big tree up-rooted, and one of my roofs was blown off. When I asked for help, the people refused. They said this happened because the spirits of their ancestors were not happy with the mission.

The wind has struck twice now. We had to replace the roof each time. Recently, the spirits have been at peace, though we still get many whirlwinds and our weather is still very hot.

After my first home leave in 1965, I was transferred to the bishop's house. From the bishop's office, I was sent to Victoria Falls at the end of 1974, and I am still there.

The parishioners spurred me to enlarge the church. I have my faith, but little money. Fortunately, I am receiving help from lots of people. But the cost of materials is ridiculous. I pray I am here to see construction through to completion.

There is little I can say about my future. A lot will depend on the new bishop. He might ask some of us to retire and leave the places to younger priests. If I am allowed to continue, I will not ask for retirement.

At present, I am paid an old age pension in Spain. I don't know the amount as the group of missionaries receives the funds. Since some of the priests get nothing, we pool our pensions. This way we all get the same when we go home for leave. I have no personal needs. I have what I need. I only ask for help for the church and for the poor.

Father Thomas del Barrio is a 40-year missionary in Africa and pastor of a church in Victoria Falls, Zimbabwe.

Memories of my visit with Father del Barrio are hard to forget. His letters of the hunger, drought, and day-to-day struggles are in sharp contrast to the life we have here in America. Their problems with AIDS, the corruption of officials, and the residual hatreds they still deal with from tribalism are very tragic and a sharp reminder of how fortunate we are in America. —Ed.

Excerpt from
Why I Am Still a Catholic

DOROTHY DAY

*I*T WAS HUMAN LOVE that helped me to understand divine love. Human love, at its best, unselfish, glowing, illuminating our days, gives us a glimpse of the love of God for man. Love is the best thing we can know in this life, but it must be sustained by an effort of the will. It is not just an emotion, a warm feeling of gratification. It must lie still and quiet, dull and smoldering, for periods. It grows through suffering and patience and compassion. We must suffer for those we love, we must endure their trials and their sufferings, we must even take upon ourselves the penalties due their sins. Thus we learn to understand the love of God for His creatures. Thus we understand the crucifixion. I pray that all who are groping for the truth will be led by the Holy Spirit from darkness into light. Even the little I see is light to me in the darkest of days and hours. And I could not breathe or live without that light which I have now—the light of faith which has been given to me by a merciful God who is the light of the world."

Dorothy Day is the founder of the Catholic Workers Movement. Her book Why I Am Still a Catholic *was published by Riverhead.*

A Reflection

Father Jack Barker

𝑇HE JOURNEY TO WHOLENESS and holiness is a journey to fulfillment, to wisdom, and to Christ, who is all. One important lesson
that can help us attain this goal is learning that reason alone cannot
finally bring us to Christ. The three wise men who came from the
east provide a good image for this. They were the scientists of their
day, and they represented the entire world outside the Jewish household of faith. They looked at a star, a heavenly body, and believed
the very universe itself was revealing something of great importance.
They didn't have a Bible, they only had the power of human reason
and the ability to reflect on nature to find truth about life. Yet they
were motivated to act.

On the other side, there were the scribes, religious leaders of their
day, who had the revelation of God in Scripture and a powerful faith
tradition. However, they failed to read the "signs of the times," so,
while reason needs to be informed by faith, it is also true that faith
needs to reflect and use reason. Reason is a gift from God.

At this dawn of a new millennium, we can be grateful that we
have the benefit of living in a time where reason, science and learning have experienced an incredible growth in the fundamental
knowledge which is at the disposal of thinking persons. Human
knowledge is at an all time high. God is manifesting Himself
through human reason, the accumulated wisdom of human effort
and history, and God is manifesting His own self through secular, as
well as sacred, experience.

But our world today seems confused about what is right. There is
a tendency to assume that because the religious experience is an inner experience, it is purely personal and entirely subjective. Religion
has been carefully excised from our community life through a radical separation of church and state that has isolated the individual.
Yet, most social scientists will admit that community life is relevant
data for understanding the human experience. Community impacts

personal perception and reality. In the time of Isaiah the prophet, this was referred to as a world that is covered with "thick clouds and darkness," a sign of the ignorance that hung over those who had not been enlightened by the truth of revelation.

Fundamentalist faiths are growing because many people want a simple answer. This is a kind of a "faith alone" reaction that is one response to the stress of our times. Another reaction is to reject formal religion altogether and to insist on reason alone.

Our Catholic tradition says it is both/and thinking, rather than either/or thinking which will best serve the truth and the true nature of the human person. It is faith and reason, it is Scripture and tradition, it is grace and nature, it is church and world, and it is faith and works. In the healthy tradition the "and" should never be replaced by an "or." In short, tradition insists that we come to the truth by reflecting on revelation and human nature.

So, reason gives us truths about human nature through psychology, history, sociology, anthropology, cosmology, etc. And, science has its agreed-upon methods for seeking the truth. So does theology, which is the reasoned reflection on the presence of faith in the human experience. Confusion arises only when people seek shortcuts, easy answers, and absolutes. Therefore, here are some principles to live by in the years ahead which I think will serve us well:

1. Catholic intellectual life is central to Catholic identity. We do not believe blindly or slavishly. We are urged to think and to understand what we believe. Reason and faith are not antagonistic.

2. We take philosophy seriously, i.e., we adapt various systems of thought about the nature of reality and knowledge and experience and apply them to the faith that is in us. We desire to render God's revelation to the world in a way that makes sense to others.

3. Facts do not come in pristine form. Facts are abstractions from something heavier and deeper, which contains implicit ends. No facts are completely free from values.

4. Our tradition rejects reductionism: the tendency to reduce things to a mechanistic or pure cause-and-effect world. For example, myth becomes fantasy and is stripped of its ability to inspire the human imagination, and things, whether simple or complex, are re-

duced to opinion. Faith and reason are compatible, but they are not equivalent. We disagree with a fundamentalist reading of Scripture.

5. The human person is neither radically independent, nor socially determined.

6. We take mysticism seriously; we know that ordinary, everyday consciousness is not the last word about reality.

7. Finally, our tradition becomes part of the culture in which it finds itself. Because our mission is to transform the world, as it is stated in *Gaudium et Spes*, the Church, a visible organization and a spiritual community, "travels the same journey as all humankind and shares the same earthly lot with the world; it is to be a leaven and the soul of human society in its renewal by Christ and transformation into the family of God." The struggle everywhere to link faith and culture enriches human life and sheds light on the human journey.

As we move into this new millennium, we can be glad that we have as our constant companion the spiritual, and natural, resources of church and world, a living tradition which enlightens our way to fulfillment and to Christ. We can move with confidence into the future, knowing that we are moving closer to the fullness of truth and enlightenment which is intended by Christ for all people.

God's love can never be restricted to any one people. Had St. Paul, and the supreme interpreter of Paul, lived today, he might have put it this way: "In Christ Jesus, all people, black and white, male and female, young and old, rich and poor, are now co-heirs with the Jews, members of the same body and sharers of the same promise through the preaching of the gospel."

Are we who claim faith manifesting or obscuring this mystery? It is our challenge, as well as our vision.

Father Jack Barker is Vicar of the Archdiocese of San Bernadino and Pastor of St. Francis of Assisi in La Quinta, California.

On Stewardship

ROBERT MATT

THE CONCEPT OF STEWARDSHIP is closely related to another concept, discipleship. Let's begin with an illustration of this thing called discipleship.

Recall the story of Christ walking by the Sea of Galilee and meeting Peter and his friends. He said to them, "Come follow me; and if you come with me, great things will happen."

But He only chose twelve followers from among them. And to those twelve, He said, "Go, therefore, and make disciples of all nations."

Today; this week; this month! Our Father is not calling you; Jesus is. He is shouting loud and clear. The question is, are you listening? To get a better perspective on the concepts of discipleship and stewardship, I'd like to define those two terms from my perspective as a practicing Christian believer.

Discipleship is a response to the invitation of Jesus to follow His teachings and His challenges. Let us recall that in those teachings most of what Jesus said concerned our relationship to the material world. Remember that Jesus is the one who is inviting you. And do not forget that God works through you. Are you going to be an engine that is running and working for Christ or an engine that has stalled?

Stewardship involves accepting the responsibility of being a disciple of Jesus. It must focus on the spiritual, on the need for the individual giver, you, to respond to your call to be a disciple.

Some of you may say, I do not hear the call of God. Well, God has not moved! God is with you every minute of your life. God is here in the real presence, every day. Now that raises two questions: Why should we respond to God's call? And how?

In answer to the first, we must respond if we are true Christians, true believers. We should receive the gifts of God gratefully and cultivate them responsibly. We should share lovingly, with justice. And we should then return our God-given gifts to the Lord with an increase.

The need for the giver to give, in response to God's call, is much greater than the church's or God's need to receive. The church, this parish, will go on forever. But we have only one chance to be a part of it. That chance is now, in this life.

That brings up the second question: How do we respond to God's call? Our response must be based on our faith: Do we believe? Do we accept Jesus as our God? This demands a conversion, a new way of living. Stewardship is a lifestyle, one that results in three things: first, and most importantly, a greater gathering of spiritual resources. The greatest spiritual benefit goes to the giver, you. You are the one who reaps the benefits.

The second result is an increase in human resources, specifically your energy and talent, required to build up God's kingdom. This brings Christ to the people and the people to Christ. The third result is an addition to the financial resources necessary to build up the kingdom of God. The stewardship lifestyle must be conceived and implemented in this order.

The stewardship lifestyle must also be rooted in gratitude and thanksgiving to our God, who is the giver of all gifts. It reflects both our relationships to God and with each other.

In the secular, materialistic world we live in, we tend to worship two gods: the god of money and material wealth and the god of self—I'll do it my way. Think for a moment about the decisions you make daily. Are they motivated by the worship of the god of money or the god of self? Are you worshipping either of these gods? That which motivates your major activities shows where your heart really is. Where do you want it to be? Which god do you want to worship?

The philosophy of the stewardship concept is simple. Wherever we place our prayers, our energy and talent, our material resources, and our faith is where we will find our hearts.

God gave us a free will, the power to accept or reject Him. Not accepting, not committing, or not getting involved is a rejection of the God you claim to believe in. Make the God we believe in the center of your life: Be a disciple. Adopt the lifestyle of a steward.

Be the steward of all the gifts God has given you. Follow the example that God has shown us through the teachings of Jesus.

I try hard to lead a lifestyle based on stewardship. I think I am a disciple. What led me down this path?

I started my business career working with my father. He was my mentor, both in business and in life. Out of the first paycheck I received, due to his urging, I contributed 10 percent to charity. Several years later, when my father was still a trustee of our parish, he asked me to be chairman of a fund drive to build an addition to the school. I was about thirty years old and already had five children. I simply did not want to take on this additional responsibility, and I told him so. His response was, "Bob, what is one of the easiest manual tasks you do almost on a daily basis?" He then answered the question himself: "It is writing a check. Bob," he continued, "that is only one small part of tithing."

Then came the lesson. "If you want to be a real disciple of this God we believe in," my father said, "then give 10 percent of your *time*. Further the cause of Christian living and the Christian perspective as it should be lived in this material world."

Since that time, I have tried to live that way all my life. It is why I spent the past two years as a Peace Corps volunteer in Poland. I was worried about what the introduction of our materialistic culture would do to a Socialist-Christian country. I thought I could be a role model, from the Christian perspective, of how to live in a free-market economy. I also felt that my father, now dead a long time, was keeping track of the days—I did not want to meet him and come up a day short! This is one example of how I have lived the lifestyle of stewardship.

Keep the spiritual dimension of stewardship in mind. When you make your personal commitment of time, talent, and treasure, don't just tell our Father what you are going to do—go do it! When Jesus invited the first disciples to join Him, He said something great would happen. If you respond to the invitation of Jesus, the Holy Spirit will lead the way, and you will be blessed abundantly. This is God's promise.

A Thank You to Robert Matt

J. Nelson Hoffman

$\mathcal{A}$s I've described in the Introduction, Bob delivered the talk on stewardship in 1995. One of his points really got through to me. He asked the question, "What religions competed for the hearts and souls of American in the last half of the twentieth century?" My silent answer was: Christianity, Judaism, and Islam. Bob had another perspective. His opinion was that in terms of what people did, and how they acted, *materialism* was far in front, followed by *me-ism*. Christianity and other traditional religions were at the back of the pack.

That view has stuck with me in the ensuing years. It caused me to think about my priorities. It caused cognitive dissonance. It caused me to think about what kind of an example I had set? As I reflected on my priorities, materialism issues and self-seeking had taken up more time than I cared to admit. The role of provider, husband, and father was there every day. But was there a consciousness to provide a deliberate day-to-day Christian example? My answer was not enough.

Reflecting on that question became one of the prime inspirations for this book. Had I taught my children with "Do as I say, not as I do?"

The Marines say it a different way: *He can talk the talk, but does he walk the walk?*

These were some of the questions I asked myself: How much time did I spend reading the *Wall Street Journal, Fortune,* and *Business Week?* How much time was spent reading about parenting, the Bible, or about the social and civic problems in my community? How many hours a week were spent at work (or doing work at home)? How many hours a week were spent in working for a volunteer organization or for a cause I profess?

Robert Matt has served as a good friend and mentor and a significant contributor to this book. Thanks, Bob.

On Science, Light, and Belief

J. Nelson Hoffman

*M*y early faith was built on the tales of the monumental figures who make up history, from Adam and Eve to Jesus and his disciples. The images were framed in the descriptions of earth, air, fire
and water, wine and blood, bread and flesh. I was taught that for
early man, the bloody sacrifices were man's first prayers, the first
recognition of God. As those cultures became more civilized, bread
and wine became their offering as return of the manna from heaven,
as symbols of God's abundance. As a teenager, I became a Baptist.
The water of baptism became a symbol of cleansing and purification.

This was later reinforced for me as I visited Epheses in 1957.
Among the ruins was a well preserved baptismal font: a cylindrical
well, four feet deep and four feet in diameter, with stone steps leading down one side, and up and out the other. Somehow, that font
made it clear: the role of water in cleansing and the passage from
one stage of life to another.

The millennium reminds me that the inspired book that grounds
my faith was written 2000 years ago by men of a tribal and agricultural society.

At age sixty-eight, I search for insight and understanding of the
written word recorded so long ago that it may have meaning and
guide my daily living. I wish I were blessed with the simple unquestioning faith of Father Del Barrio, Mother Theresa, and the saints.
My faith is that of a scientist, which carries the burden of challenging, questioning, and trying to understand why. I believe that all
knowledge man has now, and ever will have, is just a more detailed
description of a universe created by God. We may probe the outer
reaches of the universe, look in detail at the least comprehensible
particle or wave of matter, understand the most intricate systems
that allow the living and breathing of our lives, or duplicate parts of
our bodies. But all these discoveries will provide is another layer of
an infinite understanding we can only imagine.

Where did my notion of this universe created by God come from?

I am sure it derives from all the teaching and reading of my life. However, one image stands out most clearly: the first atomic explosions of Almagordo, Hiroshima and Nagasaki. The newsreels from that day show the power, the flash of light, and the rush of heat and air that produced such unimagined destruction. I recall the aerial pictures of the giant fireball rising through the clouds, upward and upward, and two questions rose up inside of me: Did this explosion represent all that man could create? Or was this explosion a forerunner of mankind's self-destruction?

History and mythology tell tales of man's attempt to be like the gods—to possess the power of the gods. In the fireball cloud of the atomic bomb, I saw what ultimate power both God and man possessed. The atomic bomb created awe, humility, and concern for man's ability to handle such awesome power and destructive capacity. My hope for the future was that the peaceful applications of that technology would overcome its dangers as a weapon.

For the first three years at the University of Rochester, I immersed myself in the study of physics. But I realized the world of research and a career in the development of atomic energy was not for me. I was more of an engineer than a scientist, and I became fascinated by the study of optics. I was interested in how the eye perceived the energy that entered it. The thing we describe as *light*, giving rise to sight and vision, captured my imagination. Upon reflection, I also realize I base my faith on this basic idea.

What we learn about our universe, our bodies, and the structure of matter is, metaphorically, *light* penetrating *darkness*. But man must be present. The Bible has a phrase that I appreciate more with time: *When the eye is healthy, the whole world is full of light.*

That quotation has stayed with me for fifty years and frames how I perceive of the world. In my reading and research for this book, I came across the words of one of the most powerful writers and spiritual influences of the last century, Thomas Merton. His book, *The Seven Story Mountain*, is a biography about his journey to faith, and he writes of light and faith in terms that have shaped and reinforced my perspective. He writes:

When a ray of light strikes a crystal, it gives a new quality to the crystal. When God's infinitely disinterested love plays upon a human soul, the same kind of thing takes place, and that is the life called sanctifying grace. The soul of man, left to its own natural level, is a potentially lucid crystal left in the darkness. It is perfect in its own nature, but it lacks something that it can only receive from outside and above itself. But, when the light shines in it, it becomes, in a manner, transformed into light and seems to lose its nature in the splendor of a higher nature, the nature of the light that is in it.

Later in the book, Merton speaks of the motto of Columbia University:

In lumini tuo videbimous lumen.
(In thy light, we shall see the light.)

This motto provides meaning for my daily life. The knowledge that I gain, the work that I do, and the growth of my spirit are all manifestations of this truth.

Wayne Connell wrote earlier of the trend over the past few centuries for man's concern with intellectual pursuits to push out his pursuit of things of the spirit. I lamented the trend I saw in great universities such as Harvard, Columbia, and my school, the University of Rochester. The trend I saw at these schools, all founded by men of deep and abiding faith, was that they were becoming bastions of secularism. This trend seems to be changing. Now, I see a student-led quest for matters of the spirit. Young people, regardless of faith, are not denying time for their spirit. Rather, though determined to succeed in the world, they make time for nurturing their spiritual side—to develop their spiritual awareness right along with their intellectual side. I have been told that at some universities, more that 70% of the students are involved with a charitable cause of some type, participating in a community service program. This participation is found in many high schools, churches, and communities.

This perspective is shaped in the recipe above and helped me find this suggestion for my children and grandchildren:

Regardless of how pressed you are for time, how stressed you feel, make time EVERY DAY for your spirit!

If there is one lament in my life, it is that I was "always busy." Now, in retirement, I make time for prayer, meditation, and reflection. And I suggest you do too, every day. Like the lucid crystal in

Thomas Merton's book, be a crystal, a prism to receive the light that will come into you. It will make you glow with an Inner Light, and your light will shine in the world.

The word "reflection" will have two meanings for you: the concentration and focus will bring inner thoughts to the surface, and taking light in will become part of you, and it will shine out.

My granddaughter Sara Clark recently asked for our support when she fasted for 30 hours to support World Vision. I can think of no a better example of nurturing spirit, of true reflection, than this example from my granddaughter. In this selfless act of hers, I see so much of what I have come to understand, and believe in, about my faith.

— FAVORITE PRAYERS —

There is little couplet buried deep in my earliest memories—something that my mother must have taught me, "There are two little magic words that will open any door with ease, one little word is *thank you*, and the other little word is *please*."

Later, when I was taught more about prayer, this was expanded to prayers of Thanksgiving, Petition, and Adoration.

Several favorite prayers of mine follow. Pastor Robert Grochau submitted "The Evening Reflection" from *A Diary of Private Prayer*, and we have Jack McKearin to thank for two prayers and Tom Tippett for one prayer contribution.

A POST-RECOVERY VIEW

Our home in Snowmass, Colorado, sits on the side of a mountain overlooking a valley which winds its way up to the town of Aspen and beyond to Independence Pass and the heavenly peaks of the

Continental Divide. When the sun rises in the morning, I stand on the porch awestruck by the view. In that early morning light, the following words from Psalm 118 give a great start to the new day: "This is the day the Lord has made; let us be glad and rejoice in it." In 1996 I was struck by cardiac arrest while on vacation in Hawaii. By God's grace, I was in the critical care unit of Queens Hospital in Honolulu, hooked to the machines, when it happened. Unable to travel, I had to stay in the hospital and rest until I had recovered enough to fly home. It was a time of great reflection, prayer, and a reassessment of priorities. A really weird thought came to me—the day you die, your net worth goes to zero! Billionaire or beggar. That day, everyone is worth exactly the same. In the weeks following my surgery I came across a hymn which best expresses my post-recovery view. It is the last prayer in this section, "All That I Am."

The Twenty-Third Psalm— A Psalm of David

The Lord is my shepherd: I shall not want.

He maketh me to lie down in green pastures: he leadeth me beside the still waters.

He restoreth my soul: he leadeth me in the paths of righteousness for his name's sake.

Yea, though I walk through the valley of the shadow of death. I will fear no evil: for thou art with me; thy rod and thy staff, they comfort me.

Thou preparest a table before me in the presence of mine enemies; thou anointest my head with oil; my cup runneth over.

Surely, goodness and mercy shall follow me all the days of my life: and I will dwell in the house of the Lord forever.

Though scholars have altered the words over the years, I still recite the King James Version that I memorized as a young boy. —Ed.

The Serenity Prayer

REINHOLD NIEBUHER

God grant me the serenity to accept the things I cannot change,
The courage to change the things I can,
And the wisdom to know the difference.

Prayer of St. Francis of Assisi

Lord, make me an instrument of your peace; where there is hatred,
let me sow love; where there is injury, pardon; where there is doubt,
faith; where there is despair, hope; where there is darkness, light;
and where there is sadness, joy.

O Divine Master, grant that I may not so much seek to be con-
soled as to console; to be understood as to understand; to be loved,
as to love; for it is in giving that we receive, it is in pardoning that
we are pardoned, and it is in dying that we are born to eternal life.

A Diary of Private Prayer

JOHN BAILLIE

Twenty-fifth Day. Evening.

Holy God, to whose service I long ago dedicated my soul and life,
I grieve and lament before Thee that I am still so prone to sin and so
little inclined to obedience:

So much attached to the pleasures of sense, so negligent of things spiritual:

So prompt to gratify my body, so slow to nourish my soul:

So greedy for present delight, so indifferent to lasting blessedness:

So fond of idleness, so indisposed for labour:

So soon at play, so late at prayer:

So brisk in the service of self, so slack in the service of others:

So eager to get, so reluctant to give:

So lofty in my profession, so low in my practice:

So full of good intentions, so backward to fulfill them:

So severe with my neighbors, so indulgent with myself:

So eager to find fault, so resentful at being found fault with:

So little able for great tasks, so discontented with small ones:

So weak in adversity, so swollen and self-satisfied in prosperity:

So helpless apart from Thee, and yet so little willing to be bound to Thee.

O merciful heart of God, grant me yet again Thy forgiveness. Hear my sorrowful tale and in Thy great mercy blot it out from the book of Thy remembrance. Give me faith so to lay hold of Thine own holiness and so to rejoice in the righteousness of Christ my Savior that, resting on His merits rather than on my own, I may more and more become conformed to His likeness, my will becoming one with His in obedience to Thine. All I ask for His holy name's sake. Amen.

John Baillie was Chaplain to the King of England and Professor of Divinity, University of Edinburgh.

All That I Am

SEBASTIAN TEMPLE

All that I am, all that I do. All that I'll ever have, I offer now to you.

All that I dream, all that I pray. All that I'll ever make, I give to you today.

Take and sanctify these gifts for your honor, Lord. Knowing that I love and serve you is enough reward.

All that I am, all that I do. All that I'll ever have, I offer now to you.

7

THE WORLD
OF WORK

"Whether you think that you can, or that you can't, you are usually right."
—Henry Ford

"In business as in life, trust is fundamental to a successful relationship."
—Anonymous

In completing our Tocqueville approach to examining the major institutions which shape our lives, we look at how jobs and careers provide a testing ground for the moral values, attitudes, and character we learned as young people.

As Ann Ehringer so eloquently points out in the first contribution of this chapter, integrity, credibility, and values are foundations of character every successful businessperson must possess, and this formation of character does not happen overnight. It starts when children are young.

Later in the chapter, Dick Mau and Jack McKearin offer examples of the necessary character attributes they believe a business person must have to be successful; Dick Hartl and Ben VanderWerf illustrate lessons they learned in their careers; and Joseph Mack describes his experiences as CEO of one of the world's great advertising agencies.

When I look back on my business life and how my career evolved, I know that hard work, persistence, and early training were some of the responsible factors which led to success. I was also willing to take chances. Sometimes they didn't work; fortunately, more times than not, the risks paid off.

In the past, when young people have asked me how I determined what career I wanted to pursue, it was easy for me to trace that decision back to my college years.

But others came to their careers in different ways. In a letter to me for this book, my good friend Robert Parker illustrates how he made his decision:

> One of the prerequisites of application to medical school is the Medical Aptitude Test, which you usually take during the junior year of college. This allows you to file applications and go for interviews in the fall of your senior year.
>
> By an unfortunate mix up of dates (or just plain stupidity) I missed the test. As a result, my application to medical school was going to be delayed for a year.
>
> This really messed up my plans. I was in love, I was engaged, and I was planning to be married in August after graduation. I needed a way out of this dilemma.
>
> Fortunately, I mentioned my problem to a classmate who was a pre-dental student, and he suggested a plan. He was going to Buffalo in a couple of weeks to take the Dental Aptitude Test and suggested that I do the same.
>
> If I was successful and accepted to dental school that was fine, since the first year is same for both dental and medical students. And since there were always drop-outs in the first years, I could transfer over to the medical school after completing a year in the dental school.
>
> The rest is history—everything went as planned, except that I found a real niche and love for dentistry, and I never considered, or regretted, pursuing that transfer.

We begin at our look at what specific aspects of character are most significant in attaining a successful career with another contribution by Dr. Ann Ehringer.

Value and Values

DR. ANN EHRINGER

IN DOING RESEARCH for my Ph.D. dissertation at Marshall some years ago (later published as *Make Up Your Mind— Entrepreneurs Talk about Decision-Making*), I talked with 60 entrepreneurs about the significant turning point decisions of their business careers. My interest in their experiences was to understand how and why they made strategic decisions and to "map" the common themes and re-curring similarities.

Among their commonalties, I found their decisions were guided far more often by personal principles than by economic advantage or any other purpose. Their principles, their personal integrity, trustworthiness, and concern for other people were the fundamental drivers of their business decisions and their personal decisions.

The range of purposes of decisions of this group of entrepreneurs included the Golden Rule, honesty, trust, and loyalty. It included money, power, control, freedom, fun, credibility, pride, security and doing the right things for their people. Few of them acknowledged being motivated by money; most described making money primarily as a way of keeping score of their achievements. Most needed to have control but tried to be sensitive about using power. They sought freedom, by which they meant money, time and independence, and they identified much of what they did and more of what they wanted to do.

They also were drawn by opportunity, often in response to it, but more often in search of it. They rarely, and often only belatedly, understood risk. They wanted financial security, even as they put it at risk in their businesses. They did not like uncertainty, even as they were comfortable dealing with change. And they were strongly driven by fear.

They valued their integrity and credibility ahead of virtually everything else and went to great lengths to protect their reputations. They learned to value personal relationships and the support of good people. At the end of their careers, what they valued most were strong personal relationships and having done work that they felt was meaningful.

With the exception of the work they did in their communities and other helping avocations, their goals did not extend greatly beyond the parameters of their personal and business lives. They were rooted in honesty, honor, and concern for the well-being of others.

The most salient lesson to emerge from the reflective conversations of these entrepreneurs was that the key to making good decisions is conscious self-awareness of who we are and want to become, of how we think, and of what is important to us. In order to create the outcomes we want, it is imperative that we understand, at our most conscious level, what our personal principles are. These personal principles drive our most significant decisions, whether or not we are aware of their driving power. Another salient message of their recollections was that for too many of these entrepreneurs, the lessons came late, and painfully, in their careers—often too late for them to change and too late for them to achieve what they belatedly had discovered was important to them.

After years of coaching entrepreneur CEOs and leading small companies, I have an opportunity to help university students develop this fundamental awareness of self. I am privileged to teach MBA-level courses that emphasize lessons of self-awareness, humility, and patience at an early stage in peoples' careers.

My courses are based on the assumptions that the primary purpose of business ownership is to build a great, enduring company— a sustainable, successful, and successfully sustainable company. Although entrepreneurs express many personal reasons for company ownership—to make a difference in peoples lives, to produce quality goods or services, to make money, to create a legacy, to be in control, to leave a family inheritance—only by creating a company with value and values that endure beyond the entrepreneur, can any of these other goals be obtained.

The most important determinant of achieving that goal is the entrepreneur himself, the Owner/President. Whatever deep down core values and personal principles he or she has, the company will become. The Owner/President's most important skill sets are those of self-awareness, decision-making, and the ability to work with and through the efforts of other people to develop, to empower, and to lead.

Useful, simple models are available that enhance the Owner/President's effectiveness and his company's success. An entrepreneur can learn these models, much as an athlete repetitively practices the basic models of his sport or an artist those of his craft, so that they become part of his intuition and unconscious foundations. This frees him to concentrate on developing vision and strategies to achieve his and his company's potential. It frees him to work on his business rather than in it. And it frees him to build meaningful relationships and do meaningful work, the achievements by which entrepreneurs ultimately judge the quality of their lives.

In the *Role of the Owner/President In Managing New Ventures*, we explore models of how to make good decisions, develop personal and company vision and strategies, and understand and anticipate the phases of one's personal life cycle.

In the *Role of the Owner/President in Managing Growing Companies*, we study models of how decision-making and authority change through succeeding phases of a healthy company's growth and why the entrepreneur must change with them, as well as models of effectively dealing with the challenges that typically emerge at different stages of company growth.

In both courses, the touchstones are each student's personal principles and the unique resources he or she brings to creating value in an entrepreneurial company. We talk at length about personal principles, ethical values, and long-term value creation.

We learn from experienced guest entrepreneurs and from probing self-examination of our individual experiences. We apply these business models for making decisions, creating vision, developing strategies, and understanding personal and business life-cycle to help these future owner/presidents proactively manage change and growth in their companies and lives. The courses are not about the nuts and bolts, nor tools and techniques of venture management, all of which they have learned in other courses. They are about self-awareness, values, attitudes, and ways of thinking.

Over the course of the semester, my goal is to help each of my students learn to know himself deeply and well; to come to dearly understand what he believes, what he values, and what he wants to contribute; to store in his mental muscles some of the fundamental lessons of entrepreneurial value creation; and to integrate all of it into creating the life he wants to have led.

Previously published by the Marshall School of Business.

Corporate Culture: Day to Day Values

JOSEPH MACK

SOME YEARS AGO when I was working in advertising at Dancer Fitzgerald Sample, before it was acquired by Saatchi & Saatchi. I was asked by the CEO to define the agency's culture. Since I had been at DFS for at least 25 years (having worked at every level of account management from trainee to management director), I felt confident that I could easily do what our chief executive had requested. Was I wrong!

I started writing, and it became more of an explanation on how I felt about our first rate agency, rather than an objective statement on the culture. After hours and pages of enthusiastic description, I realized that I was no closer to a concise statement on culture than when I began.

I sought help from a few peers and got back more of the same. The fact was, I really didn't know what corporate culture was. Happily, it dawned on me that a corporate culture was nothing more than the set of values which guided the everyday life of the agency, no different, really, than the values that guide one's personal choices in daily life.

So what were the primary values that defined the life of Dancer Fitzgerald Sample, that excellent advertising agency that was blessed with so many blue chip clients, like General Mills, Procter & Gamble, Toyota, Best Foods, Life Savers Inc., Nabisco, and

Northwest Airlines? I believe that the number of values was relatively few:

Profit—that which the stockholders share, or as one of my early bosses said, "his slice of the melon."
Product—the effectiveness of our advertising and media.
Partnership—the way we treated our relationships with clients.
People—the way we cared for, motivated, and rewarded our employees.

For Dancer Fitzgerald Sample, the priority of these values was very clear, at least to me. First came "people." We had trained our own in all departments for years. We valued loyalty and rewarded it. We rarely fired anyone—when someone wasn't working out, we counseled him or her, provided consultant help, and then moved him or her into a different department. As a result of this regard toward their employees, DFS had the reputation as being one of the most enjoyable agencies to work for on Madison Avenue.

Second, by a nose over "product," came "partnership." We placed an unusual degree of importance on strengthening relationships with clients—partnerships which had certainly stood the test of time. On average, our clients had been with us for almost 20 years. The General Mills and Proctor and Gamble relationships date back to the 1920s.

Client service, responsiveness, involvement in marketing, sound strategic thinking, creative problem solving—all had been bred into us as ways to demonstrate that we cared about our clients' businesses.

We fought our clients when we had to, but always respected their point of view. After all. it was the client's money that we were spending. We knew that if we "sold" the client advertising that it didn't like, the commercials would ultimately have a very short life. We believed that there was always a way to satisfy the client and be true to our beliefs. From a very practical standpoint, we knew that over time our real growth—our most profitable growth—came from existing clients.

Third was the "product," i.e., our research, media and advertising for products like Cheerios, Bounty Paper Towels and Bayer Aspirin.

We were very disciplined and crafted smart strategies, with input from research, the copywriters, and the client. And, while the creative team and the account team almost always seemed to have an adversarial relationship, we almost always presented work we could all support.

When it came to spilling blood to sell a new advertising campaign, I believe we drew the line. We fought hard for what we believed in, but always did it in a gentlemanly way. Unlike other agencies who seemed to have a more arrogant "we know what's best for you" attitude, we didn't want to jeopardize the client-agency relationship.

I'm sure that at times we sacrificed great work. On the other hand, we protected the client relationships. I don't mean to suggest that we rolled over easily or that we didn't win lots of battles with our clients. We did, and we fought hard.

I remember the Wendy's meeting when we were presenting the "Where's The Beef?" storyboards. The client was convinced that it had produced something that was strategically similar in the past that did not sell, and their marketing director asked us to go back to the drawing board.

I refused, politely. Cliff Freeman, the creator of the advertising, and I talked nonstop for what had to be an hour—arguing, persuading, pleading. Finally, the client agreed, I'm convinced, only to get us to shut up. The rest is history. *TV Guide* recently named that line the "most memorable" in the history of advertising.

Fourth came "profit." Our belief was that if we did the best that we could to support and motivate our employees, if we did the best to improve client relations and turn out creative work that the client liked, and which sold product, the profits would follow. They did for many years. Though, during the years immediately preceding our acquisition by Saatchi & Saatchi, our privately held stock saw little growth.

So that was the basis of our very comfortable culture at Dancer Fitzgerald Sample. Once acquired by Saatchi & Saatchi in 1986, and subsequently forced to merge with the Compton Agency, we had the opportunity to observe two new corporate cultures. Each was quite different from ours in terms of the priorities placed on the four "P's." Also, it became clear that a fifth "P" could be factored into the value set, namely "politics."

Corporate politics are those efforts, other than performance, that are designed to further an individual's career. Even DFS had its share of internal politics. They existed, but in the long run I don't think they mattered. Ultimately, management rewarded performance.

In my experience, politics often surfaces when management is weak, or when it is not clear who is running, or will run, the show. It also appears when individual drives for power and money are so strong they overwhelm the culture of the corporation, and the organization is weakened as a result.

Of course, my knee-jerk reaction was that our culture at DFS was much better than what existed at other agencies. Our commitment to thinking of our people as our company's primary priority was the way an agency should be run, and we enjoyed an enviable industry reputation. It seemed that everyone wanted to work at DFS

But, looking back, I believe that I was wrong about our own corporate culture. Ours may have been better than the new company cultures with which we were merging. However, after acquisition, the clash of cultures led me to conclude that there might be an ideal culture that is different from all three of our agencies.

First, I believe, must come the integrity of the "product." After all, advertising agencies are hired to create the smartest strategies and the most effective creative work and media thinking possible. Anticipating what will sell to the client most easily is simply wrong, even if it makes the client happy. Unless the work is truly effective, the client will not be happy for long, and the partnership will deteriorate.

Second, comes the "partnership," which includes providing quality service, listening carefully, and respecting the client's point of view. At the same time, true partnership demands honesty and the need to fight hard for what you believe in. And, when necessary, true partnership demands that you admit when you're wrong and be willing to accept a better idea, even if that idea is the client's. There is no place for ego in a good partnership relationship.

Third comes "people." Reward people for a job well done, for creating brilliant advertising, for making a smart media buy, for strengthening the agency/client relationship, for landing a new assignment, for solving client problems and agency problems. People must be acknowledged for contributing to the success of a venture. Even the most self-confident people love to be stroked. They want to go home at night feeling that their efforts are appreciated and that they are being fairly compensated. In a culture where people come first, as I defined the DFS culture, I believe the emphasis is wrong. If it is not absolutely clear that people will be rewarded only for performance, people can easily become lazy, soft, and unrealistic about their jobs. I observed both, prior to, and after, our acquisition and merger. The DFS people often became complainers when the going got a little rough. For many, their personal comfort and compensation were the most important goals, not the clients' advertising needs or what was best for the agency. While others may disagree, I believe DFS, in being such a caring employer, inadvertently created many employees who were both soft and unrealistic.

Fourth, comes "profit." Long-term profit can be guaranteed: only if the product and service are the best they can be (given price points, of course); only when the partnership with the client is totally open and honest and focused entirely on the client's needs; and only if employees are motivated and fairly compensated for helping to produce a superior product, as well as strengthening relationships with clients. There are many factors which influence the bottom line, and unless the integrity of a company's product comes first, failure is inevitable.

I have not mentioned "politics," that insidious last "P", because I know that strong management can make it clear that politics are unacceptable and simply not a substitute for performance.

For the past six years, I have been enjoying a blossoming career as a new home developer. Thanks to an excellent economy and a superb product that is fairly priced, we have been very successful.

I have been delighted to see how similar this new career is to advertising. I'm still dealing with a product that must be positioned, named, targeted, priced, and marketed. I'm still dealing with clients, demonstrating that I care by listening, recommending better and more cost efficient ways to build, and surprising them with phone calls and status reports. I still have to motivate employees and make it clear that their compensation is based on performance.

I have to believe that every enterprise, large or small, might benefit from a review of all its "p's".

In many cases, as in advertising, it is difficult to separate the product from the partnership. This is especially true in service businesses. Nonetheless, it is critical that employees know that superior product and service are the essentials of success and that they will be rewarded by their direct contributions to that success.

Joseph Mack is the retired CEO of Saatchi and Saatchi, a leading global advertising agency. He has an active volunteer life, including his service as a trustee of the University of Rochester.

Lessons Learned

D I C K   H A R T L

*M*Y MOTHER AND FATHER were married and conceived me during the Depression, and my early learning was influenced by that era. At the time, the stories and pictures they saw of people and organizations in desperate conditions reinforced the need to prepare for the future and build a nest egg for the rainy day that would surely come. "Waste not, want not" was one of my mother's favorite expressions, and she practiced it well.

My father, who had a job with the telephone company, rose rapidly in rank from being a telephone installer to ultimately managing the plant facilities for all of Wisconsin. He worked long hours and accepted transfers of location readily. He was truly "a company man" or as my mother would say "wedded to Ma Bell."

When I was considering education alternatives, my father told me that he probably could have been president of Wisconsin Bell if he had achieved a "sheepskin." He felt that education opens doors that might be hard to open any other way, but what you do afterward ultimately determines your success. In other words, don't be enamored of the degree and the institution you attended. Indeed, I have encountered those who felt that the world should be handed to them because of the prestigious schools from which they graduated, but who did little to better the enterprises for which they were working.

During high school at a small Catholic institution, I lacked direction and inspiration until a nun who taught chemistry changed my outlook, showing me that education could lead to a rewarding future. This wonderful nun, Sister Celeste, took the time to get me excited about chemistry. She demonstrated how science improves our lives. With a solid background in science, I could choose from many different careers. That experience made me reflect on the impact dedicated teachers can have on the course of our lives and how all of us can be better teachers and guides.

In 1960 when I was working at Monsanto Chemical Company, I met the woman who has made my life truly wonderful. Joan, my wife of thirty-eight years, has given me so much and I have not recognized her enough for doing so. As I scurry around the world, she reminds me to "take the time to smell the roses." Unfortunately, I have not listened as well as I ought, and on reflection, I realize I should spend more time appreciating all the things that God has given me, particularly my wonderful family.

Joan also encourages me to actively listen to our children, as they have a perspective and wisdom that I may not readily appreciate. Not only should we listen to our children but also to all the younger people with whom we interact. There is so much to be gained by active listening.

As a scientist and engineer, I haven't always followed my "instincts." Joan encourages me to trust my instincts—on people, on projects, on direction. This has been hard for me to do, but I realize that she is right: Some things in life cannot be quantified, and we need to trust our experience, judgment, and sixth sense.

Our first daughter's doctor imparted sound advice. As new parents, we were eager to learn how we could instill good values in our children. This wise lady encouraged us to think about all of the values we wanted our children to have and then behave in a way that reflected them. What an eloquent and simple way of conveying how people learn by looking to parents, teachers, leaders, and others as role models and making that behavior part of their own lifestyles! So many problems of modern society could be solved if people recognized this wisdom.

As a bright, energetic, newly minted engineer who was going to turn the world upside down, I was determined to make my company's products the best quality, the lowest in cost, and the most profitable. I had chosen a position in production technical service so that I could use my knowledge to improve commercial operations and to interact with people in production. Little did I know that many of these people had a lot at stake in maintaining the status quo. Particularly those working in the plant did not share my zeal for improving things to make their lives better. They viewed change as negative, with lots of unknowns.

My first boss in the industrial/commercial world, Bob Frey, had a big impact on me. Bob Frey was a fantastic mentor. He showed me that in order to initiate change, I needed to see it from the perspective of those who would be affected and then be able to communicate to them why my changes would be an improvement. In effect, I had to become a "salesman" for change. Dealing with the Chemical Workers Union was the ultimate challenge to my learning that lesson, but it's one that has stood me in good stead throughout my career. Bob also taught me both the importance of planning and of the need to take on the "elephant" one bite at a time instead of trying to swallow the whole thing at once.

Another person who has had a great impact on my business life is Jack Welch, General Electric's superstar CEO. I had the pleasure to work for him for several years when the GE plastics operation was going through phenomenal growth. I was extremely impressed with the time Jack spent on recruiting quality talent. He was almost ruthless in his drive to have the best possible people working in his organization. By devoting his own time to this instead of relying on the human resources department, he effectively communicated the importance of having top-notch workers.

Perhaps the most significant lesson I learned from Jack came out of his philosophy that you will accomplish more by setting extraordinary goals and falling slightly short of them rather than by setting modest goals and exceeding them. Getting an organization to stretch by raising the bar is the key to big results.

Stan Avery, inventor of the pressure-sensitive label and founder of the Avery Dennison Company, taught me the importance of being humble. Stan was very successful because he didn't get caught up in the prestige of his position. When I worked at Avery Dennison, he would always ask my permission to come see me about his ideas. Though he certainly had the power and stature to have summoned me to his office for a command meeting, he instead came to my office and asked if I could spend a few minutes considering an idea he had. Stan also taught me the value of intense curiosity; he always asked questions and looked for new and different kinds of business opportunities.

My direct boss at Avery Dennison, Dick Pearson, also taught me many lessons. Two in particular stand out:

The first was the importance of actively listening to employees and customers, our two principal stakeholders. It's often easy to tune out people and only think about what you consider important rather than take in the real meaning of what others are saying.

The second lesson was the importance of being credible and meeting commitments. Simply put, if you agree to accomplish a task, then do it.

I'd like to conclude these reflections with some of my own observations about good leadership:

1. Direction starts at the top. Strategy, products, markets, and other important parts of an organization must be determined at and communicated from the top.

2. Actions speak louder than words. You cannot say one thing, do another, and expect things to get done in the way you'd like. People are smart and will pay more attention to what you actually do.

3. Set an example. If you want your organization to accomplish something that requires extraordinary commitment, then you had better be out in front, doing and showing and talking and listening.

4. People do not do what is expected but what is inspected. If you state, for example, that quality is important to your organization but never attempt to quantify or monitor it, your employees will realize that it's not that important after all. Put in place a system for measuring the substantial and important elements of your business and provide feedback on the actual versus expected results.

5. Those in an organization will look at what the leader spends his time on to determine what is important. Spend time on the subjects you consider most important to your organization so that others will recognize your commitment and make these same factors a high priority. Your time is a valuable resource, so allocate it wisely and make sure what you do is consistent with the values of the business.

A retired executive with global business experience, Dick Hartl was a member of the advisory board of Brice Manufacturing.

Enthusiasm: An Essential Ingredient to Successful Living

Jack McKearin

*I*T USED TO BE very disappointing to me to attend a national meeting where a reportedly distinguished executive was speaking and hear him commence like someone who has one foot in the bucket and the other on a banana peel. The talk would be as exciting as a cold grilled cheese sandwich! On the contrary, what a pick-me-up it was to listen to someone speak who was actually excited to be with your group at that moment.

Sadly, many individuals are so wrapped up and focused on themselves that they are embarrassed to get truly enthused and excited about what they are doing.

In athletics, the military, and business, I have always found myself among the smallest and shortest in stature. I was able to obtain recognition only through a display of superior coordination, higher skills, determination, hustle, and drive.

I've also learned that communicating an optimistic outlook with genuine enthusiasm proves infectious and frequently rewarding.

In an atmosphere in which enthusiasm is lacking, one often finds doubt, fear of failure, indifference, and a reluctance to move forward. Enthusiasm, on the other hand, helps create a positive attitude, promote cooperation, excitement, a willingness to try, and teamwork.

In short, enthusiasm is an emotional fuel or lubricant that can change ideas and concepts into realities and results.

Jack McKearin is a retired sales executive from the DuPont Company and Brice Manufacturing Company. He now serves as an active Catholic layman.

It's amazing how Jack's ideas on business apply in so many areas, particularly in teaching. Bill Guiffre commented that there is a huge difference in teachers who convey enthusiasm and those who don't. —Ed.

Three Generations of Doctors

DR. BEN VANDERWERF

THE VANDERWERF STORY as healers started with my father, Aegidius Johannes Herman VanderWerf. Born in 1905, he was the sixth child in a family of ten.

His father had a successful clothing store in a small town in the northeastern part of The Netherlands. Two of his older brothers eventually took over the store and added a furniture store as well. Still, there was no room in the family business for the younger sons, and they were encouraged to study and become professionals.

My father elected to become a physician and settled after graduation as a family physician in Purmerend, a small town north of Amsterdam. In this community, I was born as the second child in a family of eight children. Despite caring for a relatively large number of patients, my father found time to study and receive a doctorate in neuroanatomy. With his rapidly growing family, he needed to look for a larger income, and this led to his move to Bergen op Zoom in the south of The Netherlands. There, he was active in his community and was one of the founding members of an infant and home health care group called Wit-Gele-Kruis.

During World War II, my father became a board member of a sanitarium for tuberculosis, and, after the war, he was involved in the building of a great new facility. Because of these interests and experiences, he was asked to become the building dean of a new medical school at the Catholic University of Nijmegen. It was a sacrifice, but his and my mother's deep Catholic faith made the decision to give up his more lucrative practice much easier. He must have set a fine example because three of his sons became physicians.

The first year this new medical school opened, I became one of the medical students, and my father felt great pride. Stimulated by the pioneering spirit of the new faculty, I became interested in the immunological aspects of transplantation, culminating in my Ph.D. in 1963, on the study of pregnancy as a homograft phenomenon.

I was always interested in work with my hands and was the handyman of the family, so I don't think it came as a surprise that my interest in the field of medicine led me to surgery.

Following my graduation as a surgeon, I was fortunate to be accepted for a fellowship in transplantation at the Harvard Medical School in the Massachusetts General Hospital. I attended there from 1966 to 1967. This not only prepared me for a career in organ transplantation, but also stimulated an appetite for research, which remained with me until I retired at the end of 1997.

From Boston, I went back to The Netherlands to start my first transplant program at the Catholic University of Nijmegen. It was a difficult start, partly because at that time young faculty members, even when trained specifically for new programs, did not get much opportunity to spread their wings. This led to much frustration, and finally I moved my family back to the United States to take a job in Miami, Florida.

Soon, I moved to a position at the University of Miami where my second transplant program was started. After eight successful years in Miami it became time to move on again, and I started my third transplant program, the first in private practice in the U.S., in Phoenix, Arizona.

I continued my research programs despite the demands of private practice. I was lucky to find myself working with an excellent and dedicated laboratory staff, which enabled me to start the country's first exclusive DR-matching program for kidney transplants. Our one year graft survival of kidney transplants was 25% better than other programs at the time.

I always enjoyed taking care of my patients, no matter how demanding it was sometimes, especially on my family. It is, therefore, the more gratifying that my three sons became physicians, continuing the family tradition. My oldest son became a family physician in Colorado, my second son a transplant surgeon in Florida, and my youngest son is just starting a practice in head-and-neck surgery in California.

Following my retirement I have developed a plan for quality, affordable health care coverage for all, and I am dedicating my time to see that this plan is implemented. Hopefully, the family-dedicated healing tradition started by my father will continue for many generations of VanderWerfs to come.

———————

A retired transplant surgeon, Dr. Ben VanderWerf is spending his retirement years promoting his universal health care plan.

Leadership

DICK MAU

*D*URING THE GREAT DEPRESSION, I spent my childhood in a small Iowa town with a population of 5,000. Our family was of meager but adequate means. From that early perspective, the opportunity for a future beyond the boundaries of my hometown and home state were impossible to imagine.

But on reflection, life in the 1930s in central Iowa was actually a seedbed from which one could sprout in any of a multitude of directions. As it turns out, my route through the sixty-eight years I have now lived has been littered with temptations to take ill-advised detours. Thank goodness I was blessed with enough common sense to recognize the wisdom offered to me by my mentors. It is their influence that I wish to share, as they helped instill in me intelligence, vision, strong spiritual values, ambition, modesty, affection, industry, competitive drive, and charitable inclinations.

My experiences, I'm sure, will be comparable to yours. I only hope they have proved as reassuring to you as they have been to me. The remarkable thing, or so it now seems, is that I took so much of the advice that was so freely offered in such a matter-of-fact manner, without fully appreciating the deep wisdom of those who gave it to me.

In my early years, my father, a traveling salesman, was gone from home almost every week. My chief mentor became my mother. Her message was extremely simple. She expected my brother and me to: work hard at school and at the jobs we held to earn spending money, always tell the truth, treat others—all others—as we would have them treat us, and approach life with confidence. In addition, she was always free with praise when it was deserved, and she was not reluctant to administer stern discipline when called for.

Another guiding light during my teens was a boy's advisor at our high school. He gave me the encouragement to follow my instincts with fervor. His counsel also gave me the confidence to believe I could shape my future in any way I wanted. He shared a convincing message about believing in your ability to compete. Everyone must put on their pants one leg at a time, and by using your God-given ability in combination with dedication, you'll be able to meet any opportunity head-on. A saying this advisor used about truth and trust (borrowed from another source, I believe) has always stuck with me: *Always strive to tell the truth, for it is much simpler to remember than a fabrication of the truth.*

As I began my business career, I was fortunate to have benefited from the advice and counsel of some of the very best leaders in American industry over the past forty-six years. My relationships with these intelligent, driven, and wise executives have provided me with enlightening insights into the complex mosaic of leadership qualities. It would be difficult to distill into vignettes the value of all of these relationships, but I can say that my comprehension of the "tools of achievement" was measurably enhanced.

At one time I was in need of strong guidance in respect to my professional skills and judgment. The man who helped me achieve this direction was the chief executive of the company for which I was working. Though small, this company was dedicated to producing products and services of very high quality. Likewise, the CEO required dedication to meeting these high standards. His imprint on me was indelible. Before encountering him, I felt I was adequately disciplined in my skills, and, although eager to learn, I felt my capabilities were far more complete than he acknowledged. I went on to learn from him that though a task must at some point be completed, it can always be done better. He helped me understand what is truly required in the pursuit of excellence while recognizing that this goal is seldom fully achieved.

Another mentor in business left me with the following thought, which I have held onto for many years. Though all of us wish to be recognized for success in our work, recognition most often belongs to many people. It would be misleading to give credit on too narrow a scale. When I once expressed concern about adequate recognition for my staff on a given project, this mentor reminded me that the focus of any initiative must be on the success of the effort, not recognition for the result.

Without a doubt, the most significant influence in my life has been my wife of forty-seven years, Shirley. Her continuing wisdom and pragmatism, heavily sprinkled with good old Iowa "down-homeisms," have provided me with an invaluable moral, spiritual and professional compass. And she has never let me forget that taking out the garbage is my responsibility! Referring to herself as "Chairman of Nitty-Gritty," she is a strong leader in the family, presiding with the proverbial iron fist in a velvet glove. Without her hand on the family tiller, the relative success we have achieved together would have been far less likely.

My family, as I'm sure is yours, has been at the core of my motivation in life. Our children have provided Shirley and me with a wellspring of happiness, love, and fulfillment. But never has any experience affected us more than the untimely death of our youngest son, who passed away recently. It gave me an unfathomable sense of emptiness, desperation, and anguish, as well as, finally, the resolve to consider continually the value of life. In death, our son demonstrated the immense and admirable character that was also his in life. He gave us a momentous sense of the fragility of our lives and the importance of love in our relationships with our wonderful children and grandchildren. We reflect daily on the happiness our son gave us and on the pleasures that we never fail to appreciate from every member of our family.

A retired vice president of Public Affairs for the Rockwell Manufacturing Company, Dick Mau's most important work these days is in creating positive public policies.

Dick's son Chris worked for me briefly in organizing Summit '92. He was a remarkable, inspiring young man. When he was a graduate student, he was involved with organizing international cooperation in space. He also put together a book on leadership. We mourn with Dick and Shirley the passing of this very talented young man. We hope this book will inspire other young people to dream and achieve as Chris Mau did. —Ed.

How Is Your Vertical Alignment?

JACK McKEARIN

*B*Y WAY OF INTRODUCTION, I should advise you of certain beliefs I hold as fundamental to my way of living. First, as a Christian, I believe that Jesus Christ is my Lord and Savior. Second, I believe that man is composed of body and soul, that the soul of man is immortal, and that there is life after our earthly death. Third, I believe we have been given a free will, and, therefore, we have a choice in our moral decisions, either for good or evil.

Finally, I believe that life's journey is a stewardship. We are responsible for our actions, and when our stewardship comes to an end we must give an accounting of our performance. Nothing is hidden from God. There will be total understanding of all circumstances and the judgment of how we will spend eternity—in heaven or hell—will be known to us even before it is rendered.

With that said, I readily concede that not all men agree with my philosophy. Whatever your viewpoint, however, I hope the balance of this message may hold some value for you.

Your "vertical alignment" refers to your basic priorities, those that remain when all the details and circumstances of your actions are peeled away. My priorities, in descending order—and that's the critical point—are:

1. How is your relationship with God; are you merely a social believer or a true follower?
2. How is your relationship with your family?
3. How is your relationship with your country and community?
4. How is your relationship with your job?

My dad would periodically ask me, as a young adult, "How is your vertical alignment today?" Since my early adult days, I have always thought this to be an excellent question to raise as I frequently conducted a personal analysis and evaluation of my performance on any given day. It gets to the heart of the matter, as the French say, *tout de suite.*

Many times I found that the pressures and demands of my job caused me to place an inordinate amount of time and effort on job-related activities, at the expense of my family. These priority shifts occurred often unconsciously in my daily life. My priorities got twisted under the guise of striving to be a good family provider for my wife and seven children. For example, how often did I stay at the office late to work on a project rather than come home and have dinner with the family? Or turn down the Little League coaching job for my boys' team because I would achieve more recognition, prestige, and maybe even money by putting that time into my job?

Once my wife brought me up short, saying, "Yes, you are a conscientious provider. The family has everything we need— but you! From where I sit, your job is second only to God, and sometimes I wonder if He has to take a back seat!"

It was like being hit with a two by four. I realized then that my vertical alignment was way out of whack. Fortunately I've had the opportunity to change it.

A misalignment of priorities, like the front end of a car, usually takes place over an extended period of time. But the damage, when finally detected, is costly.

The length of our stewardship on earth, when measured against eternity, is like a drop of water in the ocean. When we will meet our Creator is known only to Him. The Bible says, "Death will come like a thief in the night." Given that prospect, we must always be vigilant.

Having the proper vertical alignment will provide you much temporal peace, understanding, and contentment, and, ultimately, eternal happiness. We must strive to keep our priorities in the correct order and perspective each day. Failure to do so will result in the loss of eternal life, an unthinkable end.

The Bureaucrat

WILLIAM A. GUIFFRE

He likes the middle road,
His soup lukewarm, his coffee half and half.
He likes the temperate zone,
So perfectly in between.
He likes each job secure,
No failures, no heights to reach.
All things he likes a little,
But nothing to extreme.

Leadership—Part Two

J. NELSON HOFFMAN

WITH A PUSH FROM MY GRANDFATHER, I looked for leadership opportunities in high school and college, and later during my stint in the Navy and in my civilian career afterwards. From Boy Scouts in the beginning, to serving as a director of public and private corporations in my adult life, I recognized two critical ingredients of effective leadership: awareness and the ability to assimilate information and act appropriately.

A key characteristic of all good leaders is awareness. They are knowledgeable about trends in their industry and their profession. If they are politicians, they are aware of changes in the thinking of their electorate. If they work with technology, they know the cutting edge of new science. In non-profit organizations, they are aware of the needs and expectations of their fellow volunteers. Above all, they are aware of the needs of all the people who surround them, and they are aware of the need to allow everyone's abilities to contribute to the cause.

The second ingredient of an effective leader is the capacity to digest and integrate information and then apply it in two time dimensions. The first period is the present. Leaders apply their insights and project vitality into the current organization. They have a great confidence in bringing their team a comprehensive picture of current reality: candid, comprehensive, recognizing strength and weaknesses, and describing significant roles for everyone. The second period is the future. They work from their knowledge base and intuition to synthesize various scenarios. They sort through those scenarios, test them with key colleagues, and select one. They have a plan that will move the job or organization forward, and they have a charismatic capacity to present that plan to those around them, and get them to buy into the leader's vision.

In my early days at DuPont, Milt Roedel was high up in the company, and his job was to help spread processes throughout the company for recognizing and launching new businesses that were the product of DuPont's prolific research efforts. To illustrate the conflict that exists in many large businesses, he described two contending cults: The first is the priests whose purpose is to crowd closer and closer together to protect the sacred fire of current profit, the status quo. They are strongly opposed to change. Outside of that circle is a fanatical group of prophets of the future. Their job is to separate the knees of the priests, blow very hard to extinguish the fire, while shouting, "The winds of change are here, and they are going to blow out your sacred fire."

That imagery stayed with me. My career path took me into the field of strategic planning. I found that in many companies, schools, and community organizations, a big part of the deliberations are centered on the choice of allocating available resources to current problems or opportunities versus allocating them to building for the future. Having a leader with the twin abilities described above is a great asset.

Let me close this reflection with one other concept that relates to a tragedy in our family—technological obsolescence. My wonderful grandfather had a blind spot—he was stubborn and resistant to change. He recognized his errors too late, and it cost him his job and much grief.

During the war, the nation's manufacturing capacity for diesel engines was expanded to build the engines to power the landing craft and landing ships that landed in Normandy and the atolls of the Pacific, propelled our submarine fleet, and powered a new generation of trucks. Hundreds of thousands of ex-soldiers and sailors were trained to service and maintain these engines. In the post World War II period, the Board of Directors of the New York Central Railroad brought Robert Young from a western railway, either the Santa Fe or Southern Pacific, to be their new CEO. He had been instrumental in leading the western company from a steam-powered railway to a diesel-powered railway.

Young guided the New York Central in a conversion from steam engines to diesel engines. In a matter of a year or two, my grandfather and all the men he had recruited and trained were obsolete. I'm not sure of the precise events, but I think Granddad was demoted five or six times during that period. Because of his years of dedicated service in keeping the engines running during the war, I don't think they dared fire him. But the very unpleasant work he had to do was fire his friends and colleagues and dismantle the facilities used to service the steam engines. My grandfather was forced to oversee the tearing down of all the work of his life.

After the last demotion, he resigned and retired to his farm in Penfield. He did not take well to retirement. My memory of him was as a physically powerful man with the body of a professional wrestler. He seemed to shrivel physically in his sadness. It was ironic that the Navy sent me to diesel school, as the LST to which I was assigned was powered by diesel engines.

I believe that the sadness I saw in my grandfather's life impressed upon me that the most important responsibility of any leader is to sense and adapt to change. The price to be paid for not reacting accordingly is technological obsolescence.

In an age of accelerating technology, there are two caveats: For corporations, they must stay abreast of and anticipate new developments or face the extreme price of obsolescence. And for individuals, lifelong education is a must. Technology drastically alters the need for specific job skills. As my grandfather learned so painfully, we must adapt to change.

SECTION THREE

Western Culture and
Traditional Values

WESTERN CULTURE IS BUILT on the concept of individual morality and individual responsibility. Western religions are built on the idea that free will is exercised in the framework of a society based on family, community, and nation or nationality. Our concepts of self are related to our relationships to our fellow human beings—*Do unto others as you would have them do unto you . . . I am my brother's keeper*, etc.

This section of the book expands upon three key ideas.

- From educator Dr. Wayne Connell: Until the 1960s, most of the methods of teaching in the Western world were based on a faith-based system that explored man's knowledge and his spirit as coincident issues. For example, the *McGuffey Reader* was as much a primer about Christianity as it was about reading.
- The second idea comes from Joseph Campbell's award-winning interviews with Bill Moyers on myth: From the be-

ginning of civilization, the moral principles of a society or ethnic group have been imparted to each ensuing generation through the telling of stories and other oral traditions.

- Finally, lessons and role models are found in many places and in many walks of life. The world of sports provides many golden opportunities to learn about character and nurture leadership skills, so in this chapter, the contributors and I look at how the world of athletics gave us this opportunity.

— *8* —

UNCHANGING
LIFE VALUES

———

Like the stock of a good soup, a successful life must begin with a few key ingredients.

—PERSONAL INTEGRITY—

Lessons from My Dad and My Grandfather

JACK MACALLISTER

I REMEMBER MY GRANDFATHER, who was a farmer, city council member, Sunday school teacher, and great God-loving man. I worked for him in the harvest season of my 12th to 15th years. One day I asked him, "I hear the neighbors are going to work in the field on Sunday to get caught up after some rain. Are we going to do that?"

He smiled and said, "If we can't get it done in six days, it won't get done. The seventh day is to rest and give thanks to God for His loving care during the rest of the week."

My dad once said, "I can't do anything about someone else's reputation, but I can have everything in the world to do with my own reputation, and I can try to influence my son." This came after a football game in which I had retaliated with great vigor because of an opponent's dirty play.

My dad continued his lesson by asking about a little kid who met me at our locker room door before each football game and always wanted to carry my helmet to the field. Dad's comment was, "Don't you think that little boy saw what you did?"

Sure enough, at the next home game, the little guy was waiting for me, and the first thing he said was, "Boy, Jack, you really knocked that guy for a loop at the last game! That was really neat!"

I had to stop, sit down with him, apologize for my behavior, try and make him understand that two wrongs don't make a right, and that it was my responsibility to act in a responsible way. Hopefully, I convinced him.

My grandfather and my dad taught me many other lessons in life. They both stressed the importance of a loving God. They both suggested that you always give your very best at work, so that you can shoulder the responsibilities of a wife and family, and they both stressed the importance of respecting every person, regardless of status in life.

One experience I can recall when I first became a senior executive for my company: I often left work late and noticed a man who cleaned the lobby. He was always working hard and the place would really shine. I stopped one day and complimented him on his work and told him how much it was appreciated. He was so appreciative and was a friend from then on.

Another experience occurred when I was President of the Board of Directors for Creighton University—we were blessed by the local union trades who banded together to build a fountain as a centerpiece of our campus. Men and women worked without pay and did a beautiful job. At its dedication, much recognition was given the unions for their help, and the top union official said that this act of giving was the most important experience he had ever had in his life. We went further and honored the workers at a special banquet. Each worker received a plaque of appreciation. As I left, I walked with a man and his wife. "Congratulations," I said. "You must be very proud."

She looked at me with a tear in her eye and said how proud she was of her husband! She went on to say she was going to put the plaque in a special place in her living room so that all their children would be reminded of their father's important gift of his work, which helped beautify Creighton University, and she hoped her children would be giving people also.

It all adds up to trying to make a positive difference in lives as well as work and being sure your behavior meets the severest test you place on yourself. I haven't always passed my own test, but I've always tried.

An effective, personable leader, Jack MacAllister is the former chief executive officer of US West.

The Guy in the Glass

ANONYMOUS

When you get what you want in your struggle for self
And the world makes you king for a day,
Then go to the mirror and look at yourself
And see what that guy has to say.
For it isn't your mother, your father or wife
Whose judgment on you must pass.
The fellow whose verdict counts most in your life
Is the guy staring back from the glass.
He's the fellow to please, never mind all the rest
For he's with you clean to the end;
And you've passed your most dangerous and difficult test
If the guy in the glass is your friend.
You may be like Jack Horner and chisel a plum
And think you are a wonderful guy,
But the guy in the glass says you are a bum
If you can't look him straight in the eye.
You may fool the whole world—down the pathway of years
And get pats on the back as you pass;
But the final reward will be heartaches and tears
If you've cheated the guy in the glass.

Your Word Is Your Bond

PASTOR ROBERT GROCHAU

*Y*OUR WORD IS YOUR BOND" is a saying I was raised with from the time I was very young. It meant that when you gave your word about something, it was true and to be kept, unless excused by the person to whom you gave it. Your honor as a truthful and trusting person was at stake.

When you pledged your word, you were honor-bound to keep it. As a Boy Scout I learned: "On my honor I will do my best to do my duty to God and my country, and to obey the Scout Law—" The first law was to be "trustworthy."

Jews and Christians alike learn the Ten Commandments which includes "not bearing false witness," which implies that your word is truthful.

In the United States, as in most western societies, people holding public office, from the president on down, take an oath of office to uphold the laws of the country and not commit perjury, which is to convey a falsehood.

In the last half of the 20th century, two U.S. presidents learned the consequences of not being entirely truthful. Over time, their word became suspect and then not trusted. They may have done many good things during their presidencies, but not being entirely truthful is how many people will remember them. This untruthfulness will be part of their legacies.

In these complicated times, it is even more important that a person pledges his word of honor and ensure that this pledge is kept. If individuals have a high standard for honor and their word, then the society and the nation in which they live will be considered honorable and trustworthy. On the other hand, if an individual does not keep his pledge or word of honor to his nation, in some circumstances, this betrayal could be so important and so vital that the individual may be considered a traitor to that nation.

In addition to the common citizenry, it is also important for our government officials to remember "their word." Politicians who freely pledge to limit their terms of office, then change their mind once elected, do so at their own risk. The vast general public re-members what was said earlier, and they lessen their regard for a candidate who has such flexible standards for the "truth."

In our own nation's history, George Washington's contention that he "never told a lie" became a moral ideal school children have been guided by for over two hundred years. It meant that George Wash-ington's word was his bond and could be believed.

In literature, one of the most picturesque and remembered char-acters is Pinocchio, whose nose grew longer when he told a lie, and then grew longer and longer as he told one lie to cover another. One lie often leads to a web of lies.

In one of the Brothers Grimm stories about the Frog Prince, the king tells his daughter, "That which thou hast promised in thy time of necessity, must thou now perform." Since she had befriended the frog, it was necessary for her to keep her word, and the frog became a handsome prince.

In 1999, a judge remarked to former Secretary of Housing and Urban Development, Henry Cisneros, "No one can lie himself into office."

In *Hamlet*, Act I, Scene iii, 79–80, Shakespeare offers wise coun-sel in Polonius' advice to his son Laertes:

> This above all: to thine ownself be true,
> And it must follow, as the night the day,
> Thou canst not then be false to any man.

Your word is your bond! Don't betray it or underestimate its im-portance or power!

Pastor Robert Grochau has served three different Lutheran congregations and has retired in Monterey, California.

— R E S P E C T —

Don't Walk on the Grass

THE VENERABLE MORRIS HOLLENBAUGH

I WAS ALMOST SEVEN YEARS OLD when the Great Crash on Wall Street happened and the Great Depression began. Until that time, we lived a fairly normal mid-western family life. We didn't have a lot in the Roaring Twenties; we didn't lack a lot either.

During those early years, my father was a great influence on me. He was a man of normal temperament and very high moral values. He was always reminding his three children that we were no better than anyone else and no one else was better than us.

I do remember one thing that has stuck with me—DON'T WALK ON THE GRASS. In those days one did not, repeat, DID NOT walk on the lawn. Sidewalks were made to walk on. Paths were made to walk on. But NOT the grass.

This probably sounds absurd to present generations as I notice that everyone walks on the grass not the sidewalk. A visit to any college campus will reveal a horrid scene as paths through the grass mar the landscape everywhere. Why not walk on the grass? I have pondered that question and wondered why it was so important to my father to impress upon me not to walk on the grass. Later in life I caught what he was really saying. When you walk on someone's grass, you violate their property. They did not give permission to walk on the grass, and if I did, I was being a person of low caliber—I didn't care about them. A sidewalk was virtually a sign that said "Please do not walk on my grass." My father was teaching me that there was a necessary sense of respect and decorum required to be a decent human being. The social order should not be violated by each person, willy-nilly, making up their own rules and forcing them upon others, whether they wanted it or not.

One did not walk on the grass. To this day, that simple rule guides me through life. It is applicable to a hundred situations. I meticulously make sure that I park properly in a parking space, making it easier for someone else to park next to me. I never take or fudge over into two parking places. I don't walk on the grass! I make sure that I use good manners in a restaurant. To make noise, or to not be decently dressed, would infringe upon other people's space and disturb their meal. Again, I don't walk on the grass!

My father would be 114 years old this year, had he lived that long. I still wouldn't think of offending him by walking on the grass. He also said one other thing that I have always remembered: Do nothing that would dishonor your family name. That's kind of like "not walking on the grass" too, isn't it?

The Venerable Morry Hollenbaugh served the Anglican Community in Cincinnati and now resides in Snowmass Village, Colorado.

—SUSTAINING RELATIONSHIPS—

Learning about Honesty and Love

J. NELSON HOFFMAN

Good name in man and woman, dear my lord,
Is the immediate jewel of their souls:
Who steals my purse steals trash; 'tis something, nothing;
'Twas mine, 'tis his, and has been slave to thousands:
But he that filches from me my good name

Robs me of that which not enriches him
And makes me poor indeed.

—William Shakespeare
Othello, Act III, Scene iii

When my dad was overseas in WW II, I got into a little trouble. In the neighborhood where we lived, there was an abandoned house with many of the windows boarded up. We passed it every day on the way to the bus stop and often kidded about the house being haunted. In reality, there was nothing more ominous about the place than the fact that an older couple had died there a few years before, leaving neither heirs nor a will.

One afternoon as my friend and I cut through the backyard of this house, we noticed an open cellar window. We decided to come back later and see what was inside. After dark, with fear and a sense of adventure, we entered the cellar and climbed up the stairs.

The house was terribly dirty—an old milk bottle and dirty pans and dishes were scattered about on the kitchen table. The place looked as if no one had ever come into the house to straighten up after the old man died.

We climbed up to the second floor and looked through all the closets and chests of drawers, fascinated by what we found. We hadn't intended to take anything, but I saw a gold chain on the bed stand and slipped it into my pocket. After this little adventure, we went off to the soda shop and laughed and talked about our courageous adventure.

After returning home, I was somewhat surprised when a police car pulled up in front of the house, and two officers knocked on the door of my Uncle Al's apartment on the first floor. When he answered, one officer asked if he knew where his son was and had he been home all evening.

Al was a bit mystified and said he had no son. The officer said they were there to investigate a burglary in the neighborhood since a neighbor lady had seen two little boys entering the abandoned house, and she was sure one of the boys lived here.

Hearing this, I was really frightened, and quietly I hurried down the back stairs, jumped on my bike, and rode off to my grandparents' house.

My grandmother was surprised to see me when I arrived and remarked I looked a little "peaked." I went right up to bed.

A short while later, my Uncle Al showed up and asked if I was there. He told my grandmother and grandfather that the police had been to the house and were looking for me.

They called me down to the kitchen, and to this day, decades later, I can remember the feeling of trudging down those stairs—afraid, ashamed, and dreading the punishment I knew would be coming.

Grandad asked what I had done. "Nothing," I lied. He looked very grim, went into the bathroom for his razor strap, and returned to the kitchen. He asked again, "Did you break into someone else's house?"

I was really feeling awful and, breaking into tears, I confessed that I had.

"Did you take anything?"

"Yes," I replied, slipping out the gold chain from my pocket.

Granddad and Uncle Al were very angry, and I was sure I was about to get strapped.

Instead, I was sternly asked, "Do you want to be known as a thief or a burglar? Didn't you know it was wrong to go in someone else's house? What would your father think if he were here?"

When they saw that their message had sunk in, Granddad softened his demeanor and sat down next to me.

"You should be punished, and we should let the police deal with you as a juvenile delinquent. But we aren't going to do that. You are going to be a young man very soon, and it's time you started acting like one."

"Do you understand that honesty is an absolute must in your life? You lied a few minutes ago, and I want you to promise me you will never lie to me again, nor to anyone! Remember, your word and your honor are precious possessions. You can keep them or throw them away. It's up to you."

"But while we are talking about honesty, there is something even more important that I want you to remember. What you did today was disappointing to those of us who love you. As you grow up, you will disappoint yourself, and you will hurt. But remember, when you disappoint those who love you, you are causing even greater hurt. Part of growing up is learning how to return the love of those who love you. So don't you do anything dumb or that disappoints your grandmother and me, OK?"

After that event, my grandfather took a special interest in making time to talk to me. Even after my father got back from the war, my grandfather remained my mentor and did his best to pass along his wisdom.

When Joan and I were married, he brought us a special gift—one of his most prized possessions. He was a railroad man and kept a gold Hamilton watch to measure the trains as they passed certain crossings in Rochester. That watch and chain were part of him, and he wanted it to be part of our new lives together.

In my adult life, I have tried to reach the standards he set for me: tough love—stern, strong, judgmental, and strict. I loved all the time my grandfather spent with me. I realize now how important his "setting limits" was and how he created an image for me of "high dreams, high achievement."

He was my idol, and I was very sad when he died, but he left me a legacy that has served well all my life.

FROM FRIENDSHIP TO LOVE AND COMPASSION

After seven years of collecting material for the book and reflecting on how that material could be presented, I came to the conclusion that love and friendship are central values that I want to see passed along. Too often we focus on contrary behavior and conduct—hatred, lack of compassion, rudeness, and cruelty.

We begin with an excerpt from our friend, Terri Ross, who writes about the enriching influence her friends have had on her life.

Friendship

TERRI ROSS

IN MY SIX PLUS DECADES, I have had the privilege of knowing many wonderful people I count as friends. The primary reason that I am so content with my very hectic job as a real estate agent is the congenial atmosphere at my office and the wonderful people with whom I work. Several of us have been colleagues and friends for years.

Sometimes friends come from unlikely places. My children used to be just my children. But through the years that has changed. Now, they and their spouses are my friends. My baby brother (five years my junior) used to be a pest, but now he is a wonderful friend. How and when did this happen? It is a welcome transition. Now I am waiting for my precious grandchildren to become my friends— but not too soon.

In 1998 my husband Herb and I celebrated a very special occasion: the fiftieth anniversary of the day we decided to go steady— November 23, 1948. I was just 15 at the time, Herb was 17. We attended rival schools. Today, we are still friends, as well as husband and wife. We have had a history of shared friends—his and mine became ours, and it still holds true today.

My definition of friendship: It makes no difference if you see a friend daily, weekly, or "not often enough." What matters is the special bond that exists—shared experiences, shared secrets, shared hopes and dreams, and all the shared memories. Nothing compares to having friends you cherish remain a part of your life.

Terri Ross is a realtor and active volunteer in civic affairs in Rochester, New York. She is a lifelong friend of my wife, Joan.

On Friendships

Let me add a few ideas to Terri's thoughts. In modern terms, we often hear *To have a friend, be one.*

To my way of thinking that is just a different way of saying *Do unto others as you would have them do unto you.*

It seems that so many of our current problems are a consequence of not living this precept. In reflecting on the things that damage friendships and destroy love, criticism of a friend or loved one is a very bad habit. —Ed.

Criticism

J. NELSON HOFFMAN

ONE OF THE TOUGHEST PROBLEMS of parenting is the fact that we pass along our bad behaviors as well as our good. Our desire to pass along only the good is not possible, unless we are able to provide continuous good example of characteristics we hope to pass to the children. Can you ever recall saying "Do as I say, not as I do."?

In my life there is one bad habit that is particularly egregious: the tendency to be critical. I dislike confessional books, but upon reflection, there is one personal trait that really bothers me. From a small boy on, I have tended to be a critical person.

This bad habit, I believe, came from my father, Joe. He had particularly poor parenting: his father was not a caring man. Grandpa Hoffman traveled a lot, and when he was home, he criticized a lot more than he praised. Grandma Hoffman was often in poor health and not a very effective mother or a buffer for her young son.

Dad brought that baggage to his concept of fathering. He thought that being the provider was his main role, and the house was his domain. Dad was a shift worker, which meant he lived a "normal" life one out of three weeks. He set very high standards and had very high expectations for me. Our relationship, as it is for many young boys, was mainly one of me trying to please him. But as I look back, he had never learned to balance criticism with praise. The continued criticism kept us from becoming close. One exception was athletics. I wanted to be a very good athlete, to be a good player like my father. In this area, he was encouraging and supporting.

Two incidents helped me become aware of the damage my critical bad habit was causing. In the early sixties, Dad attended The Dale Carnegie Course, and it had some impact on him. He was so enthused with the program that he urged me to attend the course, which I did.

The classic course was based upon *How to Win Friends and Influence People* after a book with that title. It ranks only behind the Bible in circulation and sales. One caveat from the book has stuck with me as fundamental: *Don't criticize, condemn, or complain.* Whether the validation comes from modern psychologists or the Bible, there is no doubt that this is true wisdom.

A second lesson on the value of this wisdom came in my relationship with my business partner, Bruce Greenbaum. Bruce came into the company as a talented, but relatively inexperienced, young man. He became my successor. For a number of years, it was a subordinate, teacher/student relationship, but he grew rapidly, and he both wanted and earned my respect. He wanted to be treated as a peer.

I had adjusted too slowly to his growth, and it was straining our relationship. I could have lost the greatest talent in the company. However, one of Bruce's great talents is the ability to handle conflict, and we got into a deep discussion of our relationship, our needs, strengths, and weaknesses.

He pointed out the corrosive nature of my criticism, and the negativity of that word hit me for the first time. With his keen communication skills, Bruce showed me how even the smallest criticism affects those closest to you the most—that people thrive on praise, and praise should be given far more frequently than criticism.

I walked away from that talk thinking not only about my relationship with Bruce, but how I was dealing with Joan and our children as well. I realized that I had unintentionally been causing hurt. The ability to discuss problem behaviors, without being critical, is one of the greatest skills two people can have to build an enduring friendship or love

In high school, we learned in chemistry class about the powerful corrosive capacity of sulfuric and nitric acid. The labels read "Handle with Extreme Caution." These acids were so dangerous they needed to be stored in glass bottles with tight-fitting stoppers. Our teachers demonstrated how these corrosive acids ate metals. They would burn and scar any tissue they touched. Even today, I see that image in my mind.

Like any other corrosive product, criticism can cause an enormous amount of damage. It needs to be put in an impermeable container, with the label:

CRITICISM: HANDLE WITH EXTREME CAUTION

— H O N E S T Y   A N D   T R U S T —

When in Doubt

BUDDY GREENBAUM

*M*Y FRESHMAN YEAR AT COLLEGE was the second year of World War II—1942. Money was not plentiful among most of the students, and the majority were on a set allowance which covered food, board, school supplies, and a little (very little) for entertainment.

We all tried to stretch out our weekly or biweekly stipends so they would last until the next check arrived. Most students were frugal and managed well. The food in the school cafeteria was inexpensive, relative to most off campus eateries. Though it was a boring and repetitive menu, it was adequate for breakfast or a quick snack.

Just off campus, there was a small, relatively inexpensive, "mom and pop" restaurant called "The Peter Pan Restaurant" which catered to students. The owner had a long Greek name, but was

"Pete" to everyone, and he knew all his customers by their first name.

Pete kept a large cigar box under the counter by the cash register that was used to collect the meal checks of those students who elected to pay their outstanding bills weekly, biweekly, or whenever they had the cash or received their allowance. This was an informal way of having a charge account. Students would just sign their restaurant bill and drop it into the cigar box with all the other outstanding bills.

There was a tacit agreement between Pete and the involved student, and it was strictly an "honor system." When the student had the money to settle their account, Pete or his wife would give the student the cigar box to extract his bills. The student would total them himself and make the payment. We never heard a whisper or even the slightest suggestion that any student was ever dishonest.

And now for the rest of the story.

Toward the end of my freshman year at North Carolina State, I received my draft notice and was ordered to report within a week to my home draft center in New York for military assignment. After settling other outstanding accounts and purchasing my train ticket home, I realized I did not have enough cash to totally settle my account at Pete's. Unfortunately it was a substantial amount, and I, like many other students, did not have a personal checking account while away at college. Prior to college, during my adolescent years, I had been taught to get along on my mutually agreed upon allowance and to learn to manage my finances and spend no more than what my finances would allow.

Although I did have additional funds saved from part-time jobs and etc. in a personal savings account at home, I did not want to call home for money to settle my account at Pete's. Perhaps it was pride or not wanting to bring into question my ability to manage my finances properly. In any case, I asked Pete if I could leave him an IOU. As soon as I arrived home, I would send him a money order for the full amount.

Pete's kind expression did not change. Without a moment of hesitation, he wrapped an arm around my shoulder and replied, "Now look here, young man, forget this IOU business. I want you to go home and not worry about this bill. When you come back after the war, you'll take care of it."

It is needless to mention that I forwarded my payment to Pete soon after arriving home. This was not only a lesson in humanism, but a personal experience that stayed with me and became an example of the virtues we strive to instill in our children such as sensitivity, caring, trust, honesty, responsibility, respect, and accountability.

The Fullerton Recipe

DR. RICHARD FULLERTON

I HAVE RECEIVED MY "life lessons" from a variety of sources. My father strongly stressed the importance of education in order to lead a better quality of life and, perhaps, contribute more to society. Meeting obligations, particularly financial ones, was another responsibility he liked to emphasize. Buy only what you can afford. If you can't afford it, you don't need it. (I must admit departing from this advice upon occasion.)

The four years I spent as an enlisted man in the U.S. Navy strongly reinforced some of these earlier concepts, particularly in regard to education. During this time, I could see firsthand that men and women with an education had better jobs, lived a higher quality of life, and often contributed to the well-being of others.

Through their conduct, two of my college professors taught me that patience, understanding, and the ability to encourage and compliment others are extremely valuable tools in whatever I chose to do.

When I was in medical school and during my ensuing residency, a strong work discipline was enforced until it became a way of life. It reflected the philosophy that you never abandon your ship until it is safely docked in the harbor. The chief of ob-gyn during my resident years emphasized the importance of continuing education to improve your knowledge and skills. His often-expressed advice was: *It's okay not to be first, but never be last.*

It is interesting to me that the game of golf, in a simplistic way, often reflects the game of life. Regardless of the lie, play by the rules. Your conduct is as important as the score.

The last of my "recipes" is intended for my children and grand-children. If nothing more, I hope that they will always have the sensitivity to listen to other human beings and have respect for them.

Dr. Richard Fullerton is a retired gynecologist and obstetrician in Rochester, New York.

The Scout Oath

BADEN POWELL

On my honor I will do my best
To do my duty to God and my country
and to obey the Scout Law;
To help other people at all times;
To keep myself physically strong,
mentally awake, and morally straight.

—MAINTAINING COMMITMENTS—

According to the *American Heritage Dictionary* commitment is defined as: *1. The act of committing. 2. A pledge to do something. 3. The state of being bound emotionally or intellectually to a course of action.*

In my generation, some of the most important decisions a person made in their life depended upon that one word—commitment.

It seemed to come easier to people when I was growing up, but in actuality it was only achieved with a lot of devotion and hard work. Along with pride and courage it was, and still is, a virtue to be admired and modeled.

Commitment was the consequence of falling in love, thus a successful marriage and family life were built upon a bedrock of loving commitment.

In every branch of the military, commitment to comrades and commitment to duty were the foundations of the *espirit de corp.* The concept of "once a Marine, always a Marine" exemplified a total, lifelong dedication to commitment.

Quote on Commitment

W.H. MURRAY

UNTIL ONE IS COMMITTED THERE IS HESITANCY, the chance to draw back, always ineffectiveness. Concerning all acts of initiative (and creation), there is one elementary truth, the ignorance of which kills countless ideas and splendid plans: that the moment one definitely commits oneself, then providence moves too.

All sorts of things occur to help one that would never otherwise have occurred. A whole stream of events issues from the decision, raising in one's favor all manner of unforeseen incidents and meetings and material assistance, which no man could have dreamt would have come his way.

I have learned a deep respect for one of Goethe's couplets:

> *Whatever you can do, or dream you can, begin it.*
> *Boldness has genius, power, and magic in it . . . "*

"I'll Try" Is Not Enough

BRUCE MOSES

*H*OW MANY TIMES have you heard someone say, "I'll try," in response to a request for some kind of commitment? "I'll try to improve my math grades next semester." "I'll try to make quota next month." "I'll try to be home at 6 P.M. for dinner tonight."

Do you feel assured that a commitment underlies these type of responses? Probably not, simply because there *is* no commitment in trying. If the math grades don't improve, if quota is not made next month or if the arrival time for dinner is 6:45 P.M., the response is, "Well, I tried."

A commitment to trying is really no commitment at all. Rather it's an easy way for someone to be let off the hook, simply because they tried.

The question then becomes: How do you get a commitment from someone? To start with, do not accept any response to a request that includes the words, "I'll try." There is either success or failure–trying counts for nothing, and it usually results in failure because there was no plan to succeed in the first place.

When your child says, "I'll try to improve my math grades," your response should be, "How are you going to achieve this objective? When you have a plan to improve your grades, then we'll discuss it, and no later than this weekend."

The same is true for achieving quota. Wouldn't you feel more confident if your sales rep developed a well-thought-out plan, with the names of customers and prospects, as well as products, dollar amounts, and dates for anticipated sales that add up to 150 percent of quota to allow for a little slippage? That sure sounds better than, "I'll try."

We need to remove the word "try" from our vocabulary. Don't accept a response to a request that indicates "I'll try." Insist instead on a commitment to success that includes a plan to achieve the goal.

A former college classmate, Bruce Moses is a retired chief executive officer of Uarco.

I Can't

ANONYMOUS

You may say, "I choose not to," but never say, "I can't."

— COURAGE —

A thank you to Jack McKearin for submitting the preceding quote and the following poem. When I teach, I ask the young ladies to write a feminine gender version of the poem.

If

RUDYARD KIPLING

If you can keep your head when all about you
Are losing theirs and blaming it on you,
If you can trust yourself when all men doubt you,
But make allowance for their doubting too;
If you can wait and not be tired by waiting,
Or being lied about, don't deal in lies,
Or being hated don't give way to hating,
And yet don't look too good, nor talk too wise:
If you can dream—and not make dreams your master;
If you can think—and not make thoughts your aim,
If you can meet with Triumph and Disaster
And treat those two impostors just the same;
If you can bear to hear the truth you've spoken
Twisted by knaves to make a trap for fools,
Or watch the things you gave your life to broken,
And stoop and build'em up with worn out tools;
If you can make one heap of all your winnings,
And risk it on one turn of pitch-and-toss,
And lose, and start again at your beginnings
And never breathe a word about your loss;
If you can force your heart and nerve and sinew
To serve your turn long after they are gone
And so hold on when there is nothing in you
Except the Will which says to them; "Hold on!"
If you can walk with crowds and keep your virtue,
Or talk with kings—nor lose the common touch,
If neither foes nor loving friends can hurt you,
If all men count with you, but none too much;
If you can fill the unforgiving minute
With sixty seconds' worth of distance run,
Yours is the Earth and everything that's in it,
And—which is more—you'll be a Man, my son!

Quote on Courage

THEODORE ROOSEVELT

*I*T'S NOT THE CRITIC WHO COUNTS; not the man who points out how the strong man stumbles, or where the doer of deeds could have done them better. The credit belongs to the man who is actually in the arena, whose face is marred by dust and sweat and blood; who strives valiantly; who errs, and comes short again and again; because there is not effort without error and shortcoming; but who does actually strive to do the deeds; who knows the great enthusiasms, the great devotions; who spends himself in a worthy cause, who at the best knows in the end the triumphs of high achievement and who at the worst if he fails, at least fails while daring greatly, so that his place shall never be with those cold and timid souls who know neither victory nor defeat."

The above quotation hangs in the office of Dr. Larry Dorr. I liked it so well, I got a framed copy for my office and use it frequently with high school students. —Ed.

— S E L F - D I S C I P L I N E —

Discipline, Education, and a Work Ethic

BILL GOODWIN

I APPRECIATE THE FACT that Nels considers me among those who have achieved success. I believe I have done many things well, though I have not accumulated the wealth by which most people measure success. I do, however, have a most loving and complete family, each of whom has an education, a professional career, a strong commitment to their responsibilities as a citizen, and the keen ability to relate to, understand, and care for people from other nationalities, races, creeds, and colors.

How did this success come about? It didn't just happen by chance or by luck. My older brother summarized the source of responsibility when he read from Sirach at my dad's memorial service. He attributed a good deal of our achievements to the value our father placed on discipline, education, and a work ethic. These values, coupled with the intense faith and religious education instilled by our mother, resulted in offspring who include: an attorney, a business executive, a career naval officer (who commanded a nuclear SSBN submarine), a deacon, and the holder of a doctorate in electromagnetic interference. Two grandchildren are graduates of the U.S. Naval Academy. In turn, each of us has relied on these values to nurture our own families in a similar and successful fashion.

I have been especially fortunate to have a wife full of love and life who shares these same values. Without her dedicated support of both my military and business careers, we would not have been able to create our strong family bond nor enjoy the fruits of our labors. Our commitment to, sacrifices for, and attention to our children and each other is what makes us feel good. That is how we define success.

Bill Goodwin is a retired Marine Corps Colonel and former vice president of Brice Manufacturing Company.

Self-Sacrifice and Self-Discipline:
Keys to Happiness and Freedom

J. NELSON HOFFMAN

FOR MOST OF MY LIFE, there are two virtues, two assets that would have made me more effective, more content: capacity for sacrifice and a higher degree of self-discipline.

At sixty-eight, it is clear to me that the development of self-discipline is the key to freedom. The adults I have met who demonstrated this virtue have moved into positions of authority and achieved the goals they set for themselves. They were not handicapped by the choices that limit the effectiveness of less-disciplined people.

As an only child, when I entered school I did not have much practice or skill in sharing. In contrast, all five of my children demonstrate the capacity for sharing that comes with membership in a family of five, and they have been very effective parents and teachers in passing on this virtue to my grandchildren.

I was a pampered little boy. While my parents struggled with the despair and hardships of the Great Depression, they shielded me from fear in their lives. Instead, they demonstrated sacrifice, courage, and hope every day. In retrospect, I lived a sheltered childhood—well loved, but shielded from the harsh realities of life outside my home.

For a long time, I struggled with discipline. I was well into my teen-age years before I realized that internal discipline was much more important than external discipline. As a teen-ager, I rebelled against almost all of my parents' attempts to impress upon me the importance of respect for girls, alcohol, and automobiles. My rebellion came to a end when my mother and father made it clear that the privileges I enjoyed could quickly be taken away.

Sports were a great asset in learning about teamwork and sharing. In pick-up basketball games on the playground, I learned that if you could rebound and pass the ball to open teammates, you were almost always picked to play.

Like many men of my generation, I look back on my military service as a strong learning experience. The men who came home from WWII exemplified patriotism, courage, and sacrifice. As Tom Brokaw has so aptly observed in *The Greatest Generation*, they were a generation which inspired, not only our nation, but an entire world. And in the sequel, *The Greatest Generation Speaks*, we hear the words of that WWII generation through their letters.

They had seen the horror and devastation of war, and they did not want to talk about it. Even fifty years later, they still avoid recalling the pain of that period.

One personal exception to that generality was my dad's experience in seeing the gaunt bodies he encountered when his unit entered Hitler's concentration camps. Even ten and fifteen years later, he would awake in the middle of the night, terrorized with memories he could not forget.

It is an interesting contrast to compare these times of unequaled prosperity to the times of my boyhood. Every parent wants to do right by their children. But in that desire is the seed of failure. Children now expect so much. I wonder where and how they will learn the value of self-discipline and self-sacrifice?

Find a Model and Learn from His or Her Lessons

Dr. Wayne Connell

STORIES ABOUT LIFE have always been the best teachers for those who follow. One of my thoughts is to tell how and from whom I adopted the standards that have provided substance and meaning to my life. My childrens' children will probably have a more difficult time discerning these rules because of the rapidly changing environment that constitutes their culture.

I lament the loss of simple rules in our society. Not that the old simple rules no longer apply, but they are more difficult to use today. The ascension of the intellect over the spirit has been occurring over the past three hundred years and has accelerated in the past two or three decades. During this time, the framework of our culture has changed from humanism to relativism.

The standards that have traditionally created meaning and provided support are now being discarded in favor of making up one's own rules to fit the situation. Most individuals have no basis for their actions, which leaves them with the problem of justifying their behavior.

Life is much too short to learn all of the truths by experience, and most of us aren't really equipped to do so. To be a wise person, you must find a role model or teacher and learn from his or her stories. Then you will be able to learn from your own experiences. There also needs to be a test for the model: If an honest-to-goodness real relationship with God isn't in the stories, then you are not following the right model.

My father was by far the most influential person in my life (along with my wife). However, he didn't speak simply and found no need to explain things he saw as obvious. He was a relatively silent model, and that was how he believed in passing along tradition. As best he could, he lived his life by the standards that his parents had modeled for him, which in turn reflected the influence of his grandparents and great-grandparents. Now, thanks to the Internet, we have found another family "limb" of the Connells, and, wouldn't you know it, they live in the same way.

At this time, I believe that my life somewhat mirrors a model that has been generated over at least four generations.

I can't remember my father speaking about hard work, but work hard he did, and hard work he demanded. I didn't know there was any other way. To illustrate the strong impact this has had on my life, let me cite an experience that happened a full twenty-five years after I left home. My college-age daughter asked what counsel to give to a friend who was struggling with school. All that she knew to tell him was to "work harder." What I heard her say created a picture in my mind of my father, and I clearly understood where my daughter's statement came from. I thought about it a minute and then told my daughter that she had already told her friend everything I knew.

I can't remember my father speaking about saving, but save he did, and saving he demanded. During my lifetime, I have purchased one car and one house on credit, and I paid the house off after six years. This certainly wouldn't be a popular way to do things these days, as it stands in stark contrast to our society's current negative savings rate. However, if you aren't one of those who have the ability to generate wealth, it is a good way of life.

My father found no motivation in money. As the son of a sharecropper, it was important for him to own a piece of land. However, after he had bought his first farm and became a landowner, he didn't buy a second. It just wasn't important.

I can't remember my father speaking about serving, but serve he did, and service was a way of life for the Connell family. I am intuitively comfortable in the serving mode. I don't see it as a psychological something or other, but it was modeled for me, and I believe it is the right thing to do. Now, in the latter part of life, I find satisfaction, meaning, and pleasure in service.

I can't remember my father speaking about telling the truth. It was taken for granted. I never heard my father "spin" a situation, and fifty years later, my kids don't do it either.

Throughout my early years, I wondered if I was ever going to be able to walk in my dad's shoes. Finally, I had a breakthrough. I was thirty-eight years old, a commander in the Navy, and a veteran of one very long war. I had flown home to drive to the Connell family reunion with my dad. On the way back to my airplane we were talking about our relatives. When I asked him about one in particular, my dad, completely out of character, spit out, "He only works for money."

With that one statement, all the memories of my father, all the stories about grandparents and great-grandparents, came together with one loud explosion of understanding. A model had been explained. And in one startling and revealing instant, I understood so many things about my life and about life in general.

A former Navy Squadron Commander and retired school administrator, Dr. Connell is also the former executive director of Martha's Kitchen, a home for the homeless in Indio, California.

☙ ☙ ☙

— T H R I F T —

Thank God, Learn to Juggle,
Know Thyself, and Pay Cash

R O N P I E K U N K A

I DON'T CONSIDER MYSELF A RELIGIOUS PERSON, but I frequently thank God for my blessings, for my treasures. An exercise of prioritizing my God-given gifts always places Jeannie, my lovely wife, right at the top. I can't remember riding up a ski lift (now it's a snowboard lift) when I didn't thank God for the privilege of enjoying the beauty of His creation. The same is true for standing on the top of a mountain peak, the finish of a hill climb on my bike, and the end of an exhausting hike, or jog, or swim. Giving God His just due is important to me.

Life's operating philosophy: I'll borrow a simile from David Wunderlin, Nels and Joan's son-in-law. According to David: "I've tried (not always successfully) to approach living as a juggler practices his art. Life represents many balls. Among them: job, wife, family, God, religion, hobbies, education, fitness, travel, finance, health, payback, eating. We each have our own list. Just as a juggler strives to keep all his balls in the air, I continually try to balance the various aspects of my life."

Peace of mind, personal contentment, inner satisfaction, whatever catch phrase comes to mind, are the result of what I call the process of getting to know yourself. Jeannie says I'm programmed. I think it's important to know what turns you on, short term and long term.

Years ago, I made the decision to start my own business. I recognized that I was not happy with the big corporate workplace and its restrictions. I've never looked back on that decision. When making financial choices, investment selections, you should know your "risk tolerance." This is an example of knowing yourself financially.

Pay off that credit card balance each month. In our married life, the only thing Jeannie and I bought on credit was our home. Everything else we paid in cash. Some things change. Today, the password in our house is "miles, miles, miles"—buying on credit and using that credit card to generate air miles. But, some things do not change. We pay off our credit card balances each month.

Early on my job was very important to me, often to the detriment of my relationship with my wife and family. Health and fitness came naturally. Now years later, I take a few steps back to look at myself, the juggler, and hopefully correctly assess the importance of all the aspects of living. "Have I dropped the ball?" I am continually repositioning these "balls" in my life. Today, I'm happy to say God has given me the opportunity to rearrange my priorities, and wife, health, retirement, education are now more significant. Keep juggling.

An engineer and entrepreneur, Ron is a great example of self-discipline. His message, like his life, is based upon a simple plan, marvelously executed.

— 9 —

ORAL TRADITIONS

The Value of Stories

There are only two or three human stories, and they go on repeating themselves
as fiercely as if they had never happened before.

—**Willa Cather**

O Pioneers

In his trailblazing work on mythology, Joseph Campbell found that all stories are basically the same story, endlessly retold in infinite variations. They are similar stories found in completely different cultures and in completely different time periods. The similarity is that in each story a value or a piece of heritage is being passed down from one generation to the next.

In Chapter 1, I wrote about my grandfather, Frank N. Hill, and how his mentoring in public speaking provided me with essential skills that I was able to use throughout my life. It was only later in life that I realized that my grandfather had actually been more help-ful than I first imagined. Because he was a lifelong public speaker who received a good deal of acclaim for this skill, I always traced my communication abilities and self-confidence back to his tutoring and guidance. It was only after reading the first piece in this chapter that I realized that, in addition to helping me learn how to speak, my grandfather had also given me valuable skills in demonstrating how to listen.

In this chapter, we present contributors who have learned from their mentors how values are passed down from generation to generation through stories and being a good listener.

On Being Present to People

FATHER JACK HEDGES

As A PRIEST, I live with a constant awareness of Christ's presence. I try to follow His example of being *truly present* to everyone I meet.

For example, I go to see Father Al O'Brien who is failing, dying. I go not to preach a sermon, but just to be there. Even at such a critical time, I joke with him, "You faker. You just want everyone to come see you."

Al knows I am kidding. What means the most to him is for me to just be there. To listen. He knows I want to be there. I'll ask him if he wants to receive a blessing? He'll say, "Okay, but be quick about it, and get the heck out of here."

That is his way of expressing himself. I think it is a freedom he feels with me. He always says thanks as I am leaving. After I'm gone, he says to the others on the floor, "That's my best friend."

So many times it is the presence, the being, rather than words. I think we have all had the experience when we sense that people are saying words they don't mean. People see through false words. They sense when there is sincere meaning behind the words. When we are called on to preach, people see through someone up there just saying the words. Unless our life is behind it, I think people just write off the words.

I was at St. Joseph's in Penfield, New York, a very large parish, for eleven years, ten in retirement. My duties were primarily to help out on Sunday and with the daily Eucharist. I was around all the time and people picked up on that. Although I wasn't thinking about it at the time, I now see that it was the *ministry of presence* that made a difference. The parishioners knew me, and I knew them.

It was the same way when I was Chaplain at the University of Rochester for sixteen years during the 1950s and 60s. In the office, the dining area, and around the campus, I always wore the Roman collar. Although I had many duties to keep me busy, my main job was to be available, to be present to the students and faculty who needed me. I raised my own funds to get a salary. We had raffles and scratched out the few dollars to support our programs. I was not part of the institution, and I wasn't an intellectual.

In thinking about this question of "being present", my view is that the first ingredient is to be listening in a welcoming way. It is called *active listening*. Some people have commented that I was nonjudgmental. I took that as a real compliment. I think people resent, they rebel, at being judged, and the normal perception is that priests are inherently judgmental. There is so much judging on the part of the clergy that people are afraid of us. They are surprised by our humanity.

Often times, it is not easy for them to open up. I always made sure there was a glass door on my office so I could see them, and they could see me. Every once in awhile, you'd see someone walk by a couple of times before they got enough nerve to come in. This hesitancy was also seen after Mass. This was an opportunity to show Catholics and non-Catholics my openness, my concern. I wanted to let them know I would be available later on if they had something on their mind. Even as college students, there were a lot of growing pains, questions, doubt, and like many kids that age, they needed someone older to talk to.

What made those years so fulfilling was that I was blessed with a love for kids. It is important that there be someone there—someone available and present on the campus. I remember a young Jewish boy who joined me at lunch one day. He said, "You are the first priest I have ever talked to." We didn't get into anything profound, just chatted. We had such chats a few more times before he graduated. Many years later, when I had become the Pastor at St. Charles, he came to me and asked if I'd write a reference letter. I really felt honored.

And my final thought on presence is the central teaching of the church: *Jesus is always present with us in the resurrected Christ.*

I have a painting that was painted for me by a nun when I was at St. Charles. She asked me what theme I would most appreciate. I picked the Resurrection. Her work is a beautiful combination of bright oranges and yellow, with white, the light, in an image of something breaking forth, emerging from the darkness. It was her way of reminding us that Christ is always present.

In celebrating the liturgy of our nation and the Pascal mysteries, the Liturgy of the word becomes our whole way of life. Each day, each year, we adapt ourselves to that life of Christ expressed in the Eucharist—the Pascal mystery of the suffering and death of the resurrected Christ. It is through Jesus in the monstrance that I have respect for the presence. It is through the daily celebration of this presence that I fulfill my life as a priest.

And what makes that experience all the more precious is the modern emphasis on sharing with our community. In the pre-Vatican II days, the Mass was in Latin with the priest's back to his flock. Now it is clear that the Mass is of, and for, the people and the priest. It is the responsibility of the priest to bring the people into participation in the Eucharist.

In the old days, we might hurry through the Latin. Now, we must be sure we are bringing meaning first to ourselves as the presider and to convey that meaning to the people.

I sometimes worry about the psychological costs this puts on a priest. It drains you, it wears you out when you must project yourself to the people, to bring the meaning, to prepare and deliver the gospel and your sermon at a number of masses.

Since the Council, after a number of scripture courses that I've taken, and a sabbatical that took me to the Holy Land, all these things have given me a deeper concept of scriptures. My job is to be present to people, just as Christ is present to us all, everywhere, all the time.

As the chaplain at the University of Rochester for twenty years, Father Jack Hedges was instrumental in helping me find a lifelong faith.

Tell Me a Story

Sister Elaine Kolesnick

I wanted to know God's will for me and know it exactly—no more wondering, searching, fumbling. I had thought about religious life on and off, and finally it hit me—the answer lay there! Through the vow of obedience I would know God's will exactly and be at peace.

It worked for awhile—at least for the broad outline of my life, and then along came Vatican II and in came collegiality and discernment, with obedience seen primarily as involving dialogue, listening, and searching together for God's will.

Oh, me! I was right back where I started! Or was I? The Spirit was leading me through God's ongoing revelation of God's self, and God's plan for the world, and for me—bit by bit—and continued to move me through the ensuing years. God is still continuing to move me to the fullness of life here, and then, hereafter. Oh, the wonderful agonizing search for God—and my place in God's kingdom, God's plan!

My mom and dad started it all, from the word go. Their faith had rooted me in the Catholic faith through prayer and church and their lived values. They grounded me firmly in "the hidden ground of love," and I *wanted* to be there—to "bloom where I was planted."

But there's another key thread in the fabric of my life. My mother wrote in my baby book that my first sentence was "Tell me 'tory." Tell me a story! And my parents did. They read to me and my younger brothers—mostly fairy tales filled with ugly witches, beautiful maidens, and nightmarish ogres. But they also chose "dreamstuff" stories to whet our imaginations and for us to dream on.

My mom and dad would borrow storybooks from the library, and once in awhile, they bought us a book or two if they weren't too expensive. One of the first bought books I received as a pre-teen was *Tabitha of Ivy Hall*—a Christmas gift from my parents with 25 cents still penciled in at the top of the first page. I loved it! I've kept it as a memento.

This wonderful world of books and words opened many doors for me: doors to pleasure, insight, knowledge, challenge, beauty, all of life's choices.

Rooted in my childhood, these two threads—story and God's presence—have intertwined throughout the years. God's presence or "story" in *my* life affects *my* presence in the lives of others as I relate to their "stories."

My life has been very rich, and I can recommend this formula to others—as a high school English and journalism teacher; then in publications; as a public relations and communications director for my congregation; and now as a parish visitor.

As I continue to try to be alive and alert to the growing presence of God in my life—to knowing God's will, and letting it be done in me, the searching goes on until my earthly story is completed, until I meet God face to face. Then, I will know the whole story.

Sister Elaine Kolesnick was my high school English teacher. Forty-five years after graduation, I reconnected with her at a class reunion.

My Grandfather's Storytelling

STEVEN ALLDREDGE

*Y*OU WILL NOT FIND *The Cat That Wanted To Be A Dog* on the squat screen of your local collection of multiplex movie theaters. At least not yet. It was a story told in a different tradition, in a different time, in a different "story" atmosphere.

Growing up, I had a collection of rambunctious brothers, sisters, and cousins who were all very close in age, and when the whole bunch gathered together for a holiday or special occasion, the energy accumulation could light up most big cities.

The passive, one-dimensional character of television could only cut down the noise of this group and then only until the next commercial. A different type of story was called for. That's what my grandfather delivered.

Poppa would sit in a chair and gather all of his grandchildren around him. He would snuggle one or two of the smaller ones in his lap or against a shoulder while the rest of us would try to settle down. Our nervous, eager anticipation about whatever story he was going to tell, and the comical way we knew he would tell it, made calmness mostly impossible.

My grandfather would make sure that everyone was comfortable, and then he would ask what everyone wanted to hear. Often, one or more cousins would shout out a past story favorite, and Poppa would consider their request with great weight. Bushy brows were stroked, and his trim mustache smoothed out as he measured the worthiness or the entertainment value of each story. He would launch into whatever tale was asked of him, though sometimes he would suggest an alternative which was new. His final decision was enthusiastically received by those of us chomping at his ankles. And that reaches the root of this story telling, story listening, arrangement.

It didn't matter what story my grandfather told us because we were always part of the story. I'm sure my grandfather started off with some vague notion of what the "story" was. Usually it was a title, *The Cat That Wanted To Be A Dog*, *The Screwdriver That Wanted To Be A Wrench*, *The Sheep That Lived In The Tree*. Stories that were entertaining. Stories that usually had a moral. Stories that asked for interaction between storyteller and story listener.

Joseph Campbell and others have written a great deal about "oral traditions" and how valuable and nurturing storytelling was in many earlier societies and cultures. To me, it's too bad that we've lost a great deal of this power because I don't think movies, television, and other forms of electronic media have the same type of nurturing, the same type of "soul-and-character-rejuvenation" as a live storyteller. A live storyteller connects with traditions and conveys this nurturing to a gathered collection of listeners—stories which inspire, stories which enlighten, stories which pass on the traditions and values of a culture from one generation to the next.

My grandfather would "direct" the story in a vague manner, leading his narrative and our postscripts and suggestions down the story path toward a "logical" conclusion. There was usually little logic, but lots of laughs along the way. Surprisingly, a great deal of life-affirming, lifelong lessons were found in my grandfather's silly tales that now, forty years later, I can still remember in a heartbeat.

I believe Joseph Campbell is right. The power of stories told in the way my grandfather told them had a multiple effect. Both my family and I were stronger for these stories.

Maybe a "story hour" is something we still need today, whether it is our family or friends sitting down together, our like-minded religious brothers and sisters, or our collection of online friends in an Internet chat room.

Gather them all together and tell your stories—about your family, your culture, or people that you admire. Tell them about heroes and villains entangled in awe-inspiring deeds or gut-wrenching tales of adventure and romance that keep you on the edge of your seat or take you on a roller-coaster ride of your emotions. Tell them your version of *The Cat That Wanted To Be A Dog*. It will make my grandfather proud.

A former president of the non-profit organization Aspen Filmfest, Steven Alldredge is a writer, screenwriter, and one of the editors of this book.

Raising Children in an Online World

STEVEN ALLDREDGE

IN OUR MODERN AGE there is no communications medium more popular, or more controversial, than the Internet. What danger is it to our children? Should parents and educators use filtering technology to keep our kids from accessing certain kinds of information online? What are some of the issues of privacy and free speech which arise because you have the Internet in your home? These are natural questions for parents to ask in an age where everyone is "online."

In 1998, it was estimated that 17 million children ages 2 to 18 used the Internet for communications, entertainment, and as an educational resource. By 2003, that figure is expected to grow to more than 42 million children. (*Time*, May 10, 1999). Since the Internet is not "regulated" like a broadcast network, a movie theater, or a radio station, there are not the same kinds of rules and restrictions. As a result, there are no limits or checks on the kind of information, pictures, or interactive experiences found on the Internet. This variety of content provides new challenges to parents and new opportunities for them to be the first line of support for their children.

With the use of Internet rapidly becoming commonplace, our children have vastly increased possibilities for using this new technology in their schools, in libraries, or at the home of a friend. Oftentimes, children may be more experienced and comfortable with computers than their parents. What do parents do? I believe they can become more proactive by familiarizing themselves with what the Internet is, and isn't. Parents who create a safe and knowledgeable environment at home with the computer will be less inclined to feel that they need to control and censor what their child sees and reads on the Internet. Some suggestions I've heard for doing this include: Discuss with children what they may encounter on the Internet, attend school orientations to see how children are using computers and going online; participate in Internet activities with children using computers at home or in the library, share computer experiences with their children and with other parents and teachers, create a list of approved web sites for their children to explore, and, create a list of education web sites which may cover sensitive subject matter.

Another recommendation for parents would be placing the home computer in the family room where a child's use of the Internet can be monitored. Future private access to the Internet can be an incentive for older children who demonstrate that they can follow the guidelines they agreed to on appropriate Internet use.

Navigating the Internet is like any other age-appropriate activity, and parents need to take the time to know what their options are so that they may judge what's best for their children themselves. As with learning how to swim, a child's access to the Internet should grow in degrees, from the shallow water to the deep end of the pool.

Parents may wish to use technologies that can be installed on their home computers which blocks or restricts access to the Internet. This electronic software blocks or restricts web sites by focusing on key words. It's a good idea to find out what kind of information these "filters" are blocking because what one person or group finds objectionable and blocks out others may not.

If your child is very young, it may be okay to block every web site that contains any mention of the word "sex." But this may not be appropriate if your child is twelve or thirteen and working on a book report for biology on human sexuality. Remember that it's natural for children to be curious. In an earlier day, children sneaked a look at drawings in a hygiene text or looked at pictures in *National Geographic* to get a glimpse at what an adult human reproductive system looked like. That same curiosity exists today and will exist tomorrow.

For the most part, it is not what a child sees or reads on the Internet that may get them into trouble. It is what they may write or reveal in a chat room or through e-mail to someone they have never met and do not know. To create the safest environment, children of any age should not be using the Internet without having firm parameters set by their parents or guardians. The guide *Child Safety on the Information Highway* offers information for parents to remind their children what to do, and what not to do, when using the Internet. They recommend posting the following information near your computer where your kids will see it and be reminded on a constant basis:

- I will not give out personal information such as our address, phone number, parents' work address, phone number, or the name and location of my school, without my parents' permission.
- I will tell my parents right away if I come across any information that make me feel uncomfortable.
- I will never agree to get together with someone I meet online without first checking with my parents. If my parents agree to the meeting, I will be sure that it is in a public place and bring my mother or father along.
- I will never send a person my picture or anything else without first checking with my parents.

- I will not respond to any messages that are mean or in any way make me feel uncomfortable. It is not my fault if I get a message like that. If I do, I will tell my parents right away so that they can contact the online service.
- I will talk with my parents so that we can set up rules for going online. We will decide upon the time of day that I can be online, the length of time I can be online, and appropriate areas for me to visit. I will not access other areas or break these rule without their permission.

Censoring what your child is going to come in contact with is a lot harder than giving them the proper tools to understand and deal with the wide range of experiences, emotions, information, and in some cases, the pure garbage that is out there in the world.

As it is with television, newspapers, and other media, it's important for children to think for themselves as they consider the source.

How can parents give them the proper skills to do this? Media literacy. According to the Center for Media Literacy, media researchers now report that television and the mass media have become so ingrained in our cultural lives that we should no longer view the task of media education as providing protection against unwanted messages or images. Now, our goal should be to help people, especially children, become competent, critical, and literate in all media forms to ensure that they have the necessary skills to control the interpretation of what they see or hear, rather than letting the interpretation control them.

What do children and adults need to know about the media in our modern information culture? Over time, children of all ages can learn age-appropriate skills that enable them to live in a world of powerful images, words, and sounds. The Center for Media Literacy suggests five questions that children, or adults, should ask themselves or others about any media message:

1. Who created this message and why are they sending it?
2. What techniques are being used to attract my attention?
3. What lifestyles, values, and points of view are represented in the message?

4. How might different people understand this message differently
from me?
5. What is omitted from this message?

The powerful role of the media in our modern culture is one reason why media censorship is likely to fail. Instead, our children will
be better able to take in the thousands of verbal and visual symbols
they come into contact with each day if they are able to choose and
select, challenge and question, and possess the skills to be conscious
about what's going on around them without being passive and
vulnerable.

— 10 —

LESSONS FROM
ATHLETICS

"I am just a common man who is true to his beliefs."
—John Wooden and Steve Jamison
A Lifetime of Observation and Reflection On and Off the Court

"It's what you learn after you know it all that counts."
—John Wooden

"Winners never quit and quitters never win."
—Anonymous

Like so many other life lessons and life experiences, the world of sports provides endless opportunities for teaching valuable lessons about leadership and the formation of character. Throughout history from one from culture to the next, the best and the brightest have measured themselves against each other in sports competition. The Winter and Summer Olympics continue this tradition. But the world of sports is changing, and the way we view athletes is changing with the times. Title IX legislation created a mandate for equality in collegiate women's athletics. Now, playing fields are surrounded by soccer moms watching their daughters as well as their sons.

The lessons I've learned in life would not be complete without recalling my experiences with sports—the coaches, the institutions, and the sports themselves. As Jack McAllister wrote earlier in the book, sports always holds the potential for positive learning, and at the same time, sports can show examples of values and character traits that need to be improved.

Excelling at Something While Young

BOB PLACE

FOR INDIVIDUALS TO MAXIMIZE their potential for personal development and to have the greatest opportunity for successful lifelong careers in any field, I think it is very important that they excel-at-something at a fairly early age. . . . at least by their early to middle 20s.

By "excel-at-something" I mean individuals should be secure within themselves that they have mastered a target field of endeavor at a high level. That they have performed to the best of their ability. And they have received recognition for this expertise or skill.

What this really teaches (or allows to be ingrained in an individual's make-up or lifestyle) is COMMITMENT. It is the making of a commitment to excel-at-something and then following through to make it happen that shows both the individual, and their peers and support groups, that this person is effectively focused on achieving something good in some aspect of life and is maturing in a positive way. This leads to a positive attitude within the individual and within the circle of people who know them.

The most obvious area where individuals can achieve such recognition at an early age is athletics, in both team and individual sports. There are endless opportunities for this available today, in and out of the school systems. Success stories abound where dedicated committed people overcome all sorts of obstacles to realize high levels of achievement.

Perhaps not so obvious, but every bit as viable for this purpose, are all the remaining fields of human activity where there is direct, or indirect, interaction between and among people. A short list of examples would be: voice (singing or speaking), musical instruments, various fields of study, volunteering, mechanics, crafts, cooking, gardening, fishing, animal raising/training/husbandry, sewing, inventing, teaching, writing, electronics/computers, photography, acting, movies, research—just about anything where people interact in an attempt to improve themselves and the processes by which they live.

A common thread which runs through success stories in all fields is that individuals who do their best prove to be COACHABLE. That is, they are open to and may actively seek out instructions and suggestions for improvement, and they demonstrate a willingness and ability to work new ideas and techniques into their "style".

This is not to say that the "lone wolf" is incapable of accomplishing great things, especially in the short run. However, in the longer term, I believe isolation from communications and interaction with others will likely lead to a lower level of overall achievement than would otherwise be the case.

What I think the feeling of "excelling-at-something" does for individuals is to instill a sense of confidence as they move forward with their lives. Such confidence enables a person to try new directions and things because they have the security of knowing what it feels like to be good at something.

Once a person understands the dedication and plain hard work it takes to reach a level of excellence in one thing, that understanding provides a guide for meeting and overcoming other obstacles to a happy and successful life.

In my opinion, every young person should give this thesis careful consideration (perhaps discussing it with parents, peers, teachers, and so forth), and look within themselves to identify an area in which they have a passion to succeed and excel. You may not get it exactly right the first time, but the general direction will probably be close.

So, take this thesis where it leads you, and remember: Most great coaches started as players (though many were not themselves even very good players). Some great football defensive and running backs started as quarterbacks. Some great band leaders started as pit musicians. All great teachers, researchers, and inventors started as students.

To make this idea of "excellence-in-something" a reality for you, you need to develop a plan of action or program for getting started. It has to be your own plan because you will fight the hardest to make your ideas and dreams work.

I charge you to do it.

Bob Place is a retired banking executive. He and his wife Pat have been lifelong friends.

My Lessons from Athletics

J. NELSON HOFFMAN

ONE OF THE BEST PARTS OF MY DAD'S LIFE was the success, the pleasure, he enjoyed as an athlete, and the vicarious satisfactions he drew from my efforts on the court and playing field. In his day, work meant physical labor, long hours, and drudgery. Sports, like football and baseball, were a great break from work. The men of his day were participants, not spectators.

Dad had spent some time in an orphanage. His mother was sick for an extended period, and his father, a railroad man, was frequently away on the road. My father was a loner, and he found great joy in running. He had the lithe body of a distance runner (6'1" tall, 150–160 pounds). It was something that he could do well, an area where he found real success. In the fall, he was a cross-country runner and loved the cool air, the runs through wooded terrain, and the thrill of competition. In the spring, he was one of the best milers in his high school.

In the winter, he was a natural for the role of center on the basketball team. He played briefly for East High, but the pressures from home forced him to quit and work at a grocery store after school. He was limited to club basketball on weekends. He missed the fact that he could not play high school ball and did everything he could to make sure I was able to play.

In fact, he couldn't wait for me to grow up and follow in his footsteps. Most boys get a baseball and bat at a very early age. I got a basketball-at 5! That gift caused a real crisis in the Hoffman household. At five, I wasn't a very accomplished dribbler. While practicing in my grandmother's dining room, I put the ball through the front of her treasured glass china cabinet. I probably only broke the front pane and a plate or glass or two. But I caught the full fury of my mother and grandmother's wrath. My dad got a lecture on where the appropriate places to play ball were, and together we learned the 11th commandment—No playing ball in the house!

THE PLAYGROUND

Five years later, before my dad left for WWII, he put a backboard on the garage and bought me a new basketball. He told me to practice my shooting and coached me on the finer points of two-handed set shooting.

But to play the game, I had to go to Parcells Avenue Baptist Church or the playground at the Old University of Rochester Stadium. For the next two years that playground was my second home. After school, and all summer, I was playing one sport or another.

Unlike the piano lessons I was required to take and practice every day, sports became my passion. Today, inner city playgrounds are often a threatening place. But for me, in my time, they were the venue for some valuable learning:

Ethnically and racially, the playgrounds were an effective melting pot: black and white, Christian and Jew, Irish, Italian, Polish, and Germans.

We learned all the derogatory, disrespectful, demeaning, and hateful names for each group. Being mostly German, the worst name I was called was Kraut or a damn Nazi. The names for blacks, Jews, and Italians were much worse. In our young innocence, I don't think we realized how offensive they were.

Time has suppressed the usage of those epithets in most families. But their use still exists, and they still incite bigotry and prejudice.

On the playgrounds we learned that if you could field or bat a baseball, shoot, pass, or rebound a basketball, the color of your skin or the nationality of your parents didn't make any difference.

There were lessons in self-government, with no parents around. The supervisors were high school athletes and college students who passed out the equipment and settled any disputes that came up. Most of the time, the honor system was used to call fouls in basketball, with winners continuing to play and losers sitting out. As I got older, the price of admission was 10–25 cents, my first exposure to capitalism and the free market.

I learned to fist fight, wrestle, and generally defend myself, but more importantly to negotiate. I learned the art of verbal jousting. It was a lot less painful than real fighting. Somehow, the tall guy always was the target for the tests of manhood. Knives, guns, and other weapons that plague today's inner cities weren't part of our lives. Learning to resolve conflict was much simpler, and the description of someone who was street-tough and street-smart was much less ominous than it is today.

But when it comes to lessons in tolerance, the realities of competition, leadership, and teamwork—these were all learned in the games and life on the playground.

I remember my days on the playground as good times.

HIGH SCHOOL

When Dad returned from the war in 1946, the middle of my sophomore year, we moved from the city to a small farm town outside of Rochester. Penfield was transitioning from farm town to suburbia.

The grammar and high schools were in the same building. Our class had 32 members, and it meant we competed in the smaller school leagues, Class C, with an occasional game against the big Class A and AA schools.

There wasn't enough money or students for a football team, so soccer was the fall sport. It didn't attract much support from the townsfolk. I had good coaching on the freshman team at East High School, so I had a head start on playing. The team of small-town boys matured and developed under Coach Marks, and by our senior year, we had developed enough skills and teamwork to win our sectional championship.

At Thanksgiving, we moved from soccer to basketball, and with that, the excitement and fun that goes with competing for a small town. On Friday nights the town closed down, and the caravans of team bus, student buses, and the cars of parents and fans trekked off to nearby towns.

This was serious business. Town honor was at stake. The question of which town's team was best would be debated over coffee and at volunteer fireman parades for the next year. You left every game as heroes or goats. Most of the parents and fans rehashed the plays, the ref calls, and the coach's decisions in the game postmortems.

The coach of the soccer and basketball teams was Herman Marks. He coached a number of winning teams. He is not in this book because of his coaching acumen, but rather his human side. Herm was a laconic man, and his pleas for improvements in fundamentals were brief and pointed. He wasn't much for inspirational halftime talks. I remember one game we were shooting poorly, passing worse, and playing "matador defense," which meant we were waving our arms at an opposing player as they went by us and scored, without us doing much to stop them.

At halftime, we expected a chalkboard full of X's and O's and a big chewing out for playing so poorly. We waited for coach to enter the locker room. And waited.

With about a minute remaining before we had to go out for the second half, Coach Marks entered. He paused, looked us each in the eye, and waited until the room was dead silent. He flashed us a smile that said, "You know you're screwing up!" Then said, "Just go out there and stick the ball in the basket more than they do."

I'm not sure it is the same message Dean Smith or John Wooden would have delivered, but it was very effective. We lost the tension we had in the first half and ran away from the other team in the second half.

Another well-liked coach was Elmer Peck. He was a history teacher who took great pleasure in coaching the baseball team. My skills in baseball were marginal, and I probably would not have played at a larger school. Elmer was a born teacher and coach: soft spoken, patient, and empathetic. In addition to telling us how to do something, he had great skills himself and could demonstrate the fundamentals—skills like fielding the ball with the glove down, your weight balanced over your feet, head up and your fanny down, and then you move your feet to get your body in front of the ball.

Elmer advanced from the job of assistant principal to principal and oversaw the school through a period of explosive growth. He was good at helping young people look ahead and was a big factor in my decision to attend the University of Rochester. His model served me well when I got in a position to counsel young people about their careers.

COLLEGE

My final sports role model was Coach Lou Alexander, the varsity basketball coach at the University of Rochester. Lou was not warm and fuzzy. He was a patrician who used his assistant coaches well. His forte was picking five guys who would play together and execute his offense. He didn't make a big effort to get close to his players. He ruled from on high. Yet in a time when I needed support, I saw a very understanding side of him that stuck with me a long time.

Syracuse was one of the few larger schools we scheduled, and on our home court we could give them a good game. One game, I was an early substitute against them. I missed my first shot and then went on the streak of my life, making 10 straight field goals. With less than a minute to play, we were only down by one point.

I tipped a Syracuse pass toward Bill Secor, our lightning-fast guard, and raced off by myself for our basket. Bill threw me a perfect pass and I went up for a shot. In a horrible flash, I realized I had misjudged my distance and was too far out! Struggling to hang in the air, I laid the ball up as softly as I could. It rolled around the rim, and then around again, and came out.

The ball was grabbed by a Syracuse player, and one of my teammates fouled him. He made the free throws, and we lost.

I was the goat and walking up to the locker room was one of the toughest walks I had ever taken. Only a player who has been in similar circumstances can know how rotten you feel at a time like that. I had let my teammates down. And what might have been a glorious victory became a stinging defeat.

My teammates tried to console me, but I was really down. I was the last one in the locker room other than the managers when Lou came in. He sat on the bench next to me, put his hand on my shoulder, and said, "Nels, I know you feel terrible, and it would have been marvelous if that shot had gone in. But think of it this way, supposing that you had missed one of those earlier shots instead of the last one. If you hadn't made ten straight shots, we wouldn't have had a chance to win. I'm sorry and mad that we lost, but you played a great game. Go out and forget it. You are going to have a lot more chances to be a winner."

Lou never suffered defeat easily, but I saw a side of him that I really respected and remembered long after leaving the university.

THE PRESENT DAY

I am still an ardent fan of virtually all sports, but I see behaviors and trends that I think reflect problems of society at large. Let me begin with some examples.

At most college and professional basketball games, you see players taunting the opposition, putting on self-gratifying displays over a dunked basketball or scoring a touchdown. They remind me of a peacock showing off its feathers. Now, the object seems to be to put down the opponent. What ever happened to the idea that you had respect for the opponent? That you showed sportsmanship? Is this the example of respect for your fellow man we want displayed to young adults? My parents, though ardent fans, never permitted such insulting behavior, so I never needed any coach or referee telling me how to behave in a game.

Another aspect of our present day sports scene which bothers me is an overemphasis on sports. I have a young nephew who is a volleyball fanatic and travels to other states in competition. As a junior varsity player, he practiced more than I did as a varsity player, and his weekends included tournaments that lasted all day. In contrast to when I grew up, little boys and girls now begin competing in the second or third grade, and if they don't, their chances for playing on a varsity team are decreased because they'll be competing with those who have developed their skills for an additional 5–8 year period.

I loved and still love sports. But the overemphasis on competition, and the time taken away from studies now seem out of hand. Few young people will be able to make a living competing at the professional level. My plea is that sports be kept in perspective, with a balance of study, competition, and play outside the field of competition. Sports as a focus of all family activity, at the cost of academics, or other family interests is placing too much importance on the wrong values, the wrong activities.

My third concern is the preoccupation of television sports with violence: stock car pile-ups, the replay of the quarterback sack, the hockey enforcer smashing a player into the boards, and the farce that is professional wrestling, whose principal appeal is synthetic violence (It's just pretend, right?).

While the media in our country have done a poor job of limiting the amount of simulated violence our children see, there is a group that needs to take a more aggressive stance—parents and other adults. As more and more studies show, children should not have unlimited access to television or video games. Their access should be part of the growing up process. (Remember Amatai Etzioni's suggestions earlier in the book.)

The more responsible and mature a child is, the greater the access. It is the responsibility of parents to control that access or provide some type of context to what their children are watching. When children are repeatedly stimulated by acts of violence, it has the subliminal effect of insulating their senses from the real hurt and pain of those acts. There is a difference between "playing hard" on the field of sports and inflicting real violence on someone. Children need to know the difference. They need to know what is acceptable and what is not.

In closing, let me question our elevation of sports figures to the status of national "heroes." In spite of promotional efforts to make us think of their stars as role models, I believe parents should teach their children that they are nothing more than mere mortals. They behave in both positive and negative ways. Their behaviors and transgressions are no different than any other man or woman on the street. They just have a lot more money to get into trouble, or as adults, to act like spoiled, selfish children. Recently, there has been scandal of pro athletes fathering children out of wedlock, beating their spouses, using and dealing drugs, and even murder.

Let's be thankful for the few examples whose behavior off the court or playing field can serve as a positive example to our children.

Grandma Frick

DON PUENTE

IN THE MID-1930S, in a small mining town in Arizona, a widow lived alone in a one bedroom house, with no car and no money. She was too independent and too proud to accept any form of public assistance. Her sole income was from taking in sewing and being a part-time practical nurse. When my mother passed away, this lady suddenly inherited a young grandson to raise, care for, and educate.

Grandmother Frick possessed all of the values which we try to instill in our children, i.e., independence, a hard work ethic, honesty, love, dedication, self-sufficiency, and above all, a tremendous love for our Creator. She knew that education was the only answer to achieving a better life, and I can still hear her say, "Come hell or high water, you will get an education." Life was difficult, but Grandma always had a positive attitude and never complained.

Athletics was a vehicle to education. She pushed me along, recognizing that I had abilities in sports, and she made sure I applied myself properly. In eighth grade, I made the football team. But being skinny, I was at the end of the uniform issue line. When my turn came the only football shoes left were size eleven, and I wore a size seven. Grandma Frick made a cardboard inner sole and stuffed the toes with newspaper so they would not flop when I ran.

She altered the hand-me-down uniform to fit, and I was off to a long career in football. She not only laundered my uniforms and shined my football shoes, she tutored me in studies and stressed the values she felt made people successful. Thanks to her dedication, I received a football scholarship to a major university and obtained an education which allowed me to live comfortably and provide a proper education for my four children.

God has blessed me with a wonderful wife, four great children, and five of the cutest grandchildren anyone could ask for. I pray that I can pass on to my family the example and the beliefs that Grandma Frick possessed, and if I am successful, she will be very proud of her efforts.

A former vice president of Newhall Land Company, Don Puente is an active Catholic layman.

Humility—The Tragedy of Robert Montgomery Knight

J. NELSON HOFFMAN

I AM A BASKETBALL NUT. I love the college game more than any other. Since my playing days, I have closely followed the great college basketball programs. Joan worked in the admissions office at one of these powerhouses—UCLA, and my daughter Karen graduated from another—the University of North Carolina—during the Dean Smith era.

I followed the firing of Indiana's coach Bobby Knight with mixed emotions. He ran a tough, disciplined program. He instilled in hundreds of young men a strength of character that contributed to their later successes in their professional careers, as well as their personal lives. In Bobby Knight, I saw a man doing the work for which I wrote this book—helping young people understand and develop character. At the same time, he ran one of the cleanest big-time college sports programs ever. And he pushed his athletes to become college graduates.

But, as an outsider, knowing only what I read, I believe he had two flaws which provided his downfall at Indiana: pride and anger.

We all possess some blend of humility and pride. The Bible tells us pride was the first sin. In my own life, I have always carried too much pride. So, I feel great empathy for Bobby Knight. He is good at what he does. He has been successful. It is sad to see him go.

But a university campus is, first and foremost, a place of learning. Bad examples of behavior don't serve a school's true purpose. I believe Coach Knight could have stayed to the end of his career if he had learned to walk with more humility.

The second flaw was anger. Anger is a two-edged sword. There are specific times and places where anger might be appropriate. Anger at war, poverty, ignorance, environmental destruction, and greed might be OK—but not as an example of behavior to young men.

I have too much respect for Coach Knight to judge further. In my life, I have found that people who cared, and cared deeply, often at the same time, expressed anger.

I'm sure that the young man who called out to Bob Knight might have gotten a somewhat different reaction if he had called out, "Coach Knight," rather than the disrespectful, "Hey Knight" he actually used.

Bob Knight reacted to what he heard as disrespect and angrily confronted the young man. It became the straw that broke the tolerance limit for Bob Knight's career at Indiana.

As I watched the television reporting of this tragedy, George C. Scott's portrayal of General George Patton came to mind. Two men with the strength of character to accomplish great things. Both possessing fatal tragic flaws.

Would that Bob Knight could have learned from the example of fellow Hoosier, John Wooden, whose humility continues to bring him honor long after his coaching career has ended.

Putting Professional Sports in Perspective

J. Nelson Hoffman

THE EMPHASIS OF TELEVISION SPORTS in promoting the stars over the teams has put the superstars in the same category as rock stars and Hollywood stars. Their agents negotiate contracts that reward their clients with multimillion dollar contracts to whatever extent the market will bear. The owners, in turn, raise the price of tickets and the networks award ever greater contracts. As a consequence, attendance at professional football or basketball games is becoming prohibitably expensive. And, because of the promotion of these sports stars, they become the ideals for young people.

I suppose after many professional sports franchises were run like plantations for many years, the performers have a right to make all they can. But where is the restraint on the upward spiral of costs? Ultimately, it will be the customers' resistance to inflation and excess promotion. Reality will set in.

Until that occurs, I have a pair of suggestions that may help correct the current excesses:

1) The federal and state governments could cap the deductibility of sports events entertaining at $25–50 per person. Right now, businesses deduct the expense of their skybox, season tickets, etc. So until their bottom line is of concern, sports entertaining is a great way of plying customers. The forgotten customer (read fan) now spends $100–200 to take the family to a ball game.

2) My second suggestion is for cities and towns to stop putting up bond money for stadiums to attract major league franchises. Major league franchises are a gold plated endowment. Measure how much appreciation has occurred in a baseball, basketball, hockey, or NFL franchise over the past ten years. By and large, the municipalities provide the capital and debt, and the owners, free of that investment, pay the debt service BUT KEEP ALL THE APPRECIATION OF THE FRANCHISE. That is not such a great deal for the taxpayer. I'm sure voters can negotiate better for their share of the pie!

SECTION FOUR

Renewing the
Spirit of America

Where Do We Start?

IN THE BEGINNING OF THE BOOK, I said that the main purpose of the book was to create a revolution, a spiritual renewal of America.

Through the first three sections, I have presented the experiences, inspirations, and principles that made my life and the lives of the contributors meaningful. In the last section, I address initiatives of public and private action that I believe will lead to a more cohesive and connected society.

From my early history lessons, I recall a quotation from Benjamin Franklin that best expresses my thinking on the current state of affairs in our country: *We must all hang together or most assuredly we shall all hang separately.*

Benjamin Franklin spoke those words at the signing of the Declaration of Independence. His appeal to all the contending factions was a rallying cry to unite in the battle to gain freedom from England. Now, 225 years later, there is a need for leadership that unites the country rather than divides us.

Earlier in the book, Father McNamara expressed how the media frequently conveys issues in black and white terms to emphasize controversy. My purpose is just the opposite. I wish to propose encompassing ideas that develop mutual interest and trust. My intention is to develop the need for taking proactive steps to recreate a sense of community.

In collecting, organizing, and reflecting upon the materials of the prior sections, these conclusions grow clearer:

1) The generation Tom Brokaw writes about in *The Greatest Generation* and *The Greatest Generation Speaks* endured 11 years of economic trials, then immediately engaged in a global war that killed and wounded millions. Those two trials served to unite and mobilize America as the world's leader in republican democracy and free enterprise. To oversimplify, that generation underwent a 16-year costly, difficult, painful lesson in civics, community, faith, and discipline. The sense of mutual purpose, the sense of connectedness that resulted, was greater than at any time since 1776. Now, at the beginning of the twenty-first century, we are losing the people of this "greatest generation" and their positive influence at the rate of 30,000 per month.

2) The current national awareness that we are losing the connectedness that earlier generations taught us is low, and the number of people who care about this trend is relatively small. We champion diversity, but self interest or narrow group interest dominates. The central strength of America as a cohesive people with common interest is declining. The fire under the melting pot is burning low.

3) The media, particularly television, focus more and more on profit and less on a sustained commitment to the public interest.

4) Exemplary moral leadership that inspires people seems like a vanishing commodity, and new initiatives are needed.

Looking to the future, my concern is for our children. What is the effect these conditions are having? What effect have they already had? And what effect will the current trends have on our future as a nation?

I believe there is a strong, moral core of Americans who believe they are being steamrolled in matters of law, public policy, and standards of acceptable behavior. To object to outrageous behavior is to be labeled a bigot. Do the makers of 7-Up believe I will laugh at their "Up Yours" ads, rather than boycott their product? Can I protest ads that feature moronic and violent behavior that exalt barbaric themes? Am I bigoted for concluding that there is an increasing fraction of the population who function without a moral compass? With statistics showing an increasing faction of people who are alienated from society, require social support, or imprisonment, is it time for a change?

The best possible outcome I can conceive for this book is that it precipitates a widespread discussion of the issues, problems, and viewpoints we have addressed and that positive initiatives are created as a result of these discussions.

We hope that it focuses attention on what thinking people must do to create a turnaround. That is why I have used the term *renewal*, popularized by a hero of mine, Pope John XXIII, who spoke of what he sought to achieve in the Catholic Church. Renewal suggests a two-step process: First, an individual or community must examine the past to decide what is precious and must be brought forward. And secondly, they must take stock of where they are and make decisions to proactively create a better future for themselves.

We begin with the issue of leadership.

Leadership—Part Three

J. NELSON HOFFMAN

$\mathcal{S}$OMEWHERE IN THE PAST, I learned this definition: "Leadership is getting things done through others." There are many work and play activities based in individual skills and talents. Yet, in the great majority of our life activities, our ability to work with others is an important ingredient for success. Therefore, I place top priority in rating strong leaders on the capacity to articulate what must be done and their ability to energize a team to accomplish it.

Throughout this book, our contributors have described the various skills and characteristics leaders possess. Most of our contributors place a strong moral character at the top of the list. Leaders must create and maintain a climate of trust. As pointed out by Dick Hartl and others, leaders must lead by setting a good example.

Since most of my experience was gained in the world of business, my views of good leadership are shaped by that experience. Warren Bennis wrote a book several years ago titled *Why Leaders Can't Lead*. In the book, he draws a distinction between administrators and leaders. Administrators see that things are *done right*. Leaders see that the *right things* are done.

So in concluding this book, we offer a collection of initiatives for the start of this new century. We begin with a provocative essay by Governor Lamm on ways to create a sense of common purpose—building community.

— 11 —

A MODEL FOR ACTION

Ten Commandments of Community—
Diversity and Unity

RICHARD LAMM

$\mathcal{W}$E ARE SAILING INTO A NEW WORLD of public policy—a world as strange and new as Columbus discovered. It is a world where infinite government demands have run straight into finite resources. It is an America made up increasingly of diverse people. We are the only country in history that ever deliberately changed its ethnic makeup. At current immigration patterns, there will not be a dominant ethnic group by approximately 2040. We will all be minorities. It is also an aging society. Most of our institutional memories and political culture come out of the 1960s and 1970s when America was largely European and had the industrial world's highest rate of productivity growth and was doubling its wealth every 30 to 40 years. Government had a substantial yearly growth dividend it could spend.

Now, a much more diverse America has one of the lowest rates of productivity growth (1974-1994) in the industrial world. It now takes approximately 100 years to double our national wealth. We go into debt to maintain current levels of government. Being in government, today, is like sleeping with a blanket that is too short; we do not have the resources to cover all our needs.

We already live in a time of unprecedented tension between the races, sexes, even generations and religions. Compounding this, public policy cannot count on historic revenue growth; thus, it cannot chase geometric curves of public spending. It will require us to better understand what a "community" is and how it is formed and reinforced. I suggest that this world of ever-growing public needs of an aging society will require us to reconceptualize much of what government does and how it does it. It will cause us to define what is absolutely fundamental in many of our basic institutions. It will require us to think deeply about how diverse people live together.

As Marcel Proust has said: "The real voyage of discovery consists not in seeking new lands, but in seeing with new eyes. Let us look with 'new eyes' at community. We cannot take community for granted."

A community is much more than a place on a map. It is a state of mind, a shared vision, a common fate. A community is not a state of nature. A "herd" is a state of nature, a "flock," a "covey," a "gaggle," is a state of nature, but alas—not a community. A community of different religions, races, and nationalities is against most of the lessons of history, as we see daily on our TV sets. Humans bond to families, but not necessarily with their neighbors. A community requires social architecture—bridge builders, structural engineers who build bonds, bridges, who remove barriers.

The United States (and Denver) is by definition a place on the map, but it is not intrinsically a community. Every house is not a home, and every spot on the map is not a community. Community is not where we live but how we act and feel toward each other. Communities are forged by dedication, mutual respect, work, tolerance and love. Our forefathers and foremothers built a community and passed it onto us, but it is not like the Pikes Peak or the Grand Canyon—which we will inevitably pass onto our children. We will not inevitably pass community onto our children. Community is not a guarantee, but a continuing challenge.

We have not recently tested community. It is easy to keep a community when we are dividing up the spoils of a rich continent and a growing economy. It is adversity, not success, that tests community. Do we cooperate during times of adversity—to solve, alleviate, soothe, and mitigate? Or, do we form tribes and, like ravenous dogs, fight over a static pie? Community—like friendship—is never really tested until it jointly faces adversity. A rising economic tide not only raises all ships—it keeps them from bumping into each other.

In light of these new economic and social realities we must ask: How do we build a quality community? This is an immensely important question. We see daily the results of not building a community:

- in Bosnia
- in Chechnya
- in Sri Lanka
- in Quebec
- in Rwanda

What is going on today in Azerbaijan and Bosnia is not a failure of communism. It is failure of community. The Serbs, Croats, and Muslims in Bosnia were killing each other before Marx was born. The people in Azerbaijan are far less diverse than in the United States—the secret is that we formed a community (*E Pluribus Unum*) and Azerbaijan did not.

People who share a geographic area must become a community—or they become balkanized, fragmented, and fractionalized. We all bond naturally to our families; we bond to our geographic location:

> *"If you don't know where you are, you don't know who you are."*
> —Wendell Berry

But, we do not bond easily to our neighbors. We seem instinctively to view them as competitors. Living in the same neighborhood does not make one neighbors that require certain common goals for the future and a common government authority. James Fallows warns in his essay *Nobody Wants a Melting Pot*—ethnic diversity generally around the world means division and hatred. "Most Asian countries share a belief that a society is strongest when its members all come from the same race or ethnic group." America doesn't believe that, but it cannot ignore the need to have some common dreams and beliefs among these diverse people.

A community needs a shared stake in the future. It needs a shared language, shared culture, shared norms and values. It needs some common allegiance, and it must recognize that it shares to some extent a common destiny. It needs, in short, a social glue and feeling of interrelatedness which is the essence of community. It must realize a shared fate. To say my future is not tied to your future is like saying, "Your end of the boat is sinking."

Emanuel Kant said, "Religion and language are the world's great dividers." Yet Maya Angelou counters with "We human beings have far more in common than we do in what separates us." Both could be right.

We must give more thought to those things that build community—that hold us together as a community—and how to minimize those factors that separate us—like race, religion, ethnicity, and even class. Melting pots that do not melt become pressure cookers. Diversity carried too far is divisiveness.

Building communities becomes highly important public policy and imperative to our public and private futures. I should, thus, like to give you *Ten Commandments of Community*—ten building blocks which are imperative as we try to renew and expand our sense of community.

COMMANDMENT I: *God is not an American.*

Too many Americans believe that God is an American who will watch over us no matter how hedonistic, selfish, myopic, or inefficient we become.

This is a dangerous hubris. It is always a problem when nations believe too deeply in their myths. There is clearly something exceptional about the United States, but there has also been for all other great civilizations. No great nation in history has ever withstood the ravages of time. Toynbee warns us that all great nations rise and all fall, and that the "autopsy of history is that all great nations commit suicide." God will not automatically save America anymore than God saved Greece, Rome, or the British Empire. All once great nations thought they were favored by God, but all collapsed or were eclipsed.

With God's help, we must save ourselves. This leads us to the second commandment.

COMMANDMENT II: *The future is not something we inherit—it is something we create.*

We cannot rely on past success to insure future success, and we cannot take the future for granted. Successful communities—successful countries—don't just happen. They are built by dedication and hard work. Community is not synonymous with either capitalism or democracy. Voters vote their self interest, and people generally maximize individual and family income and wealth. We are not a community because we vote or because we are wealthy. We need a "social glue" which binds us together and makes us feel common bonds and mutual trust.

Members of a community recognize a mutual interdependence, a reciprocal stake in each other. A great Amazon legend states that a priest was speaking with God about heaven and hell. "I will show you hell," said God. They went into a room which had a delicious beef stew on the table, around which sat people who looked desperately famished. They held spoons with long handles which reached into the pot, but were too long to put the stew back into their mouths. Their suffering was terrible. "Now, I will show you heaven," said God. They then went into an identical room with the savory stew on the table, around which sat people with identical spoons and handles, but they were well-nourished and joyous. The priest was baffled until God said, "Quite simply, you see, these people have learned to feed each other."

We can create chaos, as in Bosnia, or we can create community. It is up to us. But community requires us, metaphorically, to feed each other.

COMMANDMENT III: *A great community needs great leaders and great citizens.*

Leadership is important. We all know this. Churchill said, "An army of lions led by sheep will always lose to an army of sheep led by a lion." But citizens are equally important.

America, in many respects, faces more of a "followership" problem than a leadership problem. One wise historian observed:

> *"To make a nation truly great, a handful of heroes capable of great deeds at supreme moment is not enough. Heroes are not always available, and one can often do without them! But it is essential to have thousands of reliable people— honest citizens— who steadfastly place the public interest before their own."*
>
> —Pasquale Villani

John Gardner, former Secretary of the Department of Health and Human Services, similarly warns: "Democracy is measured not by its leaders doing extraordinary things, but by its citizens doing ordinary things extraordinarily well. . . ."

Our society cannot achieve greatness unless individuals at many levels of ability accept the need for high standards of performance and strive to achieve those standards within the limits possible for them. We want the highest conceivable excellence, of course, in the activities crucial to our effectiveness and creativity as a society, but that isn't enough. If the man in the street says, "Those fellows at the top have to be good, but I'm just a slob and can act like one."—then our days of greatness are behind us.

A quality community needs more than leadership; it needs quality citizens. You have to be able to trust your neighbors to do the right thing. You do not have to love your neighbors to have community, but you cannot live in fear of them. This means that community needs some level of trust and some level of safety.

If our communities are not safe, they will not be communities. It is ironic that safety was one of the main reasons cities came into being. Now, it is one of the main reasons that we flee cities.

A quality community can only be built on the bedrock of quality citizens, who feel secure and have at least a certain level of trust in their neighbors.

COMMANDMENT IV: A community must generate tolerance and yet set limits on that tolerance.

Tolerance is a word easy to say—hard to apply. Michael Walzer in his book *On Toleration* points out that toleration is essential to community but difficult where there are groups "with different histories, cultures, and identities." It is also more difficult to achieve where economic inequities are large and where upward mobility is limited. But a society such as ours must recognize tolerance as essential. "Toleration makes difference possible; difference makes toleration necessary."

What should the community tolerate and what shouldn't it tolerate? It often depends on context. It is your right to read your Bible, your Koran, your Torah. It is not your right to force these readings on others. We can tolerate almost any idea, and the community should be alive with argument.

The standards for teaching and tolerance are not coterminous. It may be that you deeply believe that it is the trees moving that makes the wind blow. This is your prerogative, but you cannot teach it to my children in public institutions. You can stage debates in your school between Republicans and Democrats because it is a subject open to debate and constantly changing, but you do not give equal time in schools to how trees moving makes the wind blow. Science and rational thought have put to rest certain arguments, and knowledge must move forward if we are to survive in a competitive world. We can tolerate many private beliefs, but should stand strong against institutionalizing non-science and scientific error into our school system.

You are entitled to believe in creationism, but we should not tolerate it to be taught as science in the public schools. With all the evidence of carbon-dating rocks, fossils, and all we know about biology and geology, the whole rational basis of science supports evolution. It is not a scientific debate. James Watson, winner of the Nobel Prize for his co-discovery of the structure of DNA, said: "Today, the theory of evolution is an accepted fact for everyone but a fundamentalist minority whose objections are based not on reasoning, but on doctrinaire adherence to religious principles."

There are some people who believe the Holocaust never happened. They are entitled to be mistaken—even gravely mistaken. They can stand on a soapbox on Main Street and profess that there was no Holocaust—but they cannot teach in our schools a viewpoint that all evidence points against. We have pictures of concentration camps and Holocaust victims. And, we have pictures in rocks (called fossils) which show us the inspiring story of evolution. Schools must struggle with knowledge, but cannot teach theology—or any minority viewpoints no matter how passionately held.

Tolerance, however, can be pushed too far. Community may need some new laws that intrude on tolerance. Jane Jacobs once said: "The bedrock attribute of a successful city, district, community is that a person must feel personally safe and secure on the street among all those strangers." Dottie and I once spent a fall in San Francisco. We saw the most aggressive begging we had ever encountered. One man told us that if we didn't give him a donation, he would rob us next time.

Aggressive begging laws were put into effect in San Francisco and have been advanced by some of the most progressive mayors, such as Maynard Jackson of Atlanta and Norman Rice in Seattle. For them, the issue was not homelessness; it was staving off urban decline and dealing with the latest reason people avoid downtowns because of aggressive panhandlers who use verbal and physical intimidation in the place of a passive palm.

Much of the begging we saw in San Francisco was not common panhandling, but a type of harassment bordering on extortion. They would chase down and browbeat vulnerable people until money was handed over. A small group of aggressive panhandlers can ruin a neighborhood; it can kill a business; and it can rob citizens of the feeling of safety they once felt.

Both in Chicago and St. Louis, groups of welfare mothers decided to clean up their housing projects. They passed tenant rules which forbade carrying guns or selling drugs within their housing projects. The ACLU predictably sued, saying the rules, which required searching each person upon entry, infringed on people's rights. The courts upheld the efforts of the welfare mothers, pointing out that the tenants of a housing project could set standards and evict people who violate those standards from the public housing community.

In short, tolerance stretched in moderation becomes a safety net. Tolerance stretched too far becomes a apathetic vacuum where the holes are larger than the strings are strong—a vacuum which invites both the criminals and the narrow moralists rather than the truly moral to rush in.

Even more important is tolerance in the area of behavior, especially where behavior does not hurt others, and/or where no societal consensus exists.

COMMANDMENT V: A community can be a Joseph's coat of many colors and creeds, but it must have more things in common than differences.

"Diversity" is a word sweeping America and, in particular, sweeping college campuses. I am suspicious of the "eulogization" of this word. I recently went around the world and in no place, with the possible exception of Hawaii, did I see "diversity" working. Diverse people worldwide are mostly engaged in hating each other—that is, when they are not killing each other. A peaceful or stable "diverse" society is against most historical precedent. It cannot be achieved with slogans or happy talk. It is much harder to achieve than most Americans acknowledge. I believe that a society can be a Joseph's coat of many diverse people, but they absolutely must have more in common than what separates them. I am sobered by how much unity it takes to hold a society together, how easy it is to come unraveled. Look at the ancient Greeks. Dorf's *World History* tells us:

> The Greeks believed that they belonged to the same race; they possessed a common language and literature; and they worshipped the same gods. All Greece took part in the Olympic games in honor of Zeus and all Greeks venerated the shrine of Apollo at Delphi. A common enemy, Persia, threatened their liberty. Yet, all of these bonds together were not strong enough to overcome two factors . . . local patriotism and geographical conditions which nurtured political divisions . . .

The Los Angeles Times, whose market area is now a seething land of ethnic tensions, warns "if ethnicity begins to replace citizenship as the basis of statehood, chaos would ensue. . . ." But, this seems to be exactly what is happening. Hispanic students demand a separate graduation at which the Mexican, not the American flag, is flown. There is more talk of "reclaiming" the Southwest for Mexico than there is of allegiance to America. Is this just a passing phase? Hopefully. The history of multiple cultures living together without assimilation is not a happy history. The United States runs the very great risk of creating a "Hispanic Quebec" if we do not develop the right "social glue." As Benjamin Schwarz wrote in *The Atlantic Monthly*, ". . . the apparent success of our own multiethnic and multicultural experiment might have been achieved not by tolerance but by hegemony. Without the dominance that once dictated ethnocentrically, and what it meant to be an American, we are left with only tolerance and pluralism to hold us together."

To me, tolerance and pluralism are not enough. We must be more than a diverse people living in the same place and sharing only a standard of living. A country is not just a rooming house where we reside while we make a living. You can't be in America just for the good parts. A country that is also a community must have shared values, language, and some degree of cultural consensus.

Citizens need to have sole allegiance to one country; they can have roots in two or more. Ethnic loyalty cannot eclipse community loyalty, and I'm skeptical that we can really have "dual nationality" as has recently been done in Mexico.

The U.S. Commission on Immigration, chaired by Barbara Jordan, used the word "Americanization" and urged it be cultivated in immigrants by stressing the American values of liberty, democracy, and equal opportunity. Those are practically fighting words among the diversity proponents. Yet I suggest we need a shared sense of Americanness. Barbara Jordan wrote and spoke eloquently about the need to "Embrace the common core of American culture." We must insure that immigrants want to join our society, our polity, our culture and way of life, and that they want to be able to speak to us. We cannot allow nations within nations.

In short "diversity" is only an asset if it is secondary to unity. Lebanon has diversity without unity. Lebanon allocates its seats in Congress on a sectarian basis (and whose President must be a Maronite Christian, Prime Minister a Sunni Muslim, and Speaker of House a Shiite) and they are constantly at each other's throats. Detente is not community, nor is an armed truce. The United States must have both diversity and unity. The emphasis must be on the "*Unum*," not the "*Pluribus*." We should respect diversity, but we should celebrate unity.

COMMANDMENT VI: A quality community develops and constantly rethinks justice and is committed to peaceful change

The members of a community must feel that they are dealt with objectively and with fairness and justice. This is indispensable. Alexander Hamilton underlined its importance: "Justice is the end of government. It is the end of a civil society. It ever has been and ever will be pursued until it is obtained or until liberty be lost in the pursuit."

We pay a price for justice, but it is worth it. Robert Briffault, a British surgeon and novelist, said a hundred years ago:

> Democracy is the worst form of government. It is the most ineffi-
> cient, the most clumsy, the most unpractical. . . . It reduces wisdom
> to impotence and secures the triumph of folly, ignorance, clap-trap,
> and demagogy. Yet democracy is the only form of social order admis-
> sible because it is the only one consistent with justice.

Strong words, but true. There is no community without justice.

But concepts of justice are not static. We must be aware of the new issues of injustice that arise out of the dynamics of history. My generation did this in the areas of race and sex. But new issues of justice are always forming, even as old ones are alleviated. The German thinker Dietrich Bonhoeffer observed during his fight against Hitler that "the ultimate question for a responsible man is . . . how the coming generation will live."

My generation has not been good trustees for America. We have not met the most basic of history's tests: We have not left our children a sustainable society. We have and are improving our standard of living at the expense of our children. We have inserted into their future a large number of fiscal time bombs. We have not maintained strong, vigorous, and sustainable institutions. Let me give you some examples:

We have hung an incredible albatross around the necks of our children. Not only the $5.4 trillion debt—which is equivalent to a $20,000 mortgage on each one us—but a wide range of unfunded and contingent liabilities. When I piece all of the creative accounting of the federal government, I suggest that our children will have to pay off between $14 and $17 trillion of our federal debt—plus interest! Under the most optimistic scenario, our children will have to take approximately $.25 out of every tax dollar they spend. One congressman called it "fiscal child abuse."

Our generation has used its political power to pick our children's pockets. Social Security, Medicare, military pensions, federal civil service pensions, state and local pensions—all these and more are chain letters to the future. Medicare is one recession away from bankruptcy. The average person retiring today will receive back in Social Security five or six times what they paid in, and our children will be lucky to even get their money back. Programs that worked and were good social policy when we had society with many children growing up and a lifespan of approximately seventy years does not make economic sense in a society which has fewer children with a less productive economy and whose lifespan is eighty years.

The elderly make up 12 percent of America, and they receive 61 percent of federal social spending, despite the fact that the elderly are no longer disproportionately poor. It is political power, not social justice, which sets priorities; and money desperately needed to prepare the next generation is being transferred to the last generation whether they need it or not. Money desperately needed by poor children in St. Paul is transferred instead to wealthy retirees in St. Petersburg.

In all cultures, in all nations, and in all religions, there is a universal theme against profligacy and urging justice for future generations. A community cares about posterity. An old Middle East proverb observes, "The beginning of wisdom comes when a person plants a tree, the shade under which he knows he will never sit." Alas, my generation has cut down the shade trees we inherited.

A viable community keeps its concepts of justice up to date. It is also dedicated to peaceful change. The procedure of change is often as important as the substance. Political scientist Richard Hofstadter states it well:

Comity exists in a society to the degree that those enlisted in its contending interests have a basic minimal regard for each other: one party or interest seeks the defeat of an opposing interest on matters of policy, but at the same time seeks to avoid crushing the opposition, denying the legitimacy of its existence or its values . . . The basic humanity of the opposition is not forgotten; civility is not abandoned; the sense that a community life must be carried on after the acerbic issues of the moment have been fought over and won is seldom very far out of mind. . . .

A community knows the difference between opponents and enemies.

COMMANDMENT VII: *A community needs a shared culture and shared language.*

John Gardner says:

If the community is lucky, and fewer and fewer are, it will have a shared history and tradition. It will have its "story," its legends and heroes, and will retell that story often. It will have symbols of group identity—a name, a flag, a location, songs, and stories. . . which it will use to heighten its members' sense of belonging.

He goes on to say: "To maintain the sense of belonging and the dedication and commitment so essential to community life, members need inspiring reminders of shared goals and values."

I am convinced that one of the "shared values" we must have is a shared language. It is a blessing for an individual to be bilingual—it is a curse for a society to be bilingual. Societies must be able to talk to each other. A sign in a New York classroom late last century warned "Learn English. Be American. Otherwise America will become like the old country." Previously in American history it was always felt that a common language was necessary to promote teamwork, recognize mutual dependency, and diminish polarization.

One scholar, Seymour Martin Lipset, put it this way:

The history of bilingual and bicultural societies that do not assimilate are histories of turmoil, tension, and tragedy. Canada, Belgium, Malaysia, Lebanon—all face crises of national existence in which minorities press for autonomy, if not independence. Pakistan and Cyprus have divided. Nigeria suppressed an ethnic rebellion. France faces difficulties with its Basques, Bretons, and Corsicans.

The United States, in my opinion, is at a crossroads. It must move toward either greater integration or toward more fragmentation. It will either have to assimilate much better all of the peoples within its boundaries, or it will see an increasing alienation and fragmentation. Alexis de Tocqueville stressed this: "The tie of language is perhaps the strongest and most durable that can unite mankind." People can be proud of where they came from, but they must identify more (as much?) with their neighbors than their ancestors. Social cohesion requires us to easily converse with each other. Bilingual and bicultural nations are inherently unstable. We found in the 1950s that "separate was inherently unequal." But, we must also find that separate is also inherently divisive.

COMMANDMENT VIII: *A great community needs a community culture and some degree of cultural consensus.*

I think more and more about culture these days. Why do certain people succeed in disproportionate numbers, and others fail in disproportionate numbers? We are all God's children, but we form different cultures.

Americans have a difficult time talking about culture. Culture, however, explains more than we care to admit. I was always amazed when I was a civil rights worker that the most economically successful people in America are minorities who have been discriminated against. While never justified we have to decide whether discrimination is a hurdle or a barrier. I suggest generally a hurdle. When you look at family income, you see the top earners in America are:

- Japanese
- Chinese
- Jews
- Koreans

Why?

I believe because they came from cultures which promote education and delayed gratification, ambition and hard work, and other traits that are most often equated with success. Daniel Patrick Moynihan states: "The central conservative truth is that it is culture, not politics, that determines the success of a society. The central liberal truth is that politics can change a culture and save it from itself."

Likewise, successful communities have a successful corporate culture. James Fallows puts it this way: "In the long run, a society's strength depends on the way that ordinary people voluntarily behave."

A successful community culture encourages certain traits:

- citizen participation
- community leadership
- volunteerism and philanthropy
- civic education
- community pride
- justice
- trust

They build an institutional capacity for cooperation and consensus building. To have a community, you must have trust. People must be able to subordinate individual interests to those of the whole community. If trust is ever lost, it is very hard to regain.

The ability to cooperate, work together, and to live together requires habits, traditions, and norms that stress community and the need to trust others in your community most of the time. There needs to be some common dreams and there must be a high degree of virtue. Community demands a profound sense of personal responsibility, and willingness to govern one's own passions, a capacity for initiative and self-reliance, a spirit of civic cooperation. Successful communities have and in turn build successful community cultures. Winston Churchill said: "We build our buildings and then they build us." Likewise, we build our community culture and then it builds us.

COMMANDMENT IX: Thou shall not ask what your community can do for you. Thou shall ask what you can do for your community.

I believe a quality community is one which balances rights and privileges with duties and responsibilities. No society can live on rights and privileges alone, and we have tried too long. Our community and our nation—which nurtured us—now needs something in return. A community must demand some duties and responsibilities from its citizens. We must ask what we can do for community.

Just as a boat needs a sail and an anchor, a community needs freedom and some restriction on that freedom. Freedom is a wonderful word, but it does not "trump" all other considerations.

Saul Bellow postulates that "America is as threatened by an excess of liberty as Russia was by the absence of liberty." Those are important words. An 18th century philosopher put it another way: "Freedom is the luxury of self-discipline."

America, the Beautiful mirrors that same thought: "Confirm thy soul in self-control by liberty and law."

A free republic demands a far higher degree of virtue than any earlier society. It demands a profound sense of personal responsibility, a willingness to govern one's own passions, a capacity for initiative and self-reliance, a taste for personal independence, and a sustained spirit of civic cooperation.

But we cannot ever pass enough laws and ordinances to substitute for a sense of civic virtue. Communities need standards as well as laws. Admiral Nelson, off Trafalgar, hoisted these words: "England expects every man to do his duty." So must every woman, and yes, every child old enough to feed a younger brother or sister with a long spoon.

Adam Smith's theory of an economy where every person seeking their own selfish interest created a prosperous economy, but the "invisible hand" model—if it works in economics—does not build a community. It leaves us a collection of disparate, autonomous, and unconnected individuals. We may have made ourselves rich, but we have not made ourselves a community. Communities must expect something in return from all men and women who make them up, and a sense of obligation and responsibility.

COMMANDMENT X:

I shall not give you a Tenth Commandment. What do you think is missing? What else is needed for community? I do know that it is an increasingly important question that needs all of our thinking. We cannot blindly hope that past successes will automatically reproduce themselves. New times present new challenges.

An old Presbyterian hymn out of my youth says: "New occasions teach new duties. Time makes ancient good uncouth."

In summary, let's go back to the beginning. We can no longer take "community" for granted in the United States. We have too much evidence that we are unraveling. There is too much tension, too much misunderstanding, too many separate tribes yelling at each other.

It is too often a "dialogue" between the blind and the deaf. It is dangerous and we must attempt to salvage that elusive concept of community.

A Commentary on the
Ten Commandments of Community

NELSON HOFFMAN

IN MY RETIREMENT YEARS, I have attempted to implement the Governor's Commandment VII: "A community needs a shared culture and a shared language." Living in California for twenty-five years, I worked with Mexicano and other Hispanic workers. I have the greatest respect and affection for them, their culture, and their heritage. I speak to young people about the value of education and the need to develop the ability to speak in public. My plea to the Latino young people is to read and speak English at home. I have seen tremendous growth in those who work at and learn English.

Virtually every nationality that came to America—Irish, Italian, Polish, German, Jews, Afro-Americans—dropped their native tongue, not out of any disrespect for the old country and its culture, but rather to assimilate themselves into our economy and society. In the Southwest, the growth in the population of Spanish-speaking people continues to increase. My fondest hope is that the leaders of the Mexicano and Hispanic communities adopt and embrace English rather than creating a splinter segment of society. If Winston Churchill's description of England and America was correct: "Two peoples separated by a common language," how much more difficult will our future be if the largest immigrant group is speaking in a different language?

— 12 —

A PUBLIC AGENDA

IN THE EARLY 1990S, Jim Ryan wrote a thoughtful article titled *A Values Imperative*. In it, Jim reviewed many of the rising trends in our country at that time—crime had increased 300% from 1960–1991, violent crime was up 500%, SAT scores were declining, and the rate of divorce was increasing, creating an increase in single-parent homes.

A Values Imperative

JIM RYAN

TODAY, MORE THAN 17 million children live in single-parent homes, and this number has more than tripled in the last several decades. In major metropolitan areas such as Detroit, Washington, D.C. or Atlanta, more than half of the children live with just one parent. According to psychologist Urie Bronfenbrenner of Cornell University: "Controlling for factors such as low income, children growing up in single-parent households are at a greater risk for experiencing a variety of behavioral and educational problems, including extremes of hyperactivity and withdrawal; lack of attentiveness in the classroom; difficulty in deferring gratification; impaired academic achievement; school misbehavior; absenteeism; dropping out; involvement in socially alienated peer groups, and the so-called "teenage syndrome" of behaviors that tend to hang together: smoking, drinking, early and frequent sexual experience, and in the more extreme cases, drugs, suicide, vandalism, violence, and criminal acts."

George Will, in his article *Our Children At Risk In Today's Culture* picks up on this theme and builds an argument that without the discipline of the family and its daily habits, particularly work, childrens' intuitive moral sense, reinforced by fears of punishment and social ostracism, will erode. According to Will, "We acquire virtues as we acquire crafts, by the practice of them." If the discipline breaks down, what happens? Crime used to be a response to material circumstances, but improved with economic growth. Now it responds to cultural circumstances that derisively mock our good old "middle class values" of industriousness, thrift, responsibility, and deferral of gratification. The result according to Will is that, "All parents are parenting against today's culture. But for disadvantaged black parents, and particularly for unmarried mothers, the lack of support from the culture is especially damaging."

If the erosion of family and the resultant loss of a cohesive discipline explains so many of our social ills, what explains the decline in the indices of educational achievement, even when looking at the "intact" families? SAT scores, long a measure of educational performance, have dropped more than 80 points in the last several decades despite a significant increase in educational dollars spent.

Is this decline related to effort? Almost assuredly. Recent studies show that immigrant students study three hours a night on average, U.S.-born children of immigrant parents spend more than two hours a night, and American kids of non-immigrant families study less than one hour per night.

"As a whole, immigrant children outperform and outwork American children in the classroom," according to Ruben Rumbaut, a Michigan State sociology professor. The reasons: strong families, a strong work ethic, and the influence of poverty. Many newcomer parents arriving in the U. S. in virtual poverty from Asia, Southeast Asia, or Latin America see education as their childrens' only chance to make it and push them to seize every opportunity for success.

In response to his own analysis of the decline of our cultural values Bill Bennett wrote a best seller entitled *The Book of Virtues.* The book is an anthology comprising hundreds of stories that both illustrate and give testimony to the moral values that are essential to good character. Bennett discusses ten characteristics in depth including compassion, friendship, work, perseverance, loyalty, and faith. I want to focus on the remaining virtues of discipline, responsibility, courage, and honesty as a setting for my ultimate action plan.

For any action plan to work there has to be a framework of discipline, starting with the individual and working successively through the family unit, schools, the workplace, and society at large.

In using the word discipline I am thinking primarily about a moral and civil discipline, one that focuses on the personal acceptance of each individual's actions. In recent years it has been easy to shift responsibility for problems of moral behavior to someone else and claim they are accountable. Whether or not a teenage girl has an abortion should be the parents' decision, but that decision now often lies in the hands of a judge or a social welfare agency. Is it because of people such as Hillary Clinton who have long advocated the right of children to sue and divorce their parents with government support? Or is it because we ask the government to regulate the entertainment industry, instead of forbidding our children to bring home vulgar music or videos, passing off to someone else our own parental responsibilities.

Howard Cosell had a saying which was his trademark—that you had to "tell it like it is." In the same fashion, if we are to promote a value system, we must be clear in its detail and resounding in its endorsement. John Major, England's former Prime Minister, said, "I feel strongly that society needs to condemn a little more and understand a little less." By convoluting our language so as not to offend, we often end up with blather and no content.

Ultimately, it will be virtue, not laws, that will defeat crime. Each year Congress passes more laws than used to be passed in the lifetime of an average citizen. But successively tougher laws have had no measurable impact. Criminals don't respect the law, and punishment has become less of a deterrent over time. In an address to the National Press Club, Norman Lear, TV producer and political activist, said, "At no time in my life has our culture been so estranged from spiritual values . . . our problem lies beyond the reach of politics alone."

Charles Colson, Richard Nixon's aide, was in harmony with Lear when he wrote, "The most terrifying thing that can happen to a society is the death of conscience in its young people." Reflecting on the Long Island commuter train massacre and President Clinton's initial response for more police and gun control laws, Colson noted, "No number of police can enforce order; no threat of punishment can create it. Crime and violence frustrate every political answer because there can be no solution apart from character and creed."

In short, the responsibility for the crisis and the ultimate solution is ours, not the government's. The virtues we honor are not concepts that we catch like a cold. They must be taught and nurtured by all of us in a climate of openness and honesty.

What we need is a movement, a powerful shared movement, a crusade to make values paramount in our lives. A crusade that can be endorsed by both religious and secular positions. A crusade that will encompass all, but be focused on children. A crusade that will change attitudes and actions, much like the Civil Rights movement that progressed from early 1950 voter registrations to ultimately encompass all sorts of people, sharecroppers, college students, business executives, politicians, and the clergy. [Italic added for emphasis. —Ed.]

This total commitment must start at the top with the President of the United States and permeate all the way down to the citizen on the street. I would propose that the President, recognizing the severity of the problem, start with his own personal pledge . . .

A Reflection on Jim Ryan's Ideas

J. NELSON HOFFMAN

*J*IM WENT ON TO SUGGEST several ways the president could exert personal leadership and how Congress, business, and other community leaders could participate in exerting personal leadership. Unfortunately, in too many cases the opposite of what Jim deemed vital happened. And now, there is an even greater need for the type of crusade Jim implored.

Are we unrealistic to expect our leaders to live by higher standards? I believe Jim's prescription was a correct one. This nation needs great men and women of strong moral character to lead it. And secondly, with the ever increasing power of the media, we need a responsible press to report accurately on their conduct.

A Community Reacts

J. NELSON HOFFMAN

*L*ET ME PROVIDE A VIVID EXAMPLE from my home in Colorado why youth need to have good and strong role models. In the summer of 1999, the laid-back calmness of our mountain town was upset by a series of armed crimes and burglaries. Uneasiness grew when a store keeper was beaten during one of the robberies. These were crimes more often associated with an urban environment rather than somewhere rural like our small, resort community.

When twelve local youths were arrested for these crimes, the reaction shook our small town to its core. The examination of how these young men went astray continues today, and the reflection and analysis fit very closely with the theme of this book.

After the arrests, *The Aspen Times* probed the facts and published a special supplement.

According to *The Aspen Times*:

[A member of the school's staff] was critical of the juvenile justice system's treatment of kids who have gotten into trouble over the years, maintaining it has often been too lenient . . . [She explained how] *the consequences of making trouble at school are not always severe enough to get the kids' attention, or convice them to change their ways . . .*

She noted that, in many cases, when parents were confronted with troublesome behavior of their child at school, the parents would get mad at the school rather than confront their child. *And, by failing to deal with their child's problems . . . they contribute to the child's confusion about how to act.* [Italic added for emphasis. —Ed.]

Later in the article, Aspen's school superintendent Tom Farrell admitted that the school had to accept some responsibility for failing to meet the needs of these twelve young adults:

". . . the main failure . . . was in not teaching them the kind of moral and ethical framework that might have kept them from committing these crimes.

. . . As a matter of policy, it is not the school's job to teach morals and ethics to the students, but it is the school's role to back up whatever is taught at home in these areas." [Italic added for emphasis. —Ed.]

These crimes and arrests reminded me of my own past mistake when I took the gold watch chain from an abandoned house. I wonder if I would have ventured into further trouble in my own youth if my grandfather and my uncle had not responded in the way that they did?

Much of this book is devoted to students who are not being taught proper behavior at home or are being taught antisocial and anticommunity values at home. Most tragically for them and for our society, it is these children without parental guidance who most often operate in a moral vacuum.

Superintendent Farrell seems to confirm this when he said:

"... I don't think we're going to be very effective if you're [not] taught *[any] morals at home, but we're trying to teach them to you at school. . . .* It is confusing for kids trying to decide what is right, if they have to choose between what is taught and done at home, and what is taught at school. . . . Draw that line in the sand and stick to it [because] some find it easier to just change the line. . . . Schools nationwide stopped teaching ethics and morals in the late 1970s as a matter of policy, because parents demanded it. . . . *Parents would say I don't want Tom Farrell teaching my kids what is right and wrong. . . . Today . . . schools are picking that responsibility up again, because of a sense that, for whatever reason, kids are not being taught these values by anyone else."* [Italic added for emphasis. —Ed.]

Excerpt from The VanderWerf Universal Health Care Plan

DR. BEN VANDERWERF

IT HAS BEEN OBVIOUS to most that the health care delivery system in the United States is straining at its seams, inadequate for a large portion of our population and very frustrating for doctors and patients alike. Several attempts to overhaul our system have failed because too much was wanted at once and too little input from our health care experts left only relatively minor, extremely expensive, patchwork improvements that amplified the enormous bureaucratic overhead.

During a recent yearly meeting assembly of the Colorado Coalition for the Medically Underserved, an overwhelming majority felt that, if politically feasible, a single-payer system would be the best solution for universal access to health care.

The VanderWerf plan offers such a single-payer system and also offers a new approach for implementation to avoid the usual objection to such system.

It proposes a gradual implementation, starting with children 0–5 years of age, thereby avoiding the massive disruption to the current system of financing and organizing care. In addition, the many insurance agents and companies are offered to continue to exist by contracting to manage the new system. By giving our young children good health care, we give them a better chance to be successful and productive citizens in our future. From time to time, additional age groups can be added so that eventually all ages will be included.

It proposes a comprehensive health care package where decisions about coverage are decided by health care professionals and not bureaucrats.

It proposes funding by a payroll deduction percentage which can be paid by employees or employers or shared by both. This way, small companies, who often have mostly low-wage employees, will now be able to afford health care for their workers and their workers' families.

It proposes that the health care funds be paid into and managed by a private health fund or series of funds, thereby avoiding the need for a new, huge government bureaucracy.

It proposes that all patients be enrolled with a primary care physician of their choice who is compensated on a capitated basis, thereby avoiding the very large overhead and administration typical for many small fees.

It proposes that the primary care will include a gatekeeper function to avoid overutilization of too specialized health care workers. This is another part of the cost control, but this feature would also keep our specialists at a higher expertise by avoiding too much "lower echelon" work. Primary care physicians can refer patient to any needed specialist for consultation and treatment. Specialists are paid on a predetermined fee for service.

It proposes that hospitals be paid on a disease-related groupings basis similar to the present Medicare reimbursement, again to keep a handle on cost.

It also proposes a co-pay from patients on a sliding scale, depending on income, to avoid overutilization.

By adopting the VanderWerf health care plan, we will have quality health care accessible to all, something that we all want and something that is long overdue.

(See Appendix A for more complete details.)

My friend Dr. Ben VanderWerf is devoting his personal funds and retirement years to gaining acceptance of his Universal Health Care Plan. I believe his plan, derived from a lifetime of experience, is the most cost-effective, patient-friendly plan I've seen.

As a member of AARP, I belong to a very large lobbying group. But where is the interest group to speak for uninsured infants? Right now, the political process is focused on making sure we senior citizens have access to the medicines we need, but too many seniors still have to make the choice between their prescription medications and paying for basic expenses such as food and rent.

Understanding Bilingual Education

J. NELSON HOFFMAN

*A*s I STATED AT THE BEGINNING, the best outcome I can dream of for this book is that it creates dialogue about a few of the important issues of our time. In our democratic system, it is vital for public debate to take place. This language issue, I believe, will become more important, more critical, in the next decade and with future generations.

In so many instances, as Father McNamara wrote earlier in the book, most issues are couched in adversarial terms—my views versus your views. In school, we sponsor debating teams to satisfy our competitive streak and provide a continuing stream of candidates for law schools. But as I listen to teachers, the current priority is to teach our children cooperation, team skills, and the capacity, as Gandhi demonstrated, to bring people together. I know good lawyers who possess this skill; they contribute by bringing factions together through negotiation, not battles in the courtroom. As any experienced leader will tell you, the capacity to bring opposing factions of their organizations together in a win/win solution is a vital skill.

It is in that spirit that the following perspectives are presented. They are written by elementary school teachers concerned about about Latino children learning and adapting to life in America.

Appreciating Hispanic Culture: The Case for Bilingual Education

Jamie Mahaffey and Shawn Rios

*A*s public school teachers, with a significant number of Spanish-speaking immigrant students from Latin America, we have observed cultural differences that influence students learning in the school environment. Our children come to school with strengths and experiences that we need to acknowledge in order to be effective teachers and meet their needs. Currently, our general school environment does not value these, and as a result, our students don't often see school as meaningful in their lives. Our challenge as educators is to understand these differences and to try and connect students and parents to school. The gap between home and school can have a negative effect on our Latino student population. As our population becomes more diverse and cultures vary within our schools, we need to evaluate all factors that may or may not contribute to the success of our students. We are all stakeholders in making schools work for children.

SOCIO-CULTURAL FACTORS

In our classrooms, we have observed that our Latino students' home culture can differ in many regards from that of the mainstream U.S.

culture. One difference we have noticed is that students come with strong extended family ties. When parents come to school functions, they bring with them many members of their extended family. Often our students talk about their cousins as siblings. In preschool and kindergarten, young children do not need to distinguish between siblings and cousins because these relationships are so close.

Children are expected to care for younger family members. Older siblings or cousins come to our rooms to meet their younger charges. When a younger sister of a student in first grade started kindergarten, she kept sneaking into her classroom to see how her sister was doing. The kindergarten teacher finally was able to reassure her that her sister would be all right and convince her not to come to her room to get her before school was ended. This example of caring and nurturing is seen in the multi-age class where the older Latino students step in and mentor the younger students without asking. When Lupita's (age 7) older brother (12) was sick, she stayed home and cared for him. To many Anglo parents, this seems inappropriate, but to Lupita and her parents it was a natural part of supporting the family. We have seen many examples of this in our classroom when someone is hurt, sick, or sad. This occurs at our grade level even when the child in need is not the most popular member of the group. There seems to be a common thread of caring and support that runs through the students we have, and it supports what we have learned through our readings about Hispanic culture.

Our students also come to us with strong cooperative social skills. They generally work and play well together in a group setting that focuses on the whole, not the individual. We see them share classroom materials peacefully with each other. At snack time, we see Latino students bring their favorite foods to share while others may only offer the foods they wish to discard. These cooperative social skills are valued in the business world because they show how you work as part of a team.

Latinos receive strong modeling and care from older family members as many of these households are made up of extended families. Our native speaking aides are very different in their support of students in our classrooms. Our norm is for the student to work independently, while our aides' norm is to give more assistance. Perhaps this type of monitoring is more culturally appropriate. We can use the strength of their mentorship to scaffold the child's learning and help them still feel connected emotionally. Individualism is a highly valued trait in our culture. Does our society want more stars or team players?

To say that our students come with more of a natural work ethic seems trite and, at best, a generalization. But there is a strong sense that our students are expected to represent their families in a certain way. Often, when they talk about their parents and family, it includes a sense of pride for the work their parents do as well as their own responsibilities in the family. Shawn recently had a student say proudly to her class, "I wash my brother's and sister's pants for them." When I mentioned this to another teacher, she perceived this as a negative childhood experience and not as an example of contributing to the work of the family.

Our parents express clear-cut expectations for their children. They want their children to learn English. They also expect their children to behave, listen to the teacher, and work hard. Latino children are expected to respect their teachers because parents view educators as a high authority.

How is my child behaving? I worry that he is not working hard enough. These are the questions and comments we hear most often at conferences. Most often, this is the only thing that parents ask. Within Latin America, school and church are ultimate authorities, and the parents look to us as the experts in doing what is best educationally for their children. Our culture expects parents to be much more assertive and participatory in their children's education. For Latino parents to do that, we need to provide the necessary information so they can make the transition between the norms and expectations they know, to the norms and expectations that we value in a mainstream U.S. culture.

Students are deterred in their schooling because many of their home experiences don't support the traditional expectations of school. Currently, the Latin American immigrants coming to our area tend to have very limited academic experiences. Many of their parents have lower literacy skills, and some are illiterate. The level of education varies, but often our parents may not have finished high school or even attended school beyond the sixth grade. The jobs most of our parents have available to them do not require higher levels of academic ability. To them, learning to speak English is the means to obtaining a good paying job. Higher education may not even be considered a possibility, much less an option when lives are focused on day-to-day survival and taking care of one's immediate and extended family.

Shawn recently had a student break down and cry when she was told she could take her project home to finish it there. The student finally blurted out that she doesn't have anything to write or color with at home. Many of these families do not organize their lives around print. They use cash instead of checks and their important papers can fit into a shoe box as opposed to a four-drawer filing cabinet. Our parents, as a rule, don't use personal planners, or databases, computers, or other mechanisms of print. Anglo children are accustomed to seeing parents use reading and writing for work and for pleasure. In the Latino home, families rely heavily on oral communication. The homes of our Anglo students are filled with an abundance of magazines, books, paper, crayons, markers, and pencils. Families value these things in their lives when they understand the meaning and importance of them in their child's education and learning.

In addition to print experience, students who come from homes with academic language have more of an advantage. This language is often referred in our grades as book talk. Most of our Anglo children come from homes where they have been read to daily. They have an internal understanding of the syntax and language structure of books. Learning to read relies on this understanding and requires a rich vocabulary and the ability to talk about the meaning of stories.

In school, discourse can be heavily weighted with teacher-directed talk—the teacher asks a question, and the student is expected to answer in a certain way. When the response does not meet the teacher's expectations, the teacher may think the student does not have basic oral language skills or the ability to answer simple questions. But Latino students are not used to answering questions about things that do not seem meaningful or important like, "What color are your shoes?" The student is probably thinking, "Why is this teacher asking me the color of my shoes? Can't she see them?! Is it a trick question?"

Students come to us as fully proficient speakers of their language, and they have spent their first 5 or 6 years communicating very effectively within family environments. [In working with Latino students,] we have learned that we need to ask more open-ended questions, allow more time, and give [them] the voice to approach an answer differently then what we may be used to hearing. We need to connect with what they know and give them the opportunity to communicate in the school environment.

Many Latino children are accustomed to being directed by an older sibling or caregiver in the home. Latino students appear to have difficulty making appropriate academic choices in the classroom. This may look like students are not doing their work. Students in classrooms are expected to be able to work independently, be self-directed, and quiet while working. In order for our students to meet these expectations, we must commit time in the beginning to model, explain, and practice these expectations so that they can work independently.

Another detriment to success we see is attendance in school. Students are missing valuable academic time that they need to make progress. Families value the time they have together and pull children out of school when they have time off work. With the seasonal employment of our resort community, families often take extended trips. Students can miss school for weeks or even months and fall behind in their academic learning and English language development.

WHAT WE HAVE LEARNED

The best way to connect with students and their culture is through their home language. School is already very different from their home environment and to walk into a building and hear their mother tongue is reassuring and comforting. Even teachers who do not speak the students' language can make sure that books, audio cassettes, and other materials are available in their native language. Other ways to honor the child is to use culturally appropriate materials. In our program, we refer to our students as language experts. The Spanish speakers help teach other students and teachers. It is very powerful to see both language groups working together to learn from each others' strengths.

First language assessment allows teachers to have a better understanding of how to direct their students' learning. Students come to us from very different school experiences. Some can read and write fluently, while others have never been to school before. Knowing where to begin and how to guide instruction is a crucial part of effective teaching. Understanding a student's ability level allows a teacher to teach to the individual, not the language.

Despite recent political changes in bilingual education, research continues to support first language instruction as the best method for academic and second language acquisition. This section does not address all the issues related to language acquisition but only mentions them because of their importance in student success. Students do not lose critical cognitive understanding of academic subjects while they are learning English. As they are gaining oral language proficiency, the academic concepts transfer to the second language. As the students advance to more cognitively challenging and abstract concepts, strong reading, writing, speaking, and math skills are essential in achieving success. When students are limited in what they are able to do, they are less motivated to achieve. When they transition to secondary schools, many of our students are tracked in special classes that have little opportunity for the kind of academic successes, advancement and/or interest available to other students. School becomes less meaningful, and students feel the pull of leaving school to earn money for themselves and their family. However, by acknowledging a student's language and culture, school becomes more meaningful. By incorporating the students' language in the classroom, we demonstrate to the children that they are a valued and welcomed part of the classroom culture. Social and cultural influences are intertwined with language. After all, language defines who we are, dictates what we do, and describes where we come from.

Jamie Mahaffey and Shawn Rios teach bilingual education in the Roaring Fork Valley in Colorado.

Bilingual Education:
The Rebirth of a Vision

Angela Ponzio

$\mathcal{D}$URING MY FIRST YEAR TEACHING second language learners, I was approached by a very noble and hopeful father of one of my very first students. With gleaming eyes and a slightly shaking voice, he told me, "Thank you for helping my son 'run in the race.' He may not 'win' yet, but at least he can 'run.'"

A door had been opened through which his son could finally pass confidently and without restraint. The pressure of acculturation or assimilation was not weighing on his character or spirit. This young boy, after only months in the country, felt that he was able, whenever necessary, to navigate through the realms of his new society, utilizing the language of the masses, without losing the self-defining bond of his own. This experience inspired me to believe in the power and potential of bilingual education.

It became startling clear to me that it was due to a bilingual educational framework and environment that did not devalue his family, culture, language, nor place in this world, that he was able to "run in the race." He had reaped the benefits of a bilingual system of education and pedagogy that has been criticized as a form of welfare and misunderstood by many. It is a system which I, along with many others, believe will propel this bilingual generation and those to come into a future of lifelong learning and opportunity. It is a system that advocates the learning of English, but not at the expense of a child's own academic potential. No child would have to "mark time" in the mainstream classroom, overwhelmed by the murmur of unfamiliar babble, nor feel deprived of the chance to learn. How could anyone look that child in the eye and argue otherwise?

Opponents of bilingual education would have students assimilate into the societal norm, despite the clear, irrefutable fact that the norms are changing demographically, linguistically, culturally, and ethnically. Now, the face of America demonstrates, now more than ever, that we are no longer a nation which adheres to the Anglocentric ideologies and echoes of the past. I am not arguing that we will or should become culturally and linguistically segregated within one nation; cohesion among the masses must exist if this nation is to experience a long-needed, positive spiritual renaissance. Yet this communal spirit cannot be thrust upon the diverse cultural and ethnic newcomers, especially upon the children, and particularly not through any educational system which devalues or depreciates their origins. What a false and pathetic depiction of the American spirit that would be!

Bilingual education is the manifestation and the preservation of values, character, and identity, which can cultivate the necessary skills that allow children to be autonomous, seek opportunity, and become lifelong learners. It provides quality academic preparation and the security of being part of a society. Strict immersion or "sink or swim" strategies have proven to be less productive. They boast a faster rate of language acquisition; however, as basic science proves, for every action, there is an equal and opposite reaction. The education is devastatingly sacrificed at the expense of language acquisition. Gaps become evident in the child's academic knowledge. The hurdles become taller. The cultural character and spiritual heritage of the child is reduced to a dying ember; the smoke from the flame is but a memory of the hopes that once were. If a child feels that he or she is incapable of winning, let alone running in the race of life, the finish line becomes a blur, and the echo of "what's the point?" reverberates resiliently.

Allow me to pause and point to the statistics of immigration. Hispanics are the largest and fastest growing immigrant population in the United States. The rates will only increase. With this in mind, think of the future of our country. Schools must work for all children, inspiring growth of character, and building the three pillars of a strong nation: family, opportunity, and individuality. If not, the generations to come will be set at a distinct disadvantage.

Through my experience as an educator in strict immersion and bilingual education, I have realized that bilingual education is symbolic of a lost heritage. Ancestrally and ideologically, the strength of this nation was constructed upon the three aforementioned pillars. Again, I have argued that bilingual education nurtures character, family values, and the opportunity to "run the race." This is essentially the glue which holds a society together. Language is the essence of a people, a culture, an identity, and a spirit, all of which I fear America is beginning to lose. Should we not try to return to the core of the American vision? Should we not reweave a fabric that will not only empower our children, but our entire nation? We cannot deny the ideologies upon which America was founded. To silence the voices of a people, whether through language or access to education, would be to render our founding fathers' vision and principles as hypocrisies.

Angela Ponzio is a bilingual education teacher in the Chicago school system.

Nature, Conserving Energy, and Preserving the Environment

JIM PRITTS

ONE VALUE INSTILLED IN ME at an early age was the appreciation and enjoyment of nature and the outdoors. Growing up, I was fortunate to live in an area where I was in close contact with nature, and I grew to value it for the rest of my life. My happiest memories as a child are associated with doing things outdoors and enjoying the best that nature has to offer—trees, creeks, mountains, lakes, animals, flowers, berries, sunshine, even rain and storms, have all contributed more enjoyment than I can express.

Today, we live in a different world environment—daycare, television, computers, air travel, single-parent families, city living, etc.—all are slowly robbing us of the connection we once had with nature. As a result of these distracting forces, our appreciation and respect for the environment have been diminished, and we, and our children, have been slowly insulated from the beauty of our natural surroundings.

A special effort is required to keep it part of our lives, and that effort depends upon only one person, each and every one of us.

_____

Jim Pritts' simple observation on his life in the outdoors in western Pennsylvania triggered a deeper look at the state of environmental awareness.

Man, Nature, and the Environment

J. NELSON HOFFMAN

*I*N REFLECTING ON THIS BOOK and the marvelous thought-provoking writings of my fellow authors, I have come to a new revelation—I am a closet Greenie. In my early adult life, I didn't think about the environmental consequences of my daily life. I was deeply involved with the plastics and manufacturing industries, and I was mostly blind to the global environmental picture and the effect of man's progress on the environment. Jim Pritts' writing about nature triggered a series of images.

As a young DuPont salesman, I traveled the hills of Pennsylvania, West Virginia, and Eastern Tennessee and Kentucky—places where the miners were striping the land layer-by-layer and extracting whatever mineral is buried. Have you ever seen an open-pit mine or been in a coal town? In the West, beautiful states like Colorado and Utah have been scarred in the pursuit of iron, copper, silver, gold, and all kinds of minerals.

While I began my life as a city dweller and never gave much thought to my natural environment, that has now changed. I live in the middle of the Rocky Mountains in Snowmass, Colorado. If you drive there from Denver, you cross the Continental Divide around

Leadville. Near there, great scars mar the natural beauty of this rugged landscape—damage created by mining practices that didn't give much thought to the natural beauty of the environment. Now, a massive restoration project is underway to reclaim this land.

My views on the environment were also changed by visits to our son Ken when he studied soils engineering in northern California at Humboldt State University. The campus sits near some of the most beautiful, awe-inspiring Redwood forests on the face of the earth. It is also the home of conflict—conflict between a construction industry fighting for the preservation of their economic life and environmental groups pleading to preserve old-growth, thousand-year-old trees which have survived through the Dark Ages, the Renaissance, the Reformation, and the founding of America.

After the desolation of forests, consider the waste of fossil fuels. Globally, oil wells are flared (wasted), and I've been told that in the Middle East the smell and the smoke can be overwhelming. Shouldn't a global leader such as OPEC bear the responsibility of investing in technology which eliminates this waste to our global fossil fuel supply? And since the U.S. is one of the world's biggest users of fossil fuels, shouldn't we also be a leading voice? Texas is home to an oil and gas industry that is one of the world's leading suppliers of refined fuel. It is also the supplier of the essential raw materials that go into making plastics by the millions of pounds each and every day. But when I'm in Texas, the flames of the gas flares bother me. I see the pollution in the atmosphere, and I wonder how much the soot-and-heat waste product from those flares contributes to this contamination?

Maybe one of the young people who read this book will be the scientist who discovers how to refine fuel with no contamination.

Around the world, you can see where man has exhausted the fertility of the soil—left it and moved on. Father Del Barrio writes of the hardships he sees every day in central Africa. The poverty he describes is exacerbated by the conflicting demands of the natives' desire to establish viable farms and the intrusion of elephants and migrating herds of wildebeests. Elephants are beautiful and inspiring. But, they are fierce competitor to the struggling people who try to live there.

Countries such as Indonesia and Maylasia are repeating the timber practices and mistakes made by the western world in the past. And my friends who have visited China speak of the frantic pace of industrial development—expansion with little or no regard for the environment. I know some people worry about the expansion of China's military, but think for a moment about the devastating effects of their increased consumption of fossil fuels. Think of the thermal and contamination load on the earth's atmosphere. And think about the effect this will have on global warming.

This wonderful nation of ours is the most profligate user of energy in the world. In the name of aesthetics, lights burn all night in empty skyscrapers and all night outside many homes. What will the world be like when the emerging industrial nations pattern their economic development on the energy consumption habits of the western industrial world? We water millions of acres of golf course and raise countless tons of grain to raise beef cattle to consume way more fat than any healthy person should eat. According to the American Medical Association, one in five American adults is obese, and the percentage of overweight children is growing rapidly.

President Jimmy Carter was right when he tried to get us to think about the world as a place with finite resources. It wasn't a message we could handle. No one likes bad news or to take strong, nasty-tasting medicine. I am one of the world's greatest optimists, but at 68, I think the next generation will reconsider the "strip-mining, harvesting-without-planting mentality" that has characterized the past century.

Joseph Campbell wrote of the harmony he saw in various religions, of the sense of man found in nature. If you live out West, you have a different perception of what the words "Native American" really mean. The white man intruded upon a civilization which found sustenance in nature and believed that nature was a fundamental part of spiritual life. The buffalo were hunted into extinction, and we squeezed the survivors of many proudly independent people onto tiny plots of land we called reservations. It is time to give them all their rights and respect their calls for help. Their lesson on how to live in peace with the environment may well be one of the most important watchwords of this century.

The words attributed to Chief Seattle may not be well known to many, and there is some controversy as to whether or not such a person even existed. But the ideas ring as true now as when they were written over one hundred and fifty years ago:

Brother Eagle, Sister Sky

CHIEF SEATTLE

How can you buy the sky?
How can you own the rain and the wind?
My mother told me,
Every part of this earth is sacred to our people.
Every pine needle. Every sandy shore.
Every mist in the dark woods.
Every meadow and humming insect.
All are holy in the memory of our people.
My father said to me,
I know the sap that courses through the trees
as I know the blood that flows in my veins.
We are part of the earth and it is part of us.
The perfumed flowers are our sisters.
The bear, the deer, the great eagle, these are our brothers.
The rocky crests, the meadows,
The ponies—all belong to the same family.
The voice of my ancestors said to me,
The shining water that moves in the streams and rivers is
not simply water, but the blood of your grandfather's grandfather.
Each ghostly reflection in the clear waters of the lakes tells of memories in
*   the life of our people.*
The water's murmur is the voice of your great-great-grandmother.
The rivers are our brothers. They quench our thirst.
They carry our canoes and feed our children.

You must give to the rivers the kindness you would give to any brother.
The voice of my grandfather said to me,
The air is precious. It shares its spirit with all the life it supports.
The wind that gave me my first breath also received my last sigh.
You must keep the land and air apart and sacred, as a place where one
can go to taste the wind that is sweetened by the meadow flowers.
When the last Red Man and Woman have vanished with their
wilderness, and their memory is only the shadow of a cloud moving
across the prairie, will the shores and forest still be here?
Will there be any of the spirit of my people left?
My ancestors said to me, This we know:
The earth does not belong to us. We belong to the earth.
The voice of my grandmother said to me,
Teach your children what you have been taught.
The earth is our mother.
What befalls the earth befalls all the sons and daughters of the earth.
Hear my voice and the voice of my ancestors,
Chief Seattle said.
The destiny of your people is a mystery to us.
What will happen when the buffalo are all slaughtered?
The wild horses tamed?
What will happen when the secret corners of the forest are
heavy with the scent of many men?
When the view of the ripe hills is blotted by talking wires?
Where will the thicket be? Gone.
Where will the eagle be? Gone!
And what will happen when we say good-bye to the swift pony and the
hunt?
It will be the end of living, and the beginning of survival.
This we know: All things are connected like the blood that unites us.
We did not weave the web of life,
We are merely a strand in it.
Whatever we do to the web, we do to ourselves.
We love this earth as a newborn loves its mother's heartbeat.
If we sell you our land, care for it as we have cared for it.
Hold in your mind the memory of the land as it is when you receive it.
Preserve the land and the air and the rivers for your children's children
and love it as we have loved it.

A Fresh Look at Our War on Drugs

J. NELSON HOFFMAN

LIKE A MELANOMA, the insidious drug trade has attached itself to American society and slowly destroys all that it touches and infects. It makes life in our cities unsafe. It corrupts the entire world, particularly the nations south of us. It infects our law enforcement apparatus. It is responsible for the United States having almost two million of its citizens in prison, where some prisoners continue to engage in the drug trade.

It is presently estimated that we are spending approximately $20 billion every year to fight this war on drugs. Now, both conservative and liberal voices are taking another look at this corrupting evil and questioning whether or not there is a better way to curb, contain, and reverse this ever-widening cancer.

Traveling abroad, I've seen two very different approaches to the problem in nations much smaller than the U.S. In Singapore, there have a zero tolerance policy. A very large, prominently placed sign announces to a visitor arriving by plane that they are very clear on what will be tolerated: *Possession of illegal drugs, in any quantity, is a mandatory death sentence.*

Singapore is one of the cleanest, crime-free, poverty-free cities in the world. We Americans value our freedom too much to accept the police state restrictions it takes to back up such a policy. But if we truly want to rid ourselves of illegal drugs, do we have to allow some diminution of our freedom?

In dramatic contrast to the way Singapore deals with the drug problem, the Netherlands approaches the problem with a different set of assumptions. I believe most Americans would describe the Netherlands as a more liberal society. The Netherlands draws a very strong distinction between drug users and drug sellers. Addiction is treated 100% as a disease, not criminal conduct. Selling or distributing drugs are still treated as crimes.

I am not sure which path defines the correct policy for America. But an increasing number of knowledgeable people whom I respect are coming down on the side of legalization of some drugs. When an experienced policy-maker such as the former Secretary of State George Schultz comes out for legalization, I must rethink my own once firmly entrenched position.

As our book was going to press, I was given *Drug Crazy—How We Got into This Mess & How We Can Get Out*, written by Mike Gray. This book details the history and politics of our drug laws and supports my notion that a critical reassessment of our current strategies and tactics is needed.

Until other alternatives are available, our laws say possession or use of illegal drugs is a crime and can mean jail time for offenders. I will pray for those who think they need them or whose addiction creates a burden for themselves or others. But at the same time, I question whether or not there are medical and law enforcement alternatives to the unsuccessful programs we've tried the last forty years. In my business career, problems that went on from year to year without solutions could be labeled "too tough." But sometimes, it was also the case that, like the drug issue, we did not have the will to solve these problems.

Restoring Religious Education in Our Public Schools—Religious Freedom and Tolerance in America

J. Nelson Hoffman

ONE OF THE MOST CONTROVERSIAL ISSUES in the public arena today concerns how education of youth is to be accomplished with so many apparently conflicting forces trying to assert their perspective. The issue is centered in the public school, but includes the interests of private schools, parochial schools, and even the growing home schooling movement.

Let me return to Superintendent Tom Farrell's point about the void teachers notice in morality brought from home. Over the past fifty years, on the heels of the Madalyn Murray O'Hair decision, a vacuum has been created by parents who do not discuss standards of moral behavior with their children. Let me propose an idea that would help fill this void.

Perhaps moral conduct can be taught in a secular setting. This deprives a very large segment of Americans with a strong faith to have their children taught the same type of moral conduct that is expected of them in their places of worship and in their homes. I accept the principle that moral conduct must be taught in such a way that it does not coerce nonbelievers. Our schools are not vehicles to proselytize others.

Over the past fifty years, America has become an ever more diverse society. With that diversity, a wider range of philosophical and religious orientations must be accommodated in that most critical and formative institution of our country: the public school. I believe it is a vital part of our country's heritage to learn about religions other than our own. Developing an understanding, compassionate outlook is among the most significant accomplishments we expect from our school system.

In supporting a tolerant society, the writing of Alexis de Tocqueville seems appropriate to our times. The following excerpt is taken from *Democracy in America* translated by Harvey Mansfield and Delba Winthrop (pp. 44 and 45):

> I have already said enough to put the character of Anglo-American civilization in its true light. It is the product (and this point of departure ought constantly to be present in one's thinking) of two perfectly distinct elements that elsewhere have often made war with each other, but which, in America have they succeeded in incorporating somehow into one another and combining marvelously. I mean to speak of the spirit of religion and the spirit of freedom.
>
> The founders of New England were at once ardent sectarians and exalted innovators. While held in the tightest bonds of certain reli-

gious beliefs, they were free of all political prejudices. Hence there are two tendencies, diverse but not contrary, traces of which it is easy to find everywhere in mores as in laws . . .

. . . Far from harming each other, these two tendencies, apparently so opposed, advance in accord and seem to lend each other mutual support.

Religion sees in civil freedom a noble exercise of the faculties of man; in the political world, a field left by the Creator to the efforts of intelligence. Free and powerful in its sphere, satisfied with the place that is reserved for it, it knows that its empire is better established when it reigns by its own strength alone and dominates over hearts without support.

Freedom sees in religion the companion of its struggles and its triumphs, the cradle of its infancy, the divine source of its rights. It considers religion as the safeguard of mores; and mores as the guarantee of laws and the pledge of its own duration. . . .

In recalling how earlier social policy depended upon a moral and religious basis, Gertrude Himmelfarb, Professor Emeritus of History, Graduate School of the City University of New York, wrote a 1995 editorial in the *Wall Street Journal* titled "Re-moralizing America":

If we want to discourage dependency, criminality, illegitimacy, drug addiction and the like, we have to do more than create a more rational system of economic and legal incentives and disincentives; we have to build into that system, the moral, social, and if possible, religious sanctions that are the most compelling part of any utilitarian calculus. We have to, in short, relegitimize morality as the basis of social policy and restore the language of virtue and vice.

How could such a monumental challenge be accomplished? I am convinced the answer lies in one rather obvious, but less recognized fact. In teaching moral principles to young people, there must be consistency between the sources of authority and instruction—parents, schoolteachers, and religious instructors. (See Tom Farrell's earlier comments).

This cohesion was present in America from our founding as a nation through the World War II period. Our founding fathers were men who professed a deep religious faith and assumed governmental authority was derived from a Supreme Being. America was founded as a nation to provide freedom of worship for those who so choose. Public education was predominately Christian, but there was an ever increasing tolerance for other religions. America grew as new waves of immigrants arrived from Europe. They brought with them a wide spectrum of religious faiths: many Jews, Catholics and a range of Protestant faiths were brought to America, As they settled in small neighborhoods, there was some conflict. But they soon realized that the friction that had caused such warfare in Europe was not what The United States was all about. This was a nation built on the notion that people of different faiths live in peace and tolerance. The animosities that still exist are the remnants of that intolerant response to religious diversity.

One of the most important documents in our nation's history was the Flushing (Quaker) Remonstrance, which was written by the people of Flushing in 1657 when state officials governing New Amsterdam forbade the townspeople to give shelter to Quakers. These peace loving people were to be shunned. The protest of the residents of Flushing became a building block for establishing religious tolerance. It became the fundamental document that our founding fathers cited in their development of the concept of separation of church and state. This concept has served our nation for over three hundred years and is a central idea of our heritage.

What is this Quaker Remonstrance? Somehow, I had never learned of it in my education. I found information about it on the Internet, and from that source I gained an entirely new perspective on what our heritage of religious freedom really means.

THE FLUSHING (QUAKER) REMONSTRANCE

In the teachers' room at John Bowne High School in Flushing, New York there is a brass plaque commemorating John Bowne and his home. Bowne became a true leader and hero in founding religious freedom in America. The plaque reads as follows:

BOWNE HOUSE—
SYMBOL OF RELIGIOUS FREEDOM IN AMERICA

Not very far from where you stand at this moment is one of the United States' oldest private dwellings, at 3701 Bowne Street, here in Flushing . . . built by John Bowne in 1661.

Just four years before it was built, thirty English-born inhabitants of the town of Flushing signed and sent to Peter Stuyvesant, Governor of the Dutch colony of New Amsterdam, a document of protest—the Quaker Remonstrance.

Its signers suffered for their protest—but John Bowne suffered even more when, in 1662, he invited the Quakers to worship in his new home. Arrested and banished to Holland, he pleaded his case so eloquently and courageously that he was acquitted and returned to his home after two years' absence with instructions to Governor Stuyvesant that *free men should be permitted to worship God as their conscience dictated. This event, together with the Quaker Remonstrance, was recognized as the origin of Freedom of Religion in America, and led directly to the First Article of the Bill of Rights—a fundamental part of our American heritage.* [Italic added for emphasis. —Ed.]

That same home was continuously owned by the Bowne family for over 275 years (seven generations, the longest ownership under one name in American history). It was dedicated in 1945 as a 'National Shrine to Religious Freedom.' Bowne House is now maintained by the Bowne House Historical Society. Colonel Frederic Bowne, present male head of the family, whose collaboration is gratefully acknowledged, cordially invites you to visit this famous shrine. Open Tuesdays, Thursdays, and Saturdays from 2 to 5. Admission free.

Text of the Flushing Remonstrance
From the New York Historical Records

Remonstrance of the Inhabitants of the Town of Flushing
To Governor Stuyvesant December 27, 1657

Right Honorable,
    You have been pleased to send up unto us a certain prohibition or command that we should not receive or entertain any of those people

called Quakers because they are supposed to be by some, seducers of the people. For our part we cannot condemn them in this case, neither can we stretch out our hands against them, to punish, banish or persecute them for out of Christ God is a consuming fire, and it is a fearful thing to fall into the hands of the living God.

We desire therefore in this case not to judge least we be judged, neither to condemn lease we be condemned, but rather let every man stand and fall to his own Master. Wee are bounde by the Law to Doe good unto all men, especially to those of the household of faith. And though for the present we seem to be unsensible of the law and the Law giver, yet when death and the Law assault us, if we have our advocate to seeke, who shall plead for us in this case of conscience betwixt God and our own souls; the powers of this world can neither attack us, neither excuse us, for is God justifye who can condemn and if God condemn there is none can justify.

And for those jealousies and suspicions which some have of the, that they are destructive unto Magistracy and Minssereye, that can not bee, for the magistrate hath the sword in this hand and the minister hath the sword in his hand, as witnesse those two great examples which all magistrates and ministers are to follow, Moses and Christ, whom God raised up maintained and defended against all the enemies both of flesh and spirit; and therefore that which is God will stand, and that which is of man will come to nothing.

And as the Lord hath taught Moses or the civil power to give an outward liberty in the state by the law written in his heart designed for the good of all, and can truly judge who is good, who is civil, who is true and who is false, and can pass definite sentence of life or death against that man which rises up against the fundamental law of the States General; soe he hath made his ministers a savor of life unto life, and a savor of death unto death.

The law of love, peace and liberty in the states extending to Jews, Turks, and Egyptians, as they are considered the sonnes of Adam, which is the glory of the outward state of Holland, soe love, peace and liberty, extending to all in Christ Jesus, condemns hatred, war and bondage. And because our Saviour saith it is impossible but that offenses will come, but woe unto him by whom they cometh, our desire is not to offend one of his little ones, in whatsoever form, name or title he appears in, whether Presbyterian, Independent, Baptist or Quaker, but shall be glad to see anything of God in any of them, desiring to doe unto all men as we desire all men should doe unto us, which is the true law both of Church and State; for our Savior saith this is the law and the prophets.

Therefore, if any of these said persons come in love unto us, wee cannot in conscience lay violent hands upon them, but give them free egresse and regresse unto our Town, and house, as God shall persuade our consciences. And in this we are true subjects both of Church and State, for we are bounde by the law of God and man to doe good unto all men and evil to noe man. And this is according to the patent and charter of our Towne, given unto us in the name of the States General, which we are not willing to infringe, and violate, but shall houlde to our patent and shall remaine, your humble subjects, the inhabitants of Vlishing.

Written this 27th day of December, in the year 1657, by mee Edward Hart, Clericus

THE MADALYN MURRAY O'HAIR CASE

I believe a pivotal change occurred with the Supreme Court decision in the Madalyn Murray O'Hair case in the 1960s. The problems associated with this decision reverberate forty years later.

I believe the decision was absolutely correct to the extent that public schools should not be used to proselytize the Christian faith to nonbelievers. But the interpretation that God and religion have no place in the curriculum of our public schools is not consistent with our traditions or our law.

I think my perspective was focused most sharply in 1962 when my first child, our daughter Karen, was about to start school. Our choices were between the local public school, with small classes, or our local parish school, with sixty students in the classroom and an inexperienced lay teacher.

I was concerned that after paying my taxes for the public school, 90–95% of our parish school's tuition dollars were paying for duplicate teaching of secular subjects. But Joan's positive past experience led us to favor the parochial school. After some reflection, we decided that the economic investment of the tuition was the penalty we had to pay for exercising our constitutional choice by choosing a religion-based education for our daughter.

In collecting the material for this book, I have concluded that when religion is taught one day a week, for a couple of hours, in a separate school, it can not be the positive force it can be, as a system which teaches religious-based values on a daily basis.

I know many people will argue that religious differences have been a historical source of conflict everywhere, every place, every time. I, too, have concerns about this. For example, in Ireland, India and Pakistan, the Middle East, Eastern Europe, Africa, and in the cold war between the U.S. and the Soviet Union, taught behavior of "them vs. us" was the norm, creating people who are, at best, unaware or insensitive, or at worst, hateful. I have visited Ireland and have Irish blood flowing in my veins. I pray for the unity of the Irish people. Tribalism and separatism are poisons more deadly than any toxin and a threat to any society. That is why I believe it is essential for youth to be taught about different religions in the public school arena.

In teaching teenagers about the historical roots of discrimination, racial intolerance, and religious hatred, I ask them to study these conflicts and many others around the world. I believe education is a positive solution of this problem. But fundamentally, I think the problem is spiritual not intellectual.

Recently, on The Freedom Forum website, I found a comprehensive dissertation on what current limitations are placed on religion and religious education in our public schools, and why it is important to our children that these limitations be altered. It is titled *Finding Common Ground—A First Amendment Guide to Religion and Public Education* edited by Charles Haynes and Oliver Thomas:

> With each new advancement, communications technology moves us closer to relationships with peoples and cultures across the globe. Considering the impact that the religions of the world will have on our future, it must be said that our public system of education is failing our children by leaving them ignorant of this important realm of human history and experience.

Groups across the political spectrum are coming together to articulate compromises which allow for schools to *teach about religion* instead of *teaching religion.*

Even the federal government is beginning to see the value of religious education. According to former Education Secretary Richard Riley: "As we enter the new century, I believe that finding a satisfactory means for satisfying people of faith within the public school arena is one of the most important issues to be resolved."

The only thing I can add to that is a grateful *amen.*

The Death of Patriotism and Heroes

J. NELSON HOFFMAN

I think the strength and shared values derived from the war have set a standard for each subsequent generation. From civil rights to technological transformation, America's younger generations have grown up with the idea that dedicated people working together can truly change the world. To me, this is the greatest and most enduring legacy that my generation passed on.

—Walter H. Shorenstein
The twenty-fifth man selected among the first hundred drafted
into WW II, from *The Greatest Generation Speaks,* by Tom Brokaw

Another consequence of the changes we've seen the last fifty years has been the erosion in our nation's attitude toward honor, courage, duty, and patriotism.

During the early drafting of this book, one of the editors, Cindy Hirschfeld, observed that I was presenting a perspective that seemed to glorify the "good old days." In her view, I was saying that the world was going to hell in a hand basket and that it took a war to instill duty, honor, etc. That is not my purpose. My purpose is to reawaken the love of country that is one of our enduring legacies.

I did a little research on her perspective and found some work that is helpful in understanding her perspective. It is the work of Morris Massey, a professor at the University of Colorado. He produced a number of video and audio tapes on the topic of how values differ from decade to decade.

One particularly relevant tape is *What You Are Is Where You Were When* by Morris Massey. His premise is that much of the way we perceive the world is programmed into us when we are very young. He also makes the point that television and the turmoil of the 1960s imprinted very different views about sex, war, the military, and drugs, on the minds of those who were growing up during that time.

So with an appreciation that younger generations probably do not share the same framework I have, I will attempt to relate my recollections and perceptions of the last half of the twentieth century. Following Massey's model, I look at four different decades and how the events of those years imprinted my values and the values of my generation. Given the times, it is not surprising that my generation's views on patriotism and heroes is greatly different from the generation that came of age in the 1960s.

1944

Nineteen forty-four was a year of great tribulation for the world. The hoodlums, the misfits, and gangsters of Germany, under the hypnotic spell of Adolph Hitler, had seized control of the country. A nation of culture, science, literature and learning had become an atheistic, totalitarian bully. Without provocation, the country attacked and conquered its neighbors. Their atrocities united the Allies in a holy war against them.

In Japan, General Tojo had established a dictatorship. Without declaring war, he attacked Pearl Harbor, adding a second front in the Pacific. Everything in America was organized around the war effort. Although the world was in a horrifying, costly war, it was easy to teach an eleven-year-old boy about duty, honor, and love of God and country.

My mother's cousins, Dunbar and Leroy Simpson, were in the Navy. Elliot Hill, son of my namesake John Hill, was an infantryman. It seemed as if all the adults in our family worked in factories to support the war effort. My thirty-three-year old dad enlisted in the Marines, but the Marines were not taking men his age, so he became a half-track driver in the 770th Tank Battalion of the U.S. Army.

After Dad joined the Army, Mom and I moved into a two-bedroom apartment above Aunt Marion and Uncle Al on Heyward Avenue in Rochester, New York. Every daily activity involved work, duty, and sacrifice—anything to help win the war and bring the soldiers back home. I got up early with Mom so she could prepare breakfast before she left for work. She was tired when she got home, and it was my job to help her. After school, my duties were to make the beds and do laundry. I learned to put a light bulb in a sock to ease mending holes in the toe or heel. Mom would leave money and a shopping list, and it was often my job to start supper before she got home. She told me my father was off doing his duty for our country, and she expected me to do my duties. I could play, goof off, read, or do what I wanted, provided my chores were done first.

The media in those days consisted of radio, the daily paper, and the movie newsreels. All of the content was about the war: our victories and defeats; the heroes—Generals Patton, MacArthur, and Eisenhower; Admirals Halsey and Nimitz; and the glorious air aces who shot down Nazi and Japanese airplanes. Every boy built models of the planes flown by our heroes. Patriotism, duty, and sacrifice infused everything. In the movies, John Wayne, Alan Ladd and Brian Donlevy portrayed the heroic deeds of our servicemen and the fight against the evil enemy.

The war effort permeated every level of society—rich and poor alike were expected to contribute. Bob Hope and other Hollywood stars entertained the troops abroad. At home, people trained as air raid wardens, rolled bandages for the Red Cross, or worked at the USO. Slogans were everywhere: buy bonds; grow victory gardens; save aluminum and newspapers; conserve gasoline.

When I was eleven, I joined the Boy Scouts. Fifty-seven years later, the words of the Scout Oath are still clear in my mind: "On my honor, I will do my best to do my duty to God and my country, to help other people at all times and obey the Scout's Law." The Scout's Law: "A Scout is trustworthy, loyal, helpful, friendly, courteous, kind, obedient, cheerful, thrifty, brave, clean, and reverent."

Examples of the Scout's Oath were around me daily. With many of the men away at war, neighbors helped each other with simple things like taking out the ashes from coal furnaces, swapping food stamps, and shopping together.

Church and God had not been very important in our home life until Dad went off to war. After he got his tanker's badge and was shipped to Europe, Mom made a nightly ritual of praying: for his safe return, for the safe return of all the servicemen, and for a quick end to the war.

When her two cousins were killed, Mom explained the significance of taking down the banner with the blue stars in the front window. The blue stars told everyone there was someone off in the war. The banner was replaced with a banner of gold stars when someone was killed.

Grandma Hoffman took me to mass with her on Sundays, but with the priest facing away from the congregation, I never got much out of the Latin service or her explanation that "We are here, because Christ is here."

It was at this time in my young life that an important suggestion came to me from our scoutmaster—he suggested I join the church choir. In retrospect, the experience contributed a lot more to shaping my character than I realized. The choirmaster watched to see if we had paid attention to the minister's sermons and followed the liturgy. We rehearsed the hymns many times so the Sunday performances would be good. Fifty years later, I still get a swelling in my chest when I hear the majestic words of the hymns of Thanksgiving, Christmas, and Easter. I learned to love and still sing with gusto the words of *A Mighty Fortress is Our God* and *Onward Christian Soldiers*. Being in church as a paid member of the choir became a habit, and I was earning $3.00 per week. The money went to buying savings stamps and then war bonds. As I look back, I was learning about reverence and thrift, and I was being trained by a devoted group of mentors.

But I do not want you believing that I was any type of saint. I was a typical, energetic little boy, who found trouble in many ways: starting a fire in a church bathroom wastebasket after choir practice; entering an abandoned house and stealing a piece of jewelry; petty shoplifting. I am not proud of any of these things. But a young boy, frequently left alone, with a hard-working mother and absentee father, learns some of his lessons on the street. If it had not been for my grandfather stepping in and placing his very positive example firmly in my path, I might have gotten into serious trouble. For the young people growing up in that era, we learned an indelible sense of community and patriotism that never changed, and we carried this with us throughout our lives.

1957: THE SUEZ CRISIS AND THE EISENHOWER DOCTRINE

Skipping past high school and college to 1957, I had entered the NROTC in college and was commissioned as an ensign in June of 1955. At Norfolk, Virginia, I was trained as an amphibious assault officer, and our ship, a landing ship tank, was assigned to the Mediterranean Fleet. In case of trouble, our mission was to land the company of Marines we carried. If we were called into action, they were the probable assault troops.

Arriving in Malta in January of 1957, we were in the harbor when the command ship of the Anglo-French Fleet returned from Egypt with a lot of anger and aggravation. President Eisenhower had vetoed their invasion of Nasser's Egypt. Fearing Soviet intervention in the Middle East, Eisenhower firmly asked them to withdraw.

Navy protocol required that the junior ship present visit the senior ship present as a matter of courtesy. We walked into a hornet's nest, and the resentment of U.S. power created a real atmosphere of tension.

After a couple of strong, noontime gin-and-tonics, the traditional British reserve evaporated, and their frustration erupted into a verbal torrent. The wardroom had two or three British admirals who far outranked our commanding officer, a mere lieutenant commander. One of their admirals was the picture of frustration: "You bloody Americans. You don't know what you are getting into. For 150 years, it has been the power of Great Britain's navy and armed forces that have kept peace all around the world. Now you poke your nose in where it's not wanted. You have the money. You have the industrial capacity. WE invented the steam catapult and the canted deck aircraft carrier, but we can't afford to build them! Now you do it. You keep the peace!"

He waited for our poor captain to respond. As I recall, we thanked them for their hospitality and returned to our ship.

I did not realize the impact, the historical significance, of Eisenhower's decision until years later. With our victories and the power we gained from being victorious in World War II, the United States did become sheriff to the world. We became John Wayne—the good guy with his six-shooter, ready to defend justice and right injustice, any time of the day, anywhere in the world. We remained the good guys for years. It wasn't until Vietnam, when many in our country, and many others in the rest of the world, began to question, and reject, our role as the world's sheriff.

Forty-five years later, I wonder how many adults, or high school students, could explain "The Eisenhower Doctrine" and the significance it played in stopping the growth of global communism?

THE SIXTIES

The assassinations of Jack and Bobby Kennedy and Martin Luther King marked a time of great sorrow to the nation. They were heroes, and they were gone.

In Lyndon Johnson, we had a president who was a contrasting paradox: his Great Society vision created a whole new wave of social awareness and action, while his coarse, profane personal side personified many of the characteristics that give politicians a bad name.

Several factors occurred coincidentally that, when taken together, created a separation, a crisis in the cohesion of society that hurts us today:

An Unpopular War. The unity that was present during WW II and Korea was not there during the Vietnam conflict. Americans didn't understand the causes of the French failure there, and many people perceived of the United States as the bully, beating up on an agrarian people seeking independence. Body counts became the yardstick of success, and the gulf between those who supported the war and those who opposed it grew wider and wider.

Peaceful Civil Protests. A Gandhian model of civil disobedience was adopted by Martin Luther King to rightfully gain justice for people of color. This awoke the nation's conscience and caused most people to side with the protesters.

The Drug Culture. Riding the coattails of the civil rights cause, proponents of the drug culture and advocates of a new *free love* life style exacerbated public discontent and added to the anti-government feeling as they tried to gain *public acceptance* for their unacceptable *private behavior.*

The combined effect of the antiwar movement with the civil rights movement put government in the role of the bad guy. Through the nightly newscasts, a terrible, bloody, horrible war was brought into the living room as never before. Distrust of the government meant the populace did not trust the government to serve as policeman to the world any more: We left Vietnam in defeat, and the soldiers came home. Unlike the men and women who returned from WW II as heroes, the Vietnam veterans just came home and tried to fit into civilian life.

President Nixon. Nixon led an adjustment to a peacetime economy and created the first crack in unified global communism with the initiative to China. He had created a leg-up on a presidency of accomplishment—and then Watergate. Nixon's deception, the crassness of his language, and his conniving were revealed in "The Tapes" which helped bring him down. His failure to recognize duty and honor to his office and to the nation lowered the expectations of people for our government leaders.

THE POST-NIXON ERA AND THE PRESENT

I leave it to the reader to evaluate their perceptions of Presidents Ford, Carter, Reagan, and Bush. My opinion is that all contributed to restoring the tarnished image of the office: President Reagan for his leadership in defeating communism; President Carter who, out of office, is recognized for his humanity and volunteerism.

Which brings me to President Clinton, a man who besmirched his office through infidelity and lying. *Duty, honor,* and *country* have taken another hit. This nation remains starved for political leaders who inspire us and lead by example.

We still have heroes in and out of the military. But the nation is starved for virtuous, courageous leaders. When I speak to young students, I ask them who their heroes are. The paucity of their responses is a sad testimonial to our public morals and the lamentable examples our children witness each and every day.

As I have reflected on this, a new perspective emerged, and I realized that maybe there are heroes in our society today. We just have to see them and appreciate them for what they are. For instance, there are many parents whose day-to-day living examples do inspire their children to call them heroes. Unheralded, they are heroes living their lives with duty and honor. They are ordinary people who are policemen, firemen, teachers, and parents—people who go about their daily jobs, some facing hardship or danger, but all of them overcoming problems and obstacles to create the best life they can for themselves, for their families, for their children and for their country.

This is patriotism in action.

While we usually only see or read about the few bad examples of law enforcement or politicians who betray our trust, they are the ones who get the publicity. It is the nature of the media to promote and present the evil, the scandalous, the sensational. (Some author should expand on Gresham's Law of bad driving out good and apply it to modern communications, i.e., the scuzziest news source will apply no standards of judgment or decency in publishing some bit of questionable news, thereby applying pressure on the other news media to publish this trash.)

Millions of people who do their job professionally and act admirably on a daily basis are not publicized. Given that the nation's media spends most of its time promoting sensational failure, where and when will the next generation learn about the thousands of good cops, teachers, civil servants, nurses, and doctors?

Without a war, will the next generation learn about the dedicated men and women who train daily to defend our country or go to some foreign land to risk their lives in defense of the values and ideals of freedom and democracy for which our country stands?

I found a very telling reinforcement of this notion in Stephen Ambrose's *Citizen Soldier*. Ambrose writes about the famous Word War II correspondent Ernie Pyle:

> In the fall of 1944, Ernie Pyle needed a break from the European Theatre of Operations. In explanation, he wrote: "For me, war has

become a flat, black depression without highlights, a revulsion of the mind and an exhaustion of the spirit." Pile carried with him a conviction: In the emergency of war, our nation's powers are unbelievable. [Pile continues,] "*I have heard soldiers say a thousand times, if only we could have created all this energy for something good. But we rise above our normal powers only in times of destruction.*" [Italic added for emphasis. —Ed.]

Many of the authors who have contributed to this book have been called upon to act courageously. They have demonstrated honor and duty, and they have chosen the right path in their lives. They *are* daily heroes, and I hope their experiences inspire and instill this value in a new generation of heroes and heroines.

In the past year, I have come across two communications that speak more eloquently than I ever could on the public's disregard for former servicemen, and the men and women who currently serve our country.

The first is from a doctor, an Army captain serving at a level-one medical center near San Antonio, Texas, which has one of the largest military retiree populations in the country:

As a military doctor in training for my specialty, I work long hours and the pay is less than glamorous. One tends to become jaded by the long hours, lack of sleep, food, family contact, and the endless parade of human suffering passing before you. The arrival of another ambulance does not mean more pay, only more work. Most often it is a victim from a motor vehicle crash. Often it is a person of dubious character who has been shot or stabbed. With our large military retiree population, it is often a nursing home patient.

Even with my enlisted service and minimal combat experience in Panama prior to medical school, I have caught myself groaning when the ambulance brought in yet another sick, elderly person from one of the local retirement centers that cater to military retirees. I had not stopped to think of what citizens of this age group represented. I saw *Saving Private Ryan*. I was touched deeply. Not so much by the carnage in the first 30 minutes but by the sacrifices of so many. I was touched most by the scene of the elderly survivor at the graveside asking his wife if he'd been a good man. I realized that I had seen these same men and women coming through my emergency department and had not realized what magnificent sacrifice they had made. The things they did for me and everyone else that has lived on this planet since the end of that conflict are priceless.

Situation permitting, I now try to ask my patients about their experiences. They would never bring up the subject without the inquiry. I have been privileged to [have had] an amazing array of experiences recounted in the brief minutes allowed in an emergency department encounter. These experiences have revealed the incredible individuals I have had the honor of serving in a medical capacity, many on their last admission to the hospital. There was a frail, elderly woman who reassured my young enlisted medic trying to start an IV line in her arm. She remained calm and poised despite her illness and the multiple needle-sticks into her fragile veins. She was what we call a "hard stick." As the medic made another attempt, I noticed a number tattooed across her forearm. I touched it with one finger and looked into her eyes. She simply said "Auschwitz." Many of later generations would have loudly and openly berated the young medic in his many attempts. How different was the response from this person who'd seen unspeakable suffering!

[Another patient was] a long retired colonel who as a young USN officer had parachuted from his burning plane over a Pacific island held by the Japanese. Now an octogenarian, [he cut] his head in a fall at home where he lived alone. His CT scan and suturing had been delayed until after midnight by the usual parade of high priority ambulance patients. Still spry for his age, he asked to use the phone to call a taxi to take him home then realized his ambulance had brought him without his wallet. He asked if he could use the phone to make a long distance call to his daughter who lived 70 miles away. With great pride we told him that he could not as he'd done enough for his country and the least we could do was get him a taxi home, even if we had to pay for it ourselves. My only regret was that my shift wouldn't end for several hours, and I couldn't drive him myself.

I was there the night MSG Roy Benavidez came through the emergency department for the last time. He was very sick. I was not the doctor taking care of him, but I walked to his bedside and took his hand. I said nothing. He was so sick he didn't know I was there. I'd read his Congressional Medal of Honor citation and wanted to shake his hand. He died a few days later. The gentleman who served with Merrill's Marauders, the survivor of the Bataan Death March, the survivor of Omaha Beach, the 101-year-old WW I veteran, the former POW held in frozen North Korea, the former special forces medic now with non-operable liver cancer, the former Vietnam corp commander. I remember these citizens.

I may still groan when yet another ambulance comes in, but now I am much more aware of what an honor it is to serve these particular men and women. I am angered at the cut backs, implemented and proposed, that will continue to decay their meager retirement benefits.

I see the President and Congress who would turn their back on these individuals who've sacrificed so much to protect our liberty. I see later generations that seem to be totally engrossed in abusing these same liberties won with such sacrifice. It has become my personal endeavor to make the nurses and young enlisted medics aware of these amazing individuals when I encounter them in our emergency department. Their response to these particular citizens has me think that perhaps all is not lost in the next generation.

My experiences have solidified my belief that we are losing an incredible generation and this nation knows not what it is losing. Our uncaring government and ungrateful civilian populace should all take note. We should all remember that we must "earn this."

Rangers lead the way!

CPT Stephen R. Ellison, M.D.

If you know of such veterans, seek them out and hear their stories. Tom Brokaw's *The Greatest Generation Speaks* is a good opportunity to hear them. They are dying at the rate of thirty thousand per month.

The second message comes from a master sergeant in the Army. His writing addresses a few senators voting against a pay increase for the military. In addition to a 4.8% pay increase, the legislation also provided for a special subsistence bonus of $180 per month at a time it was estimated that between 8,000 and 16,000 U.S. military service members were receiving food stamps. Supporters cited low troop moral, the difficulty meeting recruitment goals, and a disparity of pay between the military and civilian work force as reasons for the benefits package . . .

Mr. Voinovich [the Republican Senator from Ohio]:

Unless you are planning on this being your last term in the Senate, I cannot for the life of me figure out why you would attempt to undermine a much deserved although paltry 4.8 percent pay raise to military men and women that make sacrifices that you cannot even comprehend! As a registered Republican voter, born and reared in the Buckeye state, I have a few questions I would like to ask you.

1. When was the last time you spent months on end in some God forsaken country, separated from family and friends?
2. Has your service to the nation ever required you to go beyond 100 days without a real shower?
3. Has [sic] any of your Senate duties required you to lie awake at night in a tent with a dozen other sweating senators, gagging at the wretched smell of oil well fires, and listening to desert winds beat your tent into submission?
4. Have you ever been neglected the basic freedoms most Americans take for granted? Have you ever forgotten what a real cheeseburger tastes like?

You are so quick to try and squash a pay raise that would still leave a large portion of military families below the poverty level in our nation. Please remind me again of the last time you voted and lobbied against a pay raise for yourself and fellow senators? Have you ever refused a pay increase to help balance the budget?

I dare to compare the percentage of pay raises voted by senators for senators since my career began in 1981! The AP article stated that between 8,000 and 16,000 military families are on food stamps. Even though I believe this to be a very conservative estimate, it is not a shame for hard working Americans to get much needed assistance. The real shame is that thousands and thousands of military families are even eligible for food stamps but are too proud to accept a hand out! The majority of our military families require both parents to work, while the military member works an additional part time job just to make ends meet.

I anxiously await the reunification with my family in mid-March. The operations [environment] and family separations are something I don't expect you to understand without experiencing it first hand. However, with our political pull I'm sure you could arrange to return to Saudi with me this November. The rotation in November will make the third time in two years I've left my family to proudly support the country that I love.

Yes, Mr. Voinovich, we could spend Thanksgiving and Christmas together, enjoying meals hard to identify by the appearance and taste. You could help me write a letter to my wife on our 19th anniversary in January. Possibly you could bring one of your speech writers and assist me with a letter to my twins explaining why dad had to miss yet another birthday, explaining it's for the good of our country. Before we go home, Valentine's Day will roll around and by now maybe even you will be missing your family. I could help you make that hand made card expressing your longing to be with them again. After all, I've had plenty of practice, and I'm sure we could come up with something appropriate.

Written from Saudi Arabia.

Master Sergeant Rocky Dunlap

— 13 —

DIFFERENT CHOICES, DIFFERENT LIVES

———

Since I began this book with my children and grandchildren in mind, it is very fitting that we close the book with the wisdom and inspiration of my wife and two letters from young adults who have made very different choices in their lives.

Joan's letter presents the fundamental principles she followed in raising our children.

The Choices You Make in Life Determine the Life That You Live

JOAN HOFFMAN

LIFE IS ALL ABOUT CHOICES. From the time we are very little, we must make them. Do we do as mommy says? Or do we fall down and potentially get hurt? As we get older, choices get more complicated. We often must decide between what feels good and what we know is right.

Some of our options have unpalatable consequences. It isn't fun, for example, to say no to something everyone else is doing. Responsibility and accountability may be old-fashioned ideas, but they are still worth adhering to.

We have always tried to instill in our children the following concept: the choices you make in life determine the life you live. If you decide not to study, you may fail your classes, and your educational future may be at risk. If you decide to follow the crowd and make choices that are not appropriate for you, there may be unpleasant consequences that you will have to deal with as a result of your choice. Sometimes you just have to live with the results. You can't blame anyone else for the choices you make.

This concept doesn't end with childhood. Adults, too, must be accountable—for career directions, for marriage choices, and, certainly, for the way in which they choose to raise their children.

It isn't easy in these times, and it isn't popular, to take the high road. But where will we be if we don't stand up for goodness, even godliness? Are we so far from traditional values that these things no longer have meaning? What about the concepts of good and evil?

We can blame society for some of the things that occur, but, really, aren't *we* society? Don't we all share in the blame when we are the ones who have allowed so much violence to exist in our lives? When we choose to ignore unsettling trends in our society, we make a choice we have to live with—the consequences.

Letter from the Inside

C O D Y   W I L L E

This next piece is a cautionary tale, illustrating the point that no matter where you live, young people struggle on a daily basis with issues of character and values. It is reprinted from the *Aspen Times*, 3/8/00. —Ed.

I HAVE BEEN DOING A LOT OF THINKING since my recent sentencing and have also begun keeping a diary of my daily life behind bars. My thinking has made me realize that maybe other kids my age know I've been sent to prison, but don't understand [in] our (kid) terms what prison/jail is really like. That's why I'm sending you copies of my diary—so that other kids can learn from my mistakes and not do stupid things without thinking about what the very real consequences can be. So, here is my first installment to the kids of Aspen.

Boom, boom, boom! I have arrived at my cell in Mesa County Detention Facility. Not to my surprise, I am unhappily received. The first thing I heard was a pounding like thunder; the pounding was coming from next door. The next thing I hear is, "What's your name, bitch?" I didn't know what to say, I was scared. Next I hear, "Where the [expletive] you comin' from, bitch? What are you in for, little bitch?" Just then I remembered what a friend had told me: *Act tough, act crazy, but don't act intimidated.* I did just that. I started yelling and screaming and acting tough. I heard the intercom click on: "Mr. Wille, if I were you, I wouldn't associate myself with those two troublemakers."

Now was a hard choice to make. Do I associate myself and run the risk of a write-up, or do I run the risk of getting my ass kicked? I weighed my options and went with shutting up and keeping to myself. I thought to myself that night about what had happened earlier in the day and where I was now. I didn't think sleep was an option because of the banging and constant verbal assault, but I closed my eyes and that was that.

"Hey! Is that bitch in fifteen up?" Bang, bang. "Wake up, bitch." I opened my eyes and there were about five people staring in my window. It was breakfast time; we had plain Cream of Wheat (what we have every morning). The day felt like two weeks. I had time to [assess] my entire life, what my worth was in this place. I had nothing. I felt that my whole life was about the loss of my childhood due to my father's drug addictions, then the loss of my father and finally, for the past 24 hours, the loss of myself. In those 24 hours in August, I had seemed to have lost all of my self morals and ethics; I had nothing and cared for nothing. In those 30 seconds before [the robbery], I changed my life in the most unhealthy ways possible. Now, I can't even believe that I was the same person who had committed those inexcusable acts.

I now live by Cody Wille's 10 rules of life:

1. Be yourself, never try to be what you are not.
2. Set goals and set them high. I am never coming back to jail, and I am going to break my vicious cycle of loss.
3. Resist peer pressure. If I could have done that, I wouldn't be here.
4. Respect—the more you respect others, the more they will respect you.
5. Your family and friends are the most important aspect of your life. Choose your friends well.
6. Love—there are many different types of love—love for a pet, love for family, love for your girlfriend, love for the people that help you. Everyone loves differently, but love is what unites all of us together.
7. Pride—I am not proud of some of the things I've done, but I am damn proud of the man I have become through these hard times.
8. Never take things for granted. It's the little things in life that make it so beautiful.
9. Forgiveness—forgiveness is as powerful as love. In fact, they hold each other hand in hand.
10. I may only be a 17-year-old Aspen High School senior, but I am wise enough to know that my life is only beginning, and I have had one hell of a kick start at it.

There will always be lessons to be learned and goals to achieve, but I urge you to take life one step at a time. So what is my message? We must continue to chart a course for our lives. Set goals and live every day to the fullest to achieve them. If it takes an unexpected turn, hang on to the goals that are still realistic and reassess those that are not. Our value systems must remain unchanged—it is these core values that provide a foundation for setting a new course. That course may lead us in directions that we never anticipated or dreamed of. But that new course may lead us to making contributions and accomplishment that are of more value to our society than those we had originally planned for ourselves.

My life reminds me of a story I once heard. There was this man who was stranded in a desert. He had no food or water and was on the verge of death. He kneels down and starts to pray. He says, "God, please let me make it out of this desert alive." All of a sudden he wakes up two weeks later in a city, fully refreshed. There is an angel sitting right next to him, and the man asks, "How did I get out of the desert?" The angel picks him up and shows him the path coming from the desert. In some places there are two sets of footprints and in others there is only one set. So the man says, "Where there are two sets, is that you who was walking with me?" The angel says, "Yes that was me." Then the man says, "Why did you leave me to walk the rest of the way alone?" And the angel says, "I didn't leave you. That was when I was carrying you."

I just want to say thank you to all of you that have carried me.
Love, Cody Wille

Cody Wille, a 17-year-old Aspen resident, was sentenced to three years in a prison for youthful offenders in Pueblo, Colorado for his role in an Aspen crime spree in the summer of 1999.

In the spring of 2001, Cody Wille was released from prison after serving his sentence in a positive manner. He completed his high school education and received several letters praising his behavior and attitude while he was incarcerated. He remains under strict supervision for the next several years.
—Ed.

Letter from Christina Morgan, John Bowne High School

CHRISTINA MORGAN

This letter illustrates that no matter where you live character, values, and hard work can all add up to a successful future. —Ed.

FROM THE START OF MY CHILDHOOD, my parents, Richard and Rosemary Morgan, had inculcated in me the power of positive thinking. From time to time, life has its ups and downs; however, despite how arduous an obstacle, everything works out for the best. I strongly believe and hold this to be true. If we are to live out our lives with the assurance that we will succeed in the things we desire, not just materialistically, but spiritually as well, you will see that the occurrences in life are only a reflection of your positive vision.

Throughout my entire life I have had a passion to become a successful performer. The thrill of being on stage—dancing, singing, and acting—is what I yearn for. It's amazing that one could be blessed with these talents and be given the chance to hold an audience in the palm of your hand, keeping them in such awe. I am proud and fortunate to find something that has delighted the souls of many, as well as myself. Although my family has not been able to afford to pay for the training I need to start a life in the performing arts, I continue to find opportunities to perform. In 1982 my mother was diagnosed with schizophrenia, causing her a great deal of emotional, behavioral, and intellectual imbalance. It was up to my father to try and support the family on his own while my mother was taking medication and seeking psychiatric help. It was difficult for my mother to find a stable job due to her condition and the circumstances. She was unable to find a job with flexible hours while having the ability to continue her regular hospital visits. With all the hospital bills coming in and the regular expenses, my father's carpentry work could not cover all the payments due. He is now enrolled in La Guardia Aeronautical School, receiving the education he needs to qualify for a job in aeronautical mechanical engineering, and, hopefully, it will provide the financial help we need. My family's difficulties have forced me to mature at an early age. Though it was a hardship, I am grateful for it. It motivates me even more and ignites my burning desire to overcome this obstacle and become the most successful person I can be. I am not ashamed of who I am, and I know how much I have to offer.

I was inspired by Anne Shirley's character in the story *Anne of Green Gables* written by L.M. Montgomery. Anne is an orphan girl who finds escape in books and poetry. In the movie version, Anne recites the poem *The Highwayman* by Alfred Noyes. This is a favorite of mine, and I received first place for reciting it in our sixth grade poetry contest.

In elementary school, I began to spend a lot of time on stage. I grew to love Mariah Carey, Celine Dion, and Barbra Streisand. It was their songs that I would perform, and it marked the beginning of my success on stage performing.

I participated in every talent show and multi-cultural show the school provided. In seventh grade I was introduced to the art of Indian dancing from a woman raised in Bangladesh. She saw how anxious I was to dance, and, as a result, she began to give me lessons. Ever since, I have performed with her at various functions. This intrigued many students at my junior high school. They found it odd, and yet interesting, to see someone from a Colombian/American background, so enthusiastic as to represent the Indian cultural dance.

Shortly after this, I came to know a woman who was offering her time to give free private lessons in African-American, salsa, meringue, tango, and jazz dance. You could say that was a once-in-a-lifetime opportunity. I participated in a number of shows she choreographed. Finally I was receiving the education in dance I needed to build my performing foundation.

I joined the school chorus, and not only was I learning to sing music in English, but in German and Italian as well. As you can see, I couldn't have possibly had a more fulfilling lifestyle in music compared to all that I was experiencing in junior high.

It then became time for me to audition for acceptance to a performing arts high school. I hoped that through my auditions the instructors would see my enthusiasm and potential to become a performer. However, with the lack of a stable background in private lessons, I did not compare to those who had been taking formal voice and dance lessons for many years, and I was not accepted.

The auditions were structured to see how much vocal music theory a student knew. We were set up into classroom-sized amounts of students and asked to perform uniformly in either ballet or jazz. I could not understand why the auditions were structured in a way that these schools were only looking for students who already had received lessons. What about those who had the potential and the desire to learn for the first time? A school's purpose is to teach those who want to learn.

Despite my disappointment, I continue to perform. When I achieve my career in the performing arts, I will have a goal—to instill in peoples' minds the idea that they recognize not only those who have been fortunate enough to have acquired cultivation in the arts, but also those who have the will and talent to perform if given the chance.

I am now the president of John Bowne High School student union. This school has provided many opportunities for me to perform—events such as their winter and spring concerts, multicultural shows, and assemblies. One evening at a concert I was asked to sing at Queens College for their Duke Ellington celebration. I am now a part of our school drama class and have received the leading role in our upcoming play *Stand and Deliver* by Ramon Menendez and Tom Musca. I'm currently planning for colleges where I will major in performing arts and minor in psychiatry.

All that I have experienced has shaped me into becoming the better person I am today. Spiritually and mentally, my encounters have brought me to a higher level of understanding. I am thankful for the wonderful education that I have received, and my strong faith in God has caused me to become a more knowledgeable person.

For me, an education is beneficial to all that I choose to pursue in life as a career and as a person. I have come a long way, and I look forward to the future.

Upon graduating from high school, Christina Morgan won a full scholarship to the University of Michigan.

— 14 —

LESSONS LEARNED

———

Anchoring Life's Values

NELSON HOFFMAN

IN THE SIXTIES, Joan and I lived in Wilmington, Delaware, and we were very busy raising five children. Our spiritual life was significantly impacted by the changes of Vatican II.

I remember a meeting of the Wilmington alumni of University of Rochester. The President, Dr. Allen Wallis, came to tell us about the many changes occurring at the school, including a new concept in student housing—coeducational dormitories with women on one floor and men on adjacent floors.

This plan was a source of controversy. To those of us only 10 years out of school, the concept of integrated dormitories was a truly radical (new? progressive? innovative?) step.

I recall a woman with strongly conservative values asked Dr. Wallis, "Don't you think by building these dormitories, you will be contributing to the delinquency of the students?"

As best I can recall, Dr. Wallis paused only briefly before replying, "Madam, it has been my experience that those students who come to the university with their moral values not firmly anchored will be exposed to all the temptations and forces that they will see outside the university. They will be affected. But for those with strongly embedded values, I don't think the architecture of our buildings will have much of an effect."

That response stuck a responsive chord with me. I remembered how much my college years had been a time of testing and formation, a time for making my own choices. In retrospect, I don't think my beliefs were anchored very strongly at that time. But Dr. Wallis' talk impressed on me the importance of embedding such values in our children while they are still at home with us.

This sentiment is one of the more important conclusions of this book. In Chapter Four, Melody and Bob Durham wrote about the critical importance of building trust and guiding teenagers as they make more and more of their own decisions. Parents need to blend an authoritarian approach often used with young children with a more participatory style with teenagers. They respond to trust as well as discipline. And, as Melody says, the tough task for the parents is to continue to allow them the opportunity to demonstrate good judgment, rather than taking that opportunity away.

In the limited experience I've gained working with teenagers in my retirement, I have found that a very large number of high school students are strongly influenced by a few rather obvious groups: peers, music, and celebrities. Unfortunately, the last group—celebrities—is too often the personification of "sex, drugs, and rock and roll." Rebellion and defiance are the trademark of many hard metal groups. It was amazing to me to learn how often young people list them as role models and "heroes."

As every parent of teenagers recognizes, a teenagers' desire to belong empowers the peer group and can be a significant factor working for or against family influence. In Aspen, there is a television program that gives voice to the thinking of teenagers—*Be Heard*. A young student named Gillian enumerated how good she thought it was that teenagers have a way of speaking their minds on serious topics. According to Gillian, "I think teens are more likely to listen to their peers than to grown ups."

As a word of experience to my children: Treasure those years when your children are at home. You will be amazed how rapidly the high school years pass and your young adults move on.

Faith, Family, Fulfillment, and Friendship

J. Nelson Hoffman

I REALIZE THAT MY "RECIPE" FOR SUCCESSFUL LIVING has changed over the years. The contributions from my fellow authors have sharpened my current view. Thanks to my parents, I was blessed with a very caring start in life. When I left college, my goals were to make money, get ahead in the company, and have a big family. My career took me from the field of optics, which I had studied in college, to the field of engineering plastics, where I found wonderful opportunities.

During my career years, my wife Joan carried the burden of raising our children, while I played a supporting role. Now, I see my sons and sons-in-law playing a greater role in the raising of their children. I think this one of the most positive changes to have occurred over the past few decades. But in spite of this positive trend, there is still an alarming number of children who are deprived of loving, effective parenting.

In reflecting on all the many blessings that have made my life such a joy, I think of my recipe as a circle or clock: At 12 o'clock, it begins with a basic foundation of faith and trust in God and people. At 3 o'clock, it then evolves through the love and commitment to family. At 6 o'clock, I see the activities and institutions which occupy my life. At 9 o'clock, are the friendships made along the way. By nurturing these friendships, I've gained fulfillment from them. And returning back to 12 o'clock, life reaches closure in a return to the faith with which the recipe began. The movement around this circle requires lifelong learning, lifetime giving, and the desire to stay "green and growing."

With respect for others who do not share my beliefs, the following is presented as an affirmation of the values my fellow contributors have added to those I held at the beginning of this book project.

FAITH AND TRUST: THE BEGINNING

My life is grounded in the belief that all men are created in the image and likeness of God. Our bodies are a temple for a Holy Spirit. As such, any conduct that is destructive to that body is a violation of that temple, and the use of drugs, or excessive use of alcohol, is destructive.

My intellect and all of man's accumulated knowledge are just a partial perception of all that God has created. Science and philosophy are tiny compartments of what we will learn. Beyond our bodies and minds, there is a unique spirit with free will whose purpose is to return God's love. Our every act and thought is based on the trust God has placed in us.

In early life we are takers and learn the act of giving and sharing in our *families*. As we grow up, we become providers and givers, and it is our responsibility to shepherd our children, our charges, in the skills, knowledge, character, behavior, and habits which lead to success in life.

Each of us seeks *fulfillment* in one form or another beyond our life as family members. In retrospect, there were a few organizations, a few institutions, that commanded my interests. The main groups which provided this fulfillment in my life are: *church, school, companies*, and a few, select *social* and *service organizations*.

CHURCH

While I am a Christian, I understand and respect how people of other faiths find fulfillment in their faith.

My Christian life started shortly after my birth when my parents had me baptized at the St. Paul's Episcopal Church. As a teenager, I repeated my baptism by immersion as a Baptist. After my marriage to Joan in 1955, I became a Catholic.

Attendance at church provides a continual reminder of the benefits and obligations of a believer. I love the hymns and the expression of gratitude and praise that comes with joining my fellow worshipers in song. I believe my life is richer for worshipping with others, and I have more insight into what community really means. Christ's teachings begin with how I should deal with my fellow man and woman. I've never found a more fundamental principle than "Do unto others as you would have them do unto you."

SCHOOLS

Now in my sixties, I appreciate what a wonderful system of public schools we have here in America. Though I frequently point out the need for improvement, we rely on our public schools to teach such fundamental concepts as democracy and capitalism, and we rely on school to be the place where children develop their dreams and plans for the future. Public and private schools have been critically important in the success of many of the contributors to this book. Now, many of them are finding ways to "give back" to the schools they attended.

From my earliest years, I was told I was going to go to college. I was expected to study hard and achieve the best results. The science I learned in high school and college gave me thinking skills that provided a lifetime of challenges and satisfactions.

My mother gave me a great thirst for knowledge, and I loved the competition and the teamwork I learned in school, as well as the lessons from some very skilled teachers. Now, in my retirement, teaching public speaking skills to those who may have not learned the skills at home is a true passion for me. The joy in working with young junior high, high school, and college students is one of the best parts of my life. It is a special moment to be present when a student discovers something for the first time.

MY WORK

As described by many of my fellow authors, American industry in the last half of the twentieth century provided our generation with opportunities to find work that was not backbreaking or physically tough. I worked in both big businesses and small: sales, research, and management jobs; public, private, and entrepreneurial companies. With the "Protestant work ethic" ingrained by my family, I derived a great deal of satisfaction and fulfillment from my work. (From what I've learned from history, it might better be described as "the immigrant work ethic.")

The lessons of my parents and grandparents concerning the fulfillment provided by engaging in meaningful work proved to be very true. As Ann Ehringer describes it, to find pleasure and satisfaction in the way one earns their living provides a truly "luxurious life."

In addition to the satisfaction of the work, the friendships developed in my work, as those developed at school and church, have provided lifelong relationships.

SOCIAL AND SERVICE ORGANIZATIONS

In remembering the organizations of my youth, virtually all were founded on the premise that forming the character of young children was their first purpose: Cub and Boy Scouts, Girl Scouts, the YMCA, DeMolay, and the young people's groups that are part of most places of worship. Joan speaks of the wonderful influence of the CYO and the churches that sponsored dances on the weekends. Our friend, Father Larry Solan, speaks of the powerful influence of the CYO in leading him to the priesthood.

In the suburbs and in rural areas, these organizations still flourish. But in modern urban life, many no longer hold the prominent positions they once enjoyed, and I feel our children are being robbed of something important. With more and more single-parent homes, and more homes with two working parents, these organizations could provide the training and formation that helped shape the values of my generation.

Earlier in the book, Cathy Buscher described a family life where public service was ingrained in her earliest years. In our youth, many of us learned about serving others in these organizations.

I am pleased to see that many high school and college students are engaged in volunteer programs. And yet, what about the children who receive no training or examples at home or school?

Governor Lamm sent me a book titled *Beyond the Classroom*, by Laurence Steinberg, a book that focuses on the efficacy of the school reform effort and astutely forces attention to issues in the student's life outside the classroom. As Steinberg notes in his book, "Let us agree that students need schools that provide both opportunities to learn, as well as standards to live up to and that schools can and should provide both. But, our study also shows that schools are only one of the many influences—and probably, when all is said and done, not even the most important one—that affects what students learn and how well they perform on tests of achievement."

I share his concern for that fraction of the student population which is not benefiting from our public school systems, and I hope to rally those who understand the critical nature of providing infrastructure to support and supplement home and school life. The breakdown in communal activities described in Robert Putnam's *Bowling Alone* is a major problem for our society.

Unless adults get involved in public and social organizations in the manner that earlier generations did, our society will feel serious negative effects.

FRIENDSHIP

Let me close the loop of my recipe. I can testify to the biblical promise that if you have good friends in your golden years and your children are a blessing to you, you are truly rich. My lifetime of work in my chosen field has brought me innumerable friendships. Foremost amongst them is the lifelong friendship of my loving wife, who has shared in my trials and my triumphs, as our children grew, matured, and became our best friends.

FAITH

If, as Father Michael Glenn has written, you have God as your best friend; if you have done to others as you would have them do to you; and when it comes to serving others, you can say "Whatsoever I have done to the least of my brothers (or sisters), that I have done for you," then the loop of faith is closed. My perception of faith is that my central purpose in life is to make of myself a worthwhile offering to God. That is how I define success.

Postscript

J. NELSON HOFFMAN

*I*N CLOSING THE BOOK, I am most grateful for the tremendous contribution made by the friends who provided submissions, critiques, and fresh views. On my own, I could never have created the inspiration, the personal growth, and new perspectives they contributed to this book. With this part of the project completed, my new ambition is to spread their words and ideas as widely as possible.

We began this project with the hope that the experiences of our contributors would stir a renewal of the "American spirit"—the spirit Roosevelt depicted in the inaugural address excerpted at the beginning of this book.

Let me close with a few observations that bear on reviving that spirit:

1) Jim Ryan's call for a national crusade involving all Americans seems more important every day. In the seven years taken to put this book together, we've endured a number of traumas in our country: school shootings (the California school shootings revealed that one in seven students had been bullied or threatened in the last twelve months), and the evening newscasts seem fixated on lead stories of violence, criminal acts and deviant behavior. Governor Lamm writes of our society's need to provide justice and a freedom from fear. Can our current climate foster "The Spirit of America"?

2) With multiple dimensions to the problems we face, there are no simple one-dimensional solutions. Initiatives that provide solutions will be needed from virtually every part of society: from families to the national government, civic organizations, schools, and places of worship. Our hope is that students, teachers, parents, grandparents, and all our readers will discover ideas they can put to use in their individual lives and impart to the organizations that command their loyalties.

3) My friends have recommended many wonderful books and periodicals that describe the various dimensions of the problem and offer potential solutions. My backlog of reading has reached forty or

fifty books. They range from modern interpretations of biblical texts to new analyses from academia, foundations, and religious groups. My first priority will be reading the full translation of de Tocqueville's *Democracy in America*.

4) My next priority is to reread *Leisure as a Basis of Culture* by Josef Pieper, a German religious philosopher who provides an apt closing for our work. Lecturing and writing in 1947 as Germany was rebuilding, both practically and spiritually, from the disasters of Hitler and the Nazi influence, he anticipated the events which transpired from 1950–2001. His book predicted the rise of a material, work-centered future, preempting and shrinking our spiritual core.

The book examines the meanings of work, spare time, and leisure in the 1940s. There is little ambiguity about work: it represents the activities we engage in to provide the essentials of life—food, clothing, shelter, and hopefully, a surplus to spend on other choices. Over the course of the century, intellectual work replaced manual work in many peoples' lives.

Spare time, Pieper notes, has come to mean time off from work. Pieper writes:

> If we consider the concept of spare time only in its relationship to the concept of workday, if we define spare time as a mere break from work in order to recover, a time after work to restore one's strength for more work, then again no problem will arise.

Pieper then turns to his central theme: the traditional and emerging meaning of leisure. He speaks of leisure as a time to manifest culture. He draws a distinction between holidays and holy days as present in our western, Judeo-Christian tradition. He speaks of leisure as a time for feast and celebration, a period for acting and thinking about activities that do not produce measurable results or material goods.

These issues were the starting point for our book! It seems so much of our lives is dominated by work and the hectic pace of "using" time off from work for activity-filled hours. His ideas seem right on target with the issues we have tried to illuminate in these pages.

Pieper writes of uses of leisure which center on a deeper spiritual and philosophical meaning: "How does the spirit of celebration originate in the heart of man, and how can it be fostered and preserved?"

He also comments on the work-dominated life:

> It brings about precisely that inhuman dimension so typical of the world of absolute work: it accomplishes the final bondage of man within the process of work, it makes everybody a proletarian. This is happening openly and explicitly in those totalitarian "worker states," but it is also infecting other parts of the world, at least as a danger and a temptation.

I believe his prediction was a key factor in the collapse of the Soviet Union and the current malaise in Russia. The people were not left with a hopeful, free vision in their current life or a better future. And I believe America has become one of those places he has referred to in the phrase "infecting other parts of the world." I believe we have passed the "danger" and "temptation" stage. We have been seriously "infected" and affected.

In speaking of the ultimate fulfillment of human existence, Pieper writes of the need for being quiet, for a positive, receiving attitude:

> I am only trying to express the teaching found in the Western philosophical tradition. The most important element in this teaching declares: the ultimate fulfillment, the absolutely meaningful activity, the most perfect spirit of being alive, the deepest satisfaction, and the fullest expression of human existence needs to happen in an instance of beholding, namely in the contemplating of the world's ultimate and intrinsic foundations.

In the above quotation, people of faith will find their core belief. I use it to provide a framework to ask what we mean at our deepest level by "The Spirit of America." As the standard bearer of republican democracy, human rights, and free market capitalism, what kind of community do we want for our nation? How is that vision expressed in the moral standards of our society? Are we able to serve as an example to the world?

It was in searching for the answers to such questions that we began, and it is how we conclude. As my wife, Joan, has said: "The choices you make in life determine the life you live." (And I would add that your decisions may affect all of our lives.)

My hope and prayer is that the book has provided our readers with inspiration and the will to tackle the problems they can help resolve.

This morning I walked in the brilliant sunshine admiring the majesty of the mountains and the desert and the beauty of the blooming flowers. I was listening to Beethoven's *Ode to Joy* and my spirit soared. I felt great. And then I realized that it was, as Pieper had said, a time to be quiet.

I would welcome any reactions to the ideas presented at jnelshoff@aol.com.

Via con dios!

Remember Me

ART CERRE

When I have gone to my maker, I ask
That you remember these things:
Bury my body . . . . but don't bury my beliefs.
Bury my heart . . . . but don't bury my love.
Bury my eyes . . . . but not my vision.
Bury my feet . . . . but not the path of my life.
Bury my hands . . . . but do not bury my diligent efforts.
Bury my shoulders . . . . but not the concerns I carried.
Bury my voice . . . . but not my message.
Bury my mind . . . . but do not bury my dreams.
Bury me . . . . but do not bury my life.
If you must bury something,
Let it be my faults
And my weaknesses
But let my life continue on in you.

APPENDIX A

The VanderWerf
Universal Health Care Plan

DR. BEN VANDERWERF

PHYSICIAN INVOLVEMENT

One of the most egregious mistakes made in the original development of health care insurance program—sand the resultant tinkering, fixing, and cobbling undertaken in the name of improving them—has been the astonishingly limited role physicians have played in the process.

Left to laymen and women, the result is what we have today: a health care payment system that is a patchwork of loopholes, restrictions, and regulations designed to appease actuaries and accountants, but neither physicians nor their patients.

At the center of the VanderWerf Universal Health Care Plan stands the primary care physician whose role as gatekeeper cannot be underestimated. It is the primary care physician who, especially under managed care plans, first sees the patient, diagnoses the problem and outlines the care plan.

The primary care physicians have been referred to "gatekeepers" because they control access to medical technology and resources beyond the primary care physician's office. We would be well-advised to drop the moniker, gatekeeper, because of the negative connotations (and often the reality) of blocking access to additional care.

Instead, the concept of primary care should be promoted and physicians who chose to practice as primary care providers should be generously rewarded for their efforts. The success or failure of the entire system rests on the relationship between primary care physicians and their patients, the continuity they bring to patient care, and their role as a medical first-line-of-defense against disease.

In fact, I believe it is this very lack of continuity of care that is a major shortcoming of the American health care system. And its importance cannot be understated. We must ensure that in any plan continuity of care is guaranteed—and the VanderWerf Universal Health Care Plan offers this.

Furthermore, one of the key elements of the Plan is the involvement of physicians in the ongoing oversight of the plan and the quality of care it delivers.

Such oversight will be accomplished by ensuring the presence of physicians at all levels of the Plan's management.

MAJOR ROLE FOR PRIMARY CARE PHYSICIANS

Primary care physicians in the VanderWerf Universal Health Care Plan would be paid on a capitated basis—in other words, patients, in a similar fashion to existing managed care programs would select a primary care physician from among all primary care physicians—not just those named by the particular insurance company with whom the patient is affiliated (13). Every physician who chose to could participate in the plan and each would receive a fixed payment per patient per year.

Because every citizen would be required to select a primary care physician, but not every citizen would use the services of their primary care physician at the same level, the system has, therefore built-in additional compensation to cover the costs of treating patients whose conditions require more intense case involvement, for instance, patients with diabetes or other chronic conditions which do not require the expertise of a specialist for routine management.

Capitated payments to primary care physicians would be accompanied by a feature ranked as one of the most desired by physicians: reduction of paperwork to an absolute minimum and the concomitant reduction in "hassle factor" because billing insurance companies will instantly become a thing of the past.

This benefit of the VanderWerf Universal Health Care Plan—the elimination of the physicians as collection agents—is a fact that will surely please both physician and patient.

While there is an overall emphasis on "preventive care" in the plan, when a patient's condition demands the care of a specialist, the primary care physician would now be ablewithout suffering any financial disincentive resulting from "losing" a patient—to make the appropriate referral.

And, unlike many of the contracts of current plans, selection would not be based on a list of physicians whose charges will be covered by a particular managed care plan but rather on which specialistin the estimation of the primary care physician—is best qualified to provide the care needed.

Specialists—because it would be wasteful to require all patients to "sign up" with the complete array of specialists they might need in hundreds of speculative cases—would be paid on a fee-for-service basis. The fees would be arrived at with physician input and adjusted accordingly as time and technology warrant.

The specialist's role would end after the procedure was performed or the treatment regimen had been completed. At that point, the patient would be "sent back" to his or her primary care physician for routine follow-up care.

There is an added side benefit concentrating the practice of specialists to their specialty. The burden to care for patients who required treatment falling well below the specialists' ability actually resulted in specialists "losing" some of their specialized technique and skills (14).

Under the VanderWerf Universal Health Care Plan, specialists will now be able to concentrate their attention on improving their skills—especially the ever increasing array of new skills and techniques every specialist from gastroenterology and obstetrics to neurodiagnostic radiology to pediatric renal transplantation must have to provide the best quality medicine in the new millennium.

MANAGED CARE, MILITARY, AND OTHER PROVIDER ISSUES

Because it might take as long as 20–25 years for complete integration of the VanderWerf Universal Health Care Plan into American Society, managed care and a number of other (often sacred cows) medical institutions will continue to exist in one form or another through the transition.

Ultimately, however, the Plan would eliminate the waste that comes from maintaining separate active military, veterans, senior, indigent and city, county, state and local health care programs and facilities.

Once expanded to the entire population, there would be no reason to maintain Medicare and Medicaid as separate programs. The same applies to military hospitals, V.A. hospitals, and other health care programs and facilities sponsored by such diverse organizations as the Bureau of Indian Affairs and even some small rural counties.

The potential for savings based on elimination of multiple duplicative efforts is enormous. But, until the VanderWerf Universal Health Care Plan can be fully implemented, managed care and the other special-interest providers will remain part of the system.

CAVEAT EMPTOR

But, I believe it is important to remind citizens that the plan's best chance of success is its universal enrollment. It is such an uniquely American precept that we should stress it repeatedly: United we stand. Divided we fall.

And in the case of the VanderWerf Universal Health Care Plan, all children will be covered. If parents, for religious or other reasons, choose not to avail themselves of the care for their children, then, obviously that is their decision.

When the plan is ultimately extended to all Americans, it should allow patients to seek health care outside this plan at their own expense.

MANAGED CARE MAY CONTINUE

Will managed care organizations be summarily closed down as a result of my plan? Not necessarily. I see no reason why new managed care organizations could not be formed to meet the needs of certain segments of the population.

Again, a caveat: such plans cannot be more expensive than the Universal Health Care Plan.

By allowing managed care organizations to remain a part of the system, their otherwise understood opposition may be lessened.

PAYMENT ISSUES

Under the current system, one of the arguments small businesses make against providing health care coverage to their employees is the cost of such coverage.

Under the VanderWerf Universal Health Care Plan, individuals and businesses alike will pay what they can afford—not necessarily what such coverage actually costs.

This ability to pay an "affordable" amount rather than having to provide no coverage because of excessive costs is the second of the keys to my plan. (The first key, as explained above, is its universal applicability.)

Naturally such a universal health care plan cannot be provided gratis. But it is the author's considered opinion that much of the cost of the current Gordian knot of insurance, managed care, government and private payment plans is hidden in the bureaucracy built up to establish the rules—and then enforce them.

Under the VanderWerf Universal Health Care Plan, the government would not—except for its employees—be paying for coverage.

Individual citizens and their employers would assume the role, leaving the government to other matters.

Taxes—specifically for health care—would be eliminated by the departure of the government from the role of payer. Individuals and businesses will simply re-allocate the savings to a privately managed national "Health Fund."

Ultimately, taxes now allocated to providing health care to the Veteran's Administration, retired military personnel, Medicare and Medicaid will be eliminated and individuals now receiving their care in this manner will begin to use the new Universal Health Care Plan.

AN INITIAL CALCULATION

To begin with, a working man or woman would contribute, say, two percent per child up to the first $75,000 of his or her salary. These contributions *which can be shared by employer and employee* would be deducted from payroll or benefits and entitlement checks and clearly labeled "Contribution for Universal Health Plan" to reinforce that while Americans can expect their employers and fellow citizens to help provide health care, it is anything but free.

Similar contributions will come from self-employed Americans, unemployed Americans, and even Social Security beneficiaries.

HOSPITAL PAYMENT SYSTEM

Hospitals, one of the keystone elements in the American health care system, would be reimbursed with a system that resembles the current one based on the concept of diagnosis related groups (DRGs). The DRG system sets usual, customary, and reasonable (UCR) rates for hundreds of procedures, and hospitals are reimbursed based on those rates (15) .

The DRG system, as is the case with procedural coding for physician services, has worked well because the parties most affected—hospitals and doctorsplay a significant role in determining, arbitrating, and changing rates as times, techniques, technology, and circumstances change.

SPEED CRITICALLY IMPORTANT

One of the primary reasons the VanderWerf Universal Health Care Plan does not call for immediate implementation for all Americans is the simple fact that it would be impossible to impose such a new system on so many with such short notice. Furthermore, political expediency—not to mention reality—dictates a slow, steady, methodical, one phase at a time approach.

Nevertheless, that does not mean that Americans and their leaders should revert to the habits of the past and "debate to death" the overarching vision of this plan.

As an ancient philosopher once observed, "a journey of a thousand miles begins with a single step." Americans and their leaders should move with alacrity to implement the first phases of this plan. Immediately—if not sooner, as the saying goes.

The very act of doing something, regardless of whether it's perfect, regardless of whether it has been so politically sanitized as to be innocuous and ineffective and pleasing to absolutely everyone will accomplish nothing (except to increase already intolerably high levels of frustration).

And because the first phases involve our children's health care, political resistance, while certain to be present, may be somewhat lessened because of the altruistic nature of the Plan. Because this young population generally requires less service from the health care system, the costs are considerably reduced for taxpayers and businesses.

But we must act. And act now.

CONCLUSION

This is the most powerful nation on Earth. It is a land of bountiful richness and resources. It is the center of the world's medical achievements and, by all signs, remain as far into the future as the author can see.

It is inexcusable not to provide quality care to all citizens throughout all of their lives. There is but one thing to do: convince our national legislators and other elected officials to support the concept of the VanderWerf Universal Health Care Plan and enact—without another moment's delay—enabling legislation.

That done, we can begin the ongoing process of monitoring—with physician input—the beginning phases of the plan, making minor modifications to it when and where needed, building on it when appropriate, and then basking in the pride of living in not only the richest, most powerful country in the world, but the healthiest one, too.

REFERENCES

1. Physician Opinion on Health Care Issues, 1996. American Medical Association. Chicago, IL, 1997. See also Editorial: "Doctor Discontent," *The New England Journal of Medicine* (November 19, 1998, Vol. 339, No. 21) 1543–45.

2. Source Book of Health Insurance Data. Health Insurance Association of America. Washington, DC, 1998.

3. G. Anders, *Health Against Wealth—HMOs and the Breakdown of Medical Trust* (Boston, MA: Houghton Mifflin Company, 1996). See also Samuelson, "HMO Backlash," *The Washington Post* (March 4, 1998) A21.

4. D. Eisenberg, R. Davis, S. Ettner, S. Appel, S. Wilkey, M. Van Rampay, and R. Kessler, "Trends in Alternative Medicine Use in the United States,

1990–1997," *The Journal of the American Medical Association* (November 11, 1998): 1569–75.

5. W. A. Zelman, *The Changing Health Care Marketplace* (San Francisco, CA: Jossey-Bass Publishers, 1997); "Dollar Value of Health Care Mergers and Acquisitions Reaches a Record Level," Irving Levin Associates, Inc., PR Newswire, February 19, 1999.

6. Weiss Ratings, Inc., August 31, 1998.

7. S. Findlay and J. Miller, "Down a Dangerous Path—The Erosion of Health Care Insurance Coverage in the United States," National Coalition on Health Care. Washington, DC, March 1999.

8. W. A. Glaser, *Health Insurance in Practice: International Variations in Financing, Benefits and Problems* (San Francisco, CA: Jossey-Bass Publishers, 1991).

9. Changes in Employee Health Coverage by Small Businesses, The Henry J. Kaiser Family Foundation 1999.

10. European Health Care Reforms, Analysis of Current Strategies, World Health Organization, Regional Office for Europe 1996.

11. P.B. Ginsburg and J.R. Gabel, "Tracking Health Care Costs: What's New in 1998?" *Health Affairs* (September/October 1998): 141–46.

12. The Towers Perrin 1999 Health Care Cost Survey. New York, NY, 1999.

13. J. D. Wilkerson, JK, J. Devers, and R. S. Given, *Competitive Managed Care* (San Francisco, CA. Jossey-Bass Publishers, 1997).

14. D. L. Sackett, et al., Evidenced-based Medicine (New York: Churchill Livingstone, 1997).

15. K. L. Thorpe, *Health Care Cost Containment Results and Lessons from the Past 20 Years in Improving Health Policy and Management* (Ann Arbor, MI; Health Administration Press, 1992).

APPENDIX B

The Circles Exercise

THE WUNDERLIN COMPANY

An article in the local newspaper carried a line that applies to this book: If you want to find out where a person's values are, look at his Daytimer and his charge card statement. The following exercise was developed by the Wunderlin Company to assist individuals in analyzing the priorities of their life.

1. Make a list of the seven or so major areas in your life over which you have some degree of control. For example:

Health	Spirituality	Family
Employment	Marriage	Wealth
Friendships	Hobbies	Growth
Career	Property	Education
Self-Development	Community Service	

2. Representing each one as a circle, draw a diagram of how your "life circles" relate to each other, both in terms of size, overlap, and distance from one another. Several circles can overlap and/or touch, but this is not necessary. You may want to use different colors, and you may want to edit or rewrite the drawing to give an accurate picture of your configuration. Be honest and fair!

Example
If your hobby is boating and your work is selling boats, there is a heavy overlap of those 2 circles.

If your employment requires that you be on the road and unable to spend time with your family, those two circles do not even touch. However, if you and one of your 3 children work and travel together, the two overlap somewhat.

If you work 80 hours per week, allowing no time for anything else, the work is the largest, presumably much larger than any other, and doesn't overlap the others, except possibly wealth, if you make a lot of money in your work.

3. After drawing the circles, reflect on them and be prepared to discuss why they appear the way they do, and what you like or don't like about your current "Balance."

This is an interesting exercise for spouses, so they can share their drawings and discuss them with each other.

Life Circles Example

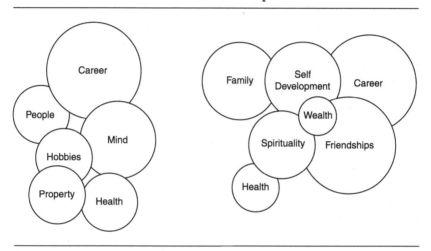

Used with permission of the Wonderlin Company, Louisville, KY.

Exit Strategies Workshop Follow-up

The most effective follow-up I know of is to redraw your circles in a configuration more the way you would like them to be. The secret is to remember that the activities that you spend time on are the controllable factor. Set the goals in specific terms with something like a six month or one year horizon. Take out your chart at some intermediate point to monitor your resolve and progress.

For background reading, see *The Third Force* by Frank Goble on Maslow's work, particularly Chapter 3, "The Study of Self-Actualization."

Basic Model	Ideal Model	Crisis Model

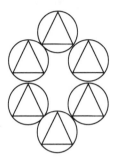 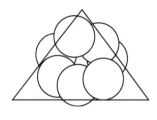 

◯ Life Areas

△ Maslow's Hierarchy
(from safety and
security to self-
actualization)

High level of functioning
Optimal performance
Compact Lifestyle
Synergy
Balanced levels of functioning

Imbalanced levels of
functioning
Dispersed Lifestyle
Frustration level
Struggling performance
Duplication of efforts

Used with permission of the Wonderlin Company, Louisville, KY.

SELECTED BIBLIOGRAPHY & SUGGESTED READING LIST

American Heritage Dictionary, Second College Edition. Houghton Mifflin Company. 1982.

Anonymous. *The Guy in the Glass*.

Ambrose, Stephen. *Citizen Soldier.* Touchstone Books. 1998.

Aristotle. *Nichomachean Ethics*. Oxford University Press. 1998.

Bellah, Robert and Richard Madsen, William Sullivan, Ann Swidler, Steven Tipton. *Habits of the Heart—Individualism and Commitment in American Life*. University of California Press. 1985.

Bellah, Robert and Richard Madsen, William Sullivan, Ann Swidler, Steven Tipton. *The Good Society*. First Vintage Books. 1992.

Baillie, John. "The Evening Reflection." *A Diary of Private Prayer*. MacMillian Publishing Company. 1984.

Bennett, William. *The Book of Virtues: A Treasury of Moral Stories*. Simon & Schuster. 1993.

Bennett, William. *The Index of Leading Cultural Indicators: American Society at the End of the 20th Century*. Broadway Books. 1999.

Bennett, William. *The Moral Compass: Stories for a Life's Journey*. Simon & Schuster. 1995.

Bennis, Warren. *Why Leaders Can't Lead: The Unconscious Conspiracy Continues*. Jossey-Bass. 1989.

Benson, Peter. *All Kids Are Our Kids*. Jossey-Bass. 1997.

Brokaw, Tom. *The Greatest Generation*. Random House. 1998.

Brokaw, Tom. *The Greatest Generation Speaks*. Random House. 1999.

Campbell, Joseph. *The Masks of God: Creative Mythology*. Arkana. 1995.

Campbell, Joseph. *The Masks of God:Primitive Mythology*. Arkana. 1991.

Cather, Willa. *O Pioneers*. Signet. 1989.

Chancellor, John. *Peril and Promise: A Commentary on America*. HarperPerennial. 1991.

Colson, John. *The Aspen Times*. 2000.

Covey, Stephen. *The Seven Habits of Highly Effective People*. Fireside. 1989.

Davis, Burke. *Black Heroes of the American Revolution*. Odyssey Books. 1913.

Day, Dorothy. *Why I Am Still a Catholic*. Riverhead.

Dinwiddie-Boyd, Elza. *In Our Own Words: A Treasury of Quotations from the African-American Community*. Avon Books. 1996.

Ehringer, Dr. Ann. *Make Up Your Mind—Entrepreneurs Talk about Decision-Making*. Merritt Publishing. 1995.

Catholic Church Encyclical. *Gaudium et Spes*.

Goodwin, Doris Kearns. *No Ordinary Times—Franklin and Eleanor Roosevelt: The Home Front in World War II*. Simon & Schuster. 1994.

Gray, Mike. *Drug Crazy—How We Got into This Mess & How We Can Get Out*. Random House. 1998.

Harrison, Lawrence E. *Who Prospers?—How Cultural Values Shape Economic and Political Success*. Basic Books. 1992.

Haynes, Charles and Thomas, Oliver. *Finding Common Ground—A First Amendment Guide to Religion and Public Education*. First Amendment Center. Third Edition. 1998.

Himmelfarb, Gertrude. "Re-moralizing America." *The Wall Street Journal*. Excerpted from *The De-Moralization of Society*. Vintage Books. 1996.

Inhabitants of Flushing. *The Flushing (Quaker) Remonstrance*.

Keyes, Alan. *Our Character, Our Future—Reclaiming America's Moral Destiny*. Zondervan Publishing House. 1996.

Kipling, Rudyard. *If*.

Lasch, Christopher. *The Revolt of the Elites and the Betrayal of Democracy*. W.W. Norton & Company. 1995.

Loomans, Diane. "If I Had My Child to Raise All Over Again." *Full Esteem Ahead: 100 Ways to Build Self-Esteem in Children*. HJ Kramer. 1994.

Massey, Morris. *What You Are Is Where You Were When*. Nightingale-Conant Corporation. 1987.

Merton, Thomas. *The Seven Story Mountain*. Harcourt Brace. 1948.

Liberman, Robert and Larry W. King, William DeRisi, Michael McCann. *Personal Effectiveness*. Research Press. 1975.

Pieper, Josef. *Leisure as a Basis of Culture*. St. Augustine Press. 1948.

Pieper, Josef. *Only the Lover Sings: Art and Contemplation*. Ignatius Press. 1990.

Powell, Baden. *The Scout's Oath*.

Putnam, Robert. *Bowling Alone—The Collapse and Revival of American Community*. Simon & Schuster. 2000.

Putnam, Robert. *Making Democracy Work—Civic Traditions in Modern Italy*. Princton University Press. 1992.

Reagan, Ronald. "Farewell Address."

Roosevelt, Franklin D. "1941 Inaugural Address."

Shawcross, William. *Deliver Us From Evil—Peacekeepers, Warlords, and a World of Endless Conflict*. Simon & Schuster. 2000.

Steinberg, Lawrence. *Outside the Classroom*. Touchstone. 1996.

The Freedom Writers, Erin Gruwell. *The Freedom Writers Diary: How Teachers and 150 Teens Used Writing to Change Themselves and the World Around Them*. Main Street Publishers. 1999.

"The Twenty-Third Psalm". *The Holy Bible*. King James Version.

Tocqueville, Alexis de. *Democracy in America*. Translation by Mansfield, Harvey and Winthrop, Delba. University of Chicago Press. 2000.

Trelease, Jim. *The Read-Aloud Handbook*. Fourth Edition. Penguin Books. 1995.

Wheatley, Phillis and Merle Richmond. *American Women of Achievement*. Chelsey House Publishers. 1988.

Wooden, John and Steve Jamison. *A Lifetime of Observations On and Off the Court*. Contemporary Books. 1997.

OUR CONTRIBUTORS

Steven Alldredge

In compiling this book I have used the dedicated editorial skills of Steven All-dredge. Steven lives down the road from me in Colorado and works full-time as a writer, editor, and screenwriter. He has been greatly influenced in his life by a mother who had a tremendous joy for books and reading and by a grand-father whose values and "love of a good story" were inspiring role models.

Father Jack Barker

Father Jack Barker is our pastor at St. Francis of Assisi in La Quinta, Califor-nia. I volunteered to help with a capital campaign, and, after working with him for the past three years, he has become a wonderful friend. A graduate of UCLA, he worked as a rocket scientist before the call to the Episcopal priest-hood. He later was moved to become a Catholic. Father Barker has served on the diocesan staff, has served as the head of Catholic Charities in the dioceses, and most recently, as pastor and vicar. The life of a pastor in a large parish is an unbelievably demanding, time-consuming, multifaceted job. It provides very little time to indulge his interest in golf or the refining of his talents as a con-cert pianist. Like the other clergy in this book, he is a wonderful shepherd.

Father del Barrio

Joan and I had been in Africa on safari in the bush for three weeks and were happy to be back in civilization at the hotel in Victoria Falls. Arriving on a Saturday evening, we called down to the desk to find out when masses were held, and we were told there was an evening mass in forty-five minutes. Imag-ine our surprise when thirty minutes later we were told that the priest was there to pick us up! We found a delightful, gray-haired gentleman in the dri-ver's seat and a beautiful, young, black child in the passenger seat. The chapel was not much larger than a two-car garage with small plain windows. We were joined by 8–10 other worshipers and listened to Father del Barrio's simple, meaningful sermon. After dinner, we talked about Father's parish and the life of a missionary in central Africa. We hear from him a couple times a year and are fascinated how he ministers to such a huge territory with minimal resources. Our small contribution seems like a drop in the bucket, but we know he gets maximum mileage out of every dollar. His story of the path to his priesthood is most inspiring. We hope he will keep his health and be able to enjoy a peaceful retirement.

Cathy Buscher

Cathy and her husband, Herb, are one of the first couples we met when we moved to the Aspen/Snowmass area. Both towns are really small, and, through church activities, you get to meet wonderful people very quickly. When we needed to raise funds to redo the classrooms and kitchen of the church, we needed to find people with experience and the inclination to help. As Cathy describes in her piece, the training to public service should come early, and, once acquired, it provides a marvelous source of lifetime satisfaction. As described so well in *Habits of the Heart*, community awareness and community service are the foundations of our society. My children have begun the process of teaching their children the need for serving others, and Cathy's words are great reinforcements to all of us.

Art Cerre

I first met Art at St. Mary's Church in Aspen working on the St. Patrick's Day dinner. One of the oldest traditions on the western slope of Colorado, this event brings out some of the best characteristics in our church members. Lots of preparation and work goes into feeding 750 people in 2–3 hours: food preparation, greeting visitors, waiting tables, washing dishes, and cleaning up. Art was there early peeling potatoes and was there at the final hour cleaning up. Art and I share a history of heart difficulties, and we are both regular participants in the cardio-rehabilitation program at Aspen Valley Hospital. With his warm smile and firm handshake, Art's skills as an advertising executive are readily apparent. Radiating charm, warmth, and sincere concern, there are few people with the talent of Art if you need someone to lead a public relations effort. I am most grateful for the poem he created for this book.

Evie and Wayne Connell

My wife and I met Evie and Wayne at St. Francis Church in La Quinta, California. Wayne is active in many church activities. He chaired the Parish Council and leads a bible study faith group. He has been the executive director of Martha's Kitchen—a nonprofit organization for the homeless. It is one of the most heartwarming and successful programs in the Coachella Valley. Wayne was born and raised in a small farming community in West Texas, where his parents and the community were strong influences in shaping his character.

After college, he joined the Navy and began a twenty-one-year career as a carrier-based fighter pilot. Like many veterans of that war, his experiences in Vietnam had a profound effect on his life. After his military service, Wayne tried a brief fling in the world of small business but found "the bottom line" did not provide the satisfactions he was seeking. He turned to education, a field that was traditional in his family, and found himself in a comfortable and satisfying career. He moved from teaching to administration, in both private and public schools, and ended this phase of his life as principal of a large high school. His academic credentials include a BS., MS., MA. and Ed.D. When I use the word retirement for Wayne, it should be in quotes, as his life now includes teaching at a university level and teaching in his church. Wayne personifies the advice I received from my dad years ago—if you want a job done well, find a busy man (or woman) to do it! His beautiful wife Evie is an equally talented companion.

Dr. Larry Dorr

It is a great pleasure to have such a skilled and famous surgeon as Dr. Dorr for a friend. In 1986, the cartilage in my hips was badly worn, and I was walking with a noticeable limp. During one particular round of golf, the painkillers were not enough—the pain so bad I could not bend over to put a golf tee in the ground. I followed my friend Warren Lien's example and went to see Dr. Dorr to learn about hip replacement. On my birthday, March 11, 1986, Dr. Dorr replaced both hips. After surgery, by following his rehabilitation directions to the letter, a new, wonderful, pain-free life began. With new hips, skiing and golf were once again great pleasures. Over the years, he has replaced the hip components as wear-and-tear, and my clumsiness, caused casualties. Later, when Dr. Dorr decided to put together a business advisory group to deal with the changes wrought by Medicare and PPO's, I joined a group of grateful patients on a business advisory board to bring business skills to the world-class team of medical professionals assembled by Dr. Dorr. Like many talented men, Larry has an equally talented wife, Marilyn, who makes his productive career possible.

Melody and Bob Durham

Some people are born to be nurses, and Melody is such a woman. She shows concern and competence, warmth, and vitality. I met Melody after my 1996 heart attack, when I entered Aspen Valley Hospital's rehabilitation program. On Monday, Wednesday, and Friday mornings, my day begins with a trek into the hospital to engage in the exercise I should have been getting every week of my life. Unfortunately, in my middle years, I let job and ambition usurp my time spent on physical exercise. Melody serves as my conscience, my "Jiminy

Cricket"—a voice telling me to exercise more, eat less, and nurture my spirit. She and her husband, Bob, are great examples and mentors. They are marvelous examples of the totally balanced life, grounded in their Christian faith. Melody supervises the professional development of the nursing staff and the rehab center. Bob is a practicing therapist who has helped us organize a discussion group on the problems of heart patients. Bob emphasizes the importance of a spiritual dimension to the whole healing process, and his message has been an important help to me.

Dr. Ann Ehringer

Ann is one of the most delightful ladies I have ever met: beautiful, charming, and blessed with an engaging mind. She brings spirit and energy to all her activities. We became acquainted when I joined The Executive Committee, an organization to develop the skills of entrepreneurs in running their businesses and organizing their personal lives. For the membership fee, each member meets with a group of fellow entrepreneurs for one day each month and a half-day of one-on-one discussion with a TEC adviser. Ann was my adviser. She brought a wonderful inquiring mind and a means of communicating, both of which were helpful and challenging. Ann's business experiences, insights, and suggestions are always comprehensive. She became one of our first recruits when we put together an advisory board for my company, Brice Manufacturing. With Ann's help and Brice's management team, we developed a successful plan for Brice's future, as well as an exit strategy which enables Joan and me to enjoy a most pleasurable life in retirement. Ann describes her life as "luxurious". The freedom my wife and I have to pursue the desires of our hearts is likewise luxurious. Ann Ehringer has my thanks for her contributions to our life and for the thoughtful words she has written for this book.

Al and Colleen Fedders

Al and Colleen are new friends in California. Al is a retired executive who owned an agricultural chemical business in the Stockton area of central California. His wife, Colleen, is a fellow parishioner at our church, St. Francis of Assisi. An ardent, hearty fisherman and golfer, Al found the Murray quotation and felt it was his best contribution to the book.

Dick Fullerton

Dr. Richard Fullerton is my brother-in-law. He was married to Joan's sister Alean for ten years before she died. Dick and I were both only sons, so it was our first experience in a brother relationship, and it has been a lot of fun. In his early 70s, Dick looks as if he weighs the same as he did when he was discharged from the Navy 44 years ago. He enjoys golf, skiing, and running four miles several times a week. Like many veterans of WW II, Dick is reluctant to speak of his wartime experiences. With a busy obstetrics-gynecology practice, Dick has delivered thousands of children to countless mothers in the Rochester area. He has served on the staff of Strong Memorial Hospital, where his skills as a surgeon have aided many women to lead more healthy lives. His skills as a teacher and mentor have aided the many future doctors in his charge. Dick's contribution here reflects the discipline and sense of duty and purpose he and his peers bring to their vocation.

Father Michael Glenn

Father was the pastor at St. Mary's in Aspen and is now the rector of the seminary for the diocese in Denver. He came to Aspen after serving as secretary to Archbishop Stafford in Denver and as director of vocations for the diocese. Changeovers at a parish are always an interesting time. Each priest brings his own enthusiasms, personality, and goals to the job. My wife and I have enjoyed Father Glenn's interest in the parish youth programs and the new slants he brings to his sermons.

Bill Goodwin

For fifteen years, we built Brice Manufacturing from a small subcontract manufacturer of parts for airplane seat companies to a significant factor in the overhaul of commercial aircraft interiors. Many people contributed to that growth, but Bill Goodwin was one of the most important. A graduate of the Naval Academy and a Marine, Bill served three tours of duty in Vietnam, then retired to civilian life. He worked at two other companies before coming to Brice as our director of manufacturing. The virtues of loyalty, dedication, and his ability to lead by example were critical factors in our success. His wife, Anna, also sought to achieve a high level of responsibility in her career. They set a wonderful example for their two daughters who have now embarked on their careers: one in the administration of funds for the protection of the environment and the other as a naval officer. Although the virtues of courage, loyalty, and dedication are more appreciated in times of war than in times of peace, they are still fundamental guideposts for achieving success, whether you are in business or some other career. In writing this book, I realized that certain people embody the discipline and character of the organizations to which they belong. Bill Goodwin is such a man.

Ruth and Buddy Greenbaum

Ruth and Buddy are the parents of my business partner at Brice Manufacturing, Bruce Greenbaum. Buddy had a very successful career in the textile manufacturing field, while Ruth mentored three talented children. Bruce, the oldest, was my daughter Karen's classmate at the business school at the University of North Carolina. With Bruce and I both interested in being entrepreneurs, we soon had a working partnership. Bruce was the critical hire in Brice's history. He rose from sales manager to president and helped drive the company from a small local vendor to a world leader in our business field. My relationship with Bruce extended well beyond business. Outside of my wife, he became my closest confidant. Where my leadership style had been authoritative, he taught me the value of participatory decision making, and our relationship became one of equal partners, sharing the tough decisions. I was the beneficiary of the great values Ruth and Buddy implanted in Bruce. He is one of the brightest, most energetic men I've ever met, and I am honored to be the godfather of his youngest son, Cody. It seems difficult for some people to understand how two men, separated by 20 years, different faiths, and different motivations, worked together so long and so successfully. I give great credit to the parenting of Ruth and Buddy Greenbaum. As they say in their story, the mark of successful parenting is the product produced. Given the way their son Bruce turned out, I would say they were very successful.

Robert Grochau

Bob was one of an outstanding group of students that had joined the fraternity two years before me at the University of Rochester. As a group, they possessed strong leadership skills, were serious students, and participated in a wide variety of campus activities. They became wonderful mentors in helping us adjust to college life. Bob was from Minnesota and brought all the open, cheerful characteristics I had associated with mid-westerners. He also had the diction and speaking talents that foretold his future as a clergyman. Bob found his calling as a Lutheran minister. He has served his flocks in Delaware (ten years), Maryland (eleven years) and California (nineteen years) for a total of forty years. The last ten years were served in Monterey, California (1985–1995), as pastor of St. Timothy Lutheran. We have shared the reconciliation conferences between Catholics and Lutherans. As a convert to Catholicism, I have always carried a yearning for ecumenical activities, a sadness over the divisions in Christianity. Bob and I share the interest and passion for the biblical studies that go back to the historical roots of our beliefs. And, we are thankful that the doctrinal differences seem to grow smaller with time. As we watched President Clinton struggle with the consequences of his behavior, it was an interesting coincidence that we both recalled the words we had memorized as Boy Scouts, "On my honor, I will do my best to do my duty to God and my country, to help other people at all times and obey the Scout's Law."

Bill and Ann Guiffre

Bill and Ann Guiffre are friends from college. My wife Joan met Ann forty-five years go during their first week of school. They were constant companions, sharing studies, gossip, and all the other things young women share in college. Bill and I were in the NROTC together and then went to Norfolk for our first duty station. Bill went on to a very successful career in education and was the principal of the high school in Victor, New York, before he retired. The Catholic faith has been the center of Bill and Ann's life, and like Joan and me, they had a large family. We have followed the growth of their children and shared their lovely lakeside home in the Adirondack Mountains for vacations. In his retirement, Bill has become an author, writing children's books and poetry.

Phil Hart

Phil and I shared the struggles and joys of managing small companies together for a period of approximately 10 years. The organization that provided this opportunity is called TEC—The Executive Committee. Groups of 10–12 managers meet once per month and share their problems and solutions. The topics include information applicable to both business and personal lives. Like the team spirit that evolves from competing together athletically, the TEC groups form bonds of friendship and support that are quite meaningful and enduring. Even though geographic distance separates us, the problem solving, the sympathy, the struggles met and resolved, form a true bond of friendship. It is particularly rewarding when a friend finds peace, contentment, and fulfillment in life. Phil's thoughts for the book were a welcome gift. His ability to share both pleasure and pain is a great gift.

Dick Hartl

I met Dick Hartl at General Electric in Pittsfield, Massachusetts, in 1973. Dick was managing the phenolics plastic business and was, like me, an import from a big chemical company: Dick from Monsanto; me from DuPont. He went out of his way to help me get comfortable in the GE environment and in the process became a friend. When our company, Brice Manufacturing, grew to the point where we could benefit from the guidance of an advisory board, Dick was one of the first recruits. At the time, he was guiding a major technology company and was of tremendous value in keeping our small company on the correct path. Dick's character and intelligence have made him an especially valued friend, and I welcome his contribution to this book. In his piece, Dick's point about humility reminds me of the Easter ritual of the priest washing the feet of his parishioners. Bill Guiffre, a school principal, noted how Dick's ideas on business leadership equally apply to a public school.

Father Jack Hedges

At the start of my senior year at Rochester, Joan and I met and fell in love. When we discussed marriage, I felt I had to accept her ideas on raising children and what it meant to marry a Catholic woman. She had firmly grounded views, while mine were not very definite. For the next year, I sought out the council of the Protestant chaplain on campus, as well as the Catholic Chaplain—Father Hedges. I could not have found a more sensitive and caring spiritual guide. He made it clear I did not have to do, or accept, anything with any sense of compunction. He asked questions to understand what my Protestant upbringing had implanted in the way of belief. And, through patient listening, he pinpointed the questions that bothered me. He suggested various readings and then would discuss the issues with me. I questioned him about papal infallibility, the Inquisition, the errant popes, and birth control. Jack explained the church's views on these subjects and left it to me to consider where I stood. Looking back over the years, the writings of St. Thomas Aquinas, Cardinal Newman, and Martin Luther provided new insight. But most of all, the inner light that Father Jack possesses, the ability to be truly present to those in his care, was a marvelous example to me.

Bonnie Hirschhorn

As a high school guidance counselor in a big city school, Bonnie performs a vital function in our society: she serves as a conduit between parents, faculty, and students. Part Mother Superior, part warm friend, part gentle prodder, and sometime voice of authority, she helps young boys and girls with the struggles of their everyday lives and helps them become young men and woman. As Dr. Dorr writes in his contribution, having a sincere concern for people is a wonderful asset and makes Bonnie very effective in her job. She offered me the chance to speak to the students at John Bowne High School, and those visits have become one of the highlights of my retirement. Bonnie arranges for me to meet with the young leaders of the school and discuss their dreams, ambitions, and perceived obstacles. Each time, I come away with a renewed sense of energy and purpose, feeling new hope for the future in the bright young people at the school. Bonnie's two sons are a great source of pride and satisfaction to her, fulfilling the lessons Bonnie learned from her parents.

Morris Hollenbaugh

Morry is a retired Episcopal minister from Cincinnati, Ohio. I met him at the Aspen Men's Bible reading group. Each Tuesday morning, an interfaith group meets to read scripture and pray together. We have a quick breakfast and an hour of study and dialogue. It's an opportunity to hear how different individuals hear and interpret sacred scripture.

Don Huntsman

Don Huntsman began his career as a dentist. He dabbled in various art forms as a hobby, but it was soon obvious that his love and talents were in the field of sculpture. Joan and I met Don when we bought our house in Snowmass. We had planned to have a western/mountain theme in the house, and we loved all the paintings and sculptures in Don's gallery. We bought a few paintings and loved to browse the gallery and observe Don as he sculpted new works. When I retired, Joan surprised me with an original piece. She commissioned Don to sculpt a statue of Jedediah Smith, one of my favorite Western explorers. At my retirement party, Joan was the last speaker and when she brought out the piece Don had created, I was ecstatic. I got to know Don better after that, and we have filled our homes with art from his gallery. The sculpture on the cover of this book is titled *Apron Strings*. It was created by Don Huntsman for Joan on the occasion of our fortieth wedding anniversary.

Apron Strings captured the goal I had wanted when I commissioned Don to create the sculpture: a hard working woman who might have been a counterpart to Jedediah. The inspiration to add the young boy was all Don's. In the statue, I see all the fatigue, the effort, the love, and attention it takes to raise a child. And in the child, I see all the safety and support that a loving mother provides. The statue reminds me of all the years Joan spent in caring for our children and, as described by Ann Ehringer in Chapter One, a part of living a luxurious life.

Sister Elaine Kolesnick

One of the wonderful benefits of putting this book together has been the renewal of old, old friendships. Sister Elaine is just as bright, enthusiastic, warm, and concerned as she was as a fresh young teacher fifty years ago. Sister Elaine was my high school English teacher at Penfield High School. Fresh out of Nazareth College, she brought a freshness and a loving concern, which radiated in all her responses to those eager young teenage minds. Her talent for coaching was most evident in class and in advising our junior and senior class plays. In looking back, I must have been an obstreperous disruption in her efforts to lead us through the literature, grammar, drama, and nuances of the English language. We met again at the Penfield High 45th reunion of the class of 1950. When I sought out Father Hedges, I found he had retired to the Sisters of Mercy Motherhouse. To my great delight, I found Sister Elaine was also at the reunion. She was most helpful in assisting Father Hedges in preparing his contribution to this book. Last year, we celebrated our 50th high school reunion, and Sister Elaine was there. She personifies all the advantages and blessings of the spiritual life.

Governor Richard Lamm

I am a died-in-the-wool Republican, thus it might be somewhat of a surprise that one of the most-admired public figures I know is a Democrat. And I would describe him not as a politician, but as a statesman. He was an extremely popular and progressive Governor of Colorado. Now, he is a scholar/spokesman for the Institute for Public Policy at the University of Denver where he has written and articulated solutions for a wide array of essential issues and challenges facing our society. His national work in the areas of health care and education has brought him national renown. We met at Summit '92, when he served as our capstone speaker. During the conference, Joan and I had the pleasure of sharing dinner with the Governor and his wonderful wife Dottie. After Summit '92 and our dinner conversation, the idea for this book began to take shape. Apart from the inspiration he provided to this book, his identification and analysis of major societal issues is a mark of his continuing public service. Like President Carter, Governor Lamm continues to serve the public after his elected service is over. I read, and reread, how modern information technology can classify, organize, and categorize the most detailed feelings and preferences of the electorate. We are approaching government by real time polling. It is a refreshing contrast to have a leader who seeks first to understand major public issues, seeks out possible solutions, then courageously articulates them regardless of the resistance and political consequences. I admire his courage and leadership and am grateful for his insights on health, education, and community.

Warren Lien

Warren is a neighbor and friend from Chatsworth, California, where our children grew up together. Warren and his wife, Gabriel, are ardent UCLA fans, and we've shared twenty years of Bruin victories and defeats. We have golfed, worshipped, traveled, and worked on volunteer projects together. Warren has managed a successful manufacturing business for over thirty years. Like Robert Matt, he is an example of reverence, humor, and generosity.

John Lutz

John and I go back 44 years to 1957 when I began work in the Technical Services Laboratory of DuPont's Plastics Division. As a young trainee, I was taught how to design, tool, and manufacture parts by the injection molding process, and John was part of the "Delrin" task force charged with developing new applications and markets for this new plastic. Along with nylon, this was one of the first materials specifically targeted as a replacement for zinc, brass, and aluminum. John mentored me in the business of market and applications development, and he gladly took my money on the golf course. Over time, he became a close friend. John coped with a seriously ill wife and is the first single parent I encountered. When his daughter Sherri went off to college, John offered the "no-nonsense" guidance included in his contribution.

Jack MacAllister

My wife and I met Jack through our friend Dick Lee who lives in Castle Pines, Colorado. Known widely in the business community as an effective, personable leader, Jack retired from US West where he had served as chief executive officer. He had grown up in the Bell System and was selected to head the US West unit when the government decided to break up the Bell System. We went to Valdorama, Spain, together to see the Ryder Cup golf match, and he was a great traveling companion. We cheered loudly for the American team, but unfortunately our guys were not up to the challenge. I was pleased when Jack found time to contribute to this book. Like many of the individuals I have known who have ascended to the top of their companies, Jack's character was formed and nurtured in his early years by loving and thoughtful parents.

Joseph Mack

Joe is one of those likable, creative people who generate enthusiasm and success in every activity they undertake. I met Joe when I was rushing chairman for our fraternity, and he was one of the most sought after pledges on campus. His leadership skills were a great asset to both our fraternity and the school. He was a liberal arts major who studied English and became involved in a myriad of campus activities. In reviewing the freshman bible from Joe's years in school, it is no surprise he became a great success in business. While gaining academic honors, he served as director of the student drama group, worked on the campus newspaper, chaired the freshman week committee, as well as being involved in other student activities. After a stint in the U.S. Navy, including a year of teaching English at the Naval Academy, he returned to civilian life. He began a celebrated career in advertising on Madison Avenue that culminated in his position as the chief operating officer of the world's largest advertising agency, Saatchi and Saatchi. Joe has served as a trustee at the University of Rochester for the past ten years and was chosen by the school's president to head the 150th anniversary celebration. With his success in business and his tireless commitment to charitable causes, Joe is a modern Renaissance man, and I greatly welcomed his contribution to the book.

Father Roddy MacNamara

Every parish changes somewhat when a new pastor comes on the scene. Father Roddy MacNamara came into our lives when he became pastor of St. John Eudes, our California parish. The Irish, it seems, are blessed with a marvelous ability to project both joy and reverence. Father Roddy's sermons became a new source of inspiration and pleasure, and our parish lit up with his smiling, optimistic countenance. When the Northridge earthquake severely damaged the church structure, Father faced the challenge of rebuilding for the next century, as well as keeping the parish running day-to-day. Many of our friends were asked to assist Father Roddy in the design, fund-raising, and construction of the new sanctuary and support buildings. The new church, the vitality of the laity, the liturgical celebration, and the variety and dynamism of the parish stewardship programs are a tribute to our friend. In my forty-five years as a Catholic, I have found that the success of the pastor in involving all of his flock is a great blessing. Father Roddy has been a very successful pastor at St. John Eudes.

In discussing this book, we talked about the meaning of the word "pastor," or shepherd. In one way, I object to being thought of as a sheep because sheep don't think or make decisions. But the older I become, the more my focus shifts from the sheep to the shepherd, the more my thoughts focus on the relationship of the sheep to the shepherd. I now understand the thought of a loving God and of how he might regard me, in terms of how the shepherd cares for his flock. Both pastors and shepherds have charges that are their greatest concern, and both would lay down their lives to protect them. So I've come to regard my pastor as my human shepherd, the instrument of my God. I am a convert to Catholicism.

When I was growing up, my family did not have a warm, close relationship with our clergyman. Maybe that is why Joan and I have made a special effort to be close to our pastor—to welcome him into our home and enjoy his blessing and guidance. So I share with my children, and with other readers, my recipe for a successful spiritual family life: bring your pastor into your home and your family, and you will be unable to count all the blessings that accrue.

Robert Matt

My friendship with Bob Matt began in Aspen when he came to assist St. Mary's Church with our capital campaign to renovate the 100-year-old church. He travels to Aspen frequently as a fellow of the Aspen Institute. Besides his two-year stint in the Peace Corp in Poland teaching entrepreneurial skills and capitalism to former communists, Bob travels around this country offering his advice and experiences to churches, dioceses, and schools which face major fund raising efforts. Our pastor, Father Larry Solan, planned three presentations on consecutive Sundays to explain our financial needs. It was Bob's task to develop the concept of stewardship, and his talk had a very profound effect on me. I realized that too many of the actions and decisions of my life had been grounded by a materialistic perspective rather than a Christian perspective. His talk caused me to rethink my own life and to look at things in a new light. I asked Bob if I might use that talk in this book. His life, as a living profession of his beliefs, serves as a marvelous example. Bob Matt is one of those rare individuals who "walks the walk."

Dick Mau

While planning for Summit '92, a conference on the competitiveness of U.S. companies in global markets, I met Dick through his son, Chris—a student at The Anderson School of Business at UCLA. There was a great deal of organizational and administrative work that went into planning a national conference, so I had asked Al Osbourne, Dean of the School, to recommend a student who might be interested in the subject of global competitiveness. Chris was able to work two days per week and helped me put the program together, make contacts, and sort ideas for the agenda. He had good organizational skills, a lot of imagination, and the ability to think broadly. He was a wonderful young man. Dick, Vice President of Public Affairs for Rockwell International, provided help and direction in shaping our public relations activities for the conference. Dick's understanding of public policy and the societal impact of various programs have been very helpful to me. Before we retired, we shared our thinking on school reform and how public education might be improved. Even in retirement, Dick maintains an active interest in public affairs and participates in various charitable groups. We share the wonderful weather of summers in Aspen and the pleasures of the golf course.

John J. (Jack) McKearin

In the middle 1960s, Jack and I met as salesmen assigned to the Philadelphia district of DuPont's Plastics Division. Jack's experience had been in several field assignments and in advertising, areas in which I had no experience, while I had come from tech service and marketing, areas where I could help Jack. We became close friends. Jack is the classic optimist, a friendly extrovert who achieved great success in sales because he knew how to gain insight into the customer's perspective. When Jack retired from DuPont in the late 1980s, he joined me at Brice Manufacturing the next week, where he helped build our sales of seat parts to airlines headquartered in the East. Jack and his wife Pauline had seven children, including a set of twins, so our affinity for large families became a source of friendship and commiseration. My wife, Joan, and Pauline shared their experiences of rearing a family with business husbands who were often on the road. Our families share an interest in skiing, and we play golf together. The best way to describe Jack is a straight arrow. In my opinion, his rendition of *The Music Man* is second only to Robert Preston's performance, and at 70, Jack's voice and enthusiasm remain undiminished.

Bruce Moses

Bruce was a college fraternity brother of mine at the University of Rochester. He came from Oak Park, Illinois, and was a talented football player, as well as an active member of the fraternity. He chose a career in sales and rose to be president and chief executive officer of UARCO, a large Chicago business forms company. We renewed our friendship while participating in University of Rochester alumni activities. Bruce bought a home near us in Palm Desert, California, and he and his wife, Betty Jean, are also neighbors in Snowmass, Colorado.

Robert "Pink" Parker

Robert "Pink" Parker is a fellow graduate of the University of Rochester. He practiced dentistry for over thirty-five years and now has time to indulge his passion for golf and skiing. We share the joy of large families, sports, and reminiscing about times past.

Ron Piekunka

Like myself, Ron attended school in Rochester, New York, and he is also a fellow engineer and entrepreneur. He graduated from Aquinas High School in Rochester and Rensselaer Polytechnic Institute. Ron began his career with W.R. Grace and became an expert in the materials and equipment used to manufacture wire, cable, and fiber optics. He developed a wonderful business as a manufacturer's representative and achieved notable success. Ron is a great example of self-discipline: he keeps his body fit, manages his time well (as he says he knows "how to juggle"), and has traveled the world with his wife, Jeannie, for business and pleasure. Ron's message, like his life, is based upon a simple plan, marvelously executed.

Pat and Bob Place

Bob and I began competing against each other in high school, and we were teammates in college. Bob's story about learning to do something well while young is based, in part, on his experience as a skilled basketball player. He was one of the best shooters in the history of the University of Rochester and was second in the country in free throw accuracy. Bob and I were both NROTC students and officers at Little Creek, Virginia. Our wives worked together at the Social Services Bureau while Bob and I learned the life of an amphibious sailor. After the Navy, he joined Lincoln Rochester Bank in Rochester and after moving through a series of operational assignments he headed the bank's development of a credit card program. On our trips to Rochester, the Places have been cordial hosts. They are truly wonderful friends. Pat's civic awareness and enthusiastic bent for volunteer work has benefited the Junior League, the Pittsford Historical Society, and the Chatterbox Club.

Bob and Theda Pile

From early childhood, almost everybody can relate the story of the "good Samaritan." Joan and I met two modern versions in the tiny town of Fridens, Pennsylvania, which is just off the Somerset exit of the Pennsylvania Turnpike. The blizzard of 1966 had closed the turnpike from one end to the other, and some of the local townspeople pitched in to help out with the stranded travelers. Bob and Theda Pile were total strangers. They not only took us in off that highway, they put us up for three days until the roads were cleared. We became close friends and visited back and forth as our families grew up. And even though we moved west, and a continent separated us from our old friends such as the Piles, we've managed to continue our visits in each others' homes. The Piles' three children are a tribute to their parents' outstanding examples of hard work, strong love, and the ability to avert the traps of materialism. Their son Jim is a minister in the San Fernando Valley, and their daughters, Barbara and Linda, have followed the model of their mother in providing stable homes and love for their children.

Jim Pritts

I met Jim Pritts when he was a senior in high school. Bob Pile asked me to watch Jim play basketball, and I discovered a good athlete and a promising scholar. Bob and I counseled Jim on future academic and career opportunities and were pleased when he attended the University of Rochester. He not only played varsity, but also followed my path into the field of optics. He was a very fine student, and after completing his undergraduate studies, he received an MBA from the Simon School. Jim has had a wonderful career at Bausch and Lomb Optical company, serving as the marketing manager for Rayban sunglasses and as executive vice president of Revo. Jim was one of the first young men from whom I learned a bit about mentoring, and it is great to see the bountiful life he has developed for himself and his family. He and his wife Pat are blessed with a beautiful daughter who is the light of their life.

Don Puente

We met through the men's club at St. Francis Church. Don and his wife, Miki, had just moved into the parish, and my wife and I were among the greeters to welcome them and explore their interests. Don had just retired from a successful career as vice-president of Newhall Land Company and was expanding his charitable work. His experience in putting together fund-raising golf tournaments was a talent that we recruited immediately. Through working together and the sharing of our beliefs, our families have become good friends. Along with Evie and Wayne Connell, we hope to support the wonderful work Don is doing with The Martha's Village and Kitchen in nearby Indio, California.

Carol Quinn

Carol is a college friend of my wife's, and along with Anne Guiffre, one of the women described in Terri Ross's piece *Friendship*. Her husband, Mike, died early, so Carol has lived the life of a single parent, while building her career as a talented elementary school teacher. In addition to heading her local chapter of the teacher's union, she has been recognized in the roster of distinguished educators by being included in the 1998 edition of *Who's Who Among America's Teachers.* Her contributions to this book provide insight into the imaginations of five to eight year old children and show us the joys of parenting and teaching.

Terri Ross

Terri Ross is one of my wife's best friends, and as a consequence, one of mine. Their friendship began the first week in college and has continued unabated through our lifetime. Terri was a very good student and took part in a number of campus activities. It is no surprise she has given back so strongly to civic activities in Rochester, New York. Terri's success in her career in real estate is notable enough to be included in this book, but instead we have included her writing on the value of friendships. It details Terri's own warm friendship with her lifelong friends, and her contribution nicely illustrates a wise, old axiom— "To have a friend, be one."

James D. Ryan

I'm not sure exactly when Jim and I first met. I think it was on the basketball court behind the grammar school at the Four Corners in Brighton, N.Y. Jim went on to Hamilton College, while I went to the University of Rochester. We were both guards, so we competed against each other in basketball all through college. Jim's wife, Joan, had been a classmate of my sister-in-law Alean at Nazareth High School. Over the years, I occasionally saw Jim when we returned to Rochester, and our home in ski country has provided an opportunity to renew our friendship when Jim, his family, and friends come to Aspen to ski. Jim has belonged to a group in Rochester called the Philosophers and had been recording his thinking about the same time I began putting this book together. His views, written four years after those of Governor Lamm, provide additional insight on our problems and offer potential solutions.

Jay Thompson

As with many of our contributors, Jay had the blessing of growing up in a small, close-knit town, which created a foundation that has lasted a lifetime. Jay was a classmate of mine at Penfield High School near Rochester, New York. When I transferred from East High School in the middle of my sophomore year, Jay was one of the first to welcome me to town. After high school and college, he stayed in the Rochester area and spent his career teaching elementary school. Over the years, we have seen each other infrequently, mostly at the school reunions he organizes. Jay's writing is a valuable contribution to this book. Like most teachers, Jay offers a valuable insight on the realities of our society. His commentary on the tendency to value things over people is very close to my own views on the subject.

Tom Tippett

Tom is one of the new friends my wife and I met after we moved to La Quinta, California. We met Tom and his wife Barbara on the golf course. Tom and I share a number of similarities—his grandfather, like mine, was a marvelous example and mentor. Like myself, Tom joined the Theta Delta Chi house in college (in his case at Berkeley) then served in the Navy and found business success as an entrepreneur. Tom also believes strongly in giving something back to the next generation, so he devotes his retirement energies in the Service Corp of Retired Executives, and he serves on the board of Martha's Village and Kitchen. Tom's wife Barbara is a close friend of my wife Joan, and we enjoy our time together playing golf and traveling.

Ben VanderWerf

After a long and successful career, Ben and his wife Miki selected Colorado for their retirement, and this is where my wife and I met them. As with many of our friendships, we met them at St. Mary's Church, and a new and wonderful friendship began. Ben is a transplant surgeon who was trained in the Netherlands and at Harvard. He founded transplant clinics in Florida and Arizona and performed numerous surgeries himself. He has trained other physicians in the art of transplanting and has researched and published widely in the field to advance the science. I have a great admiration for Ben. His great cause now is to create a financially sound universal health care plan. Of the many plans I have heard suggested, Ben's ideas sound like the most easily implemented, since it begins with infant children, then adds recipients year by year. (See Appendix.) Like all the healers who have offered their thoughts for this book, Ben's empathy and concern for patients is very apparent. He is a wonderful example of a noble profession.